Being Mother Courage

The Whistling Girls & Crowing Hens Series
Book 4

Jan Anthony

Published by Mother Courage Press
https://www.mothercouragepress.com

ISBN: 979-8-3303-5486-3
Library of Congress Preassigned
Control Number 2024913992

Being Mother Courage

I'll be a key to help you unlock the door
to your side of that closet.

The Whistling Girls & Crowing Hens Series
Book 4
A creative memoir based on letters,
prose, poetry, journals, diaries and imagination

Jan Anthony

Mother Courage Press
Publisher, Jeanne Arnold

The Whistling Girls & Crowing Hens Series

Two straight married women risk families and careers, leave society's compulsory heterosexuality in 1972, and boldly thrive in an unchartered, intimate relationship. Jan and Bea experience historic events in the women's movement and gay/lesbian world in their 39 years together. Each book presents deeper levels on major topics and adventures.

The stand-alone books in this Whistling Girls & Crowing Hens Series will appeal to:

- readers to experience straight and lesbian lives,
- young adults to appreciate what has come before them,
- adults and elders to remember what they've survived and
- women-loving-women who've defied society's rules.

DEDICATION

Dedicated to the women in my life,
especially Bea for her love, her poems
and journals,
and to those who love her and them

Prologue

Science enough?
Poetry enough?
There can be no love
without a beloved.
Barren life.
Winter always.
Desert always.
But once at least once
in a lifetime, I hope,
a person crosses
your comet path
and because
of chemistry,
of atomic number
or critical mass,
of affinity,
of electron lack
or gain,
begins this profound
chain reaction of love,
then and only then,
oh rational one,
will you know
the magnitude
of infinite feeling,
joyous, renewing,
vibrant, incredible love!
By Bea

CHAPTER 1

Jan on August 11, 1976

We did it. So far Bea Lindberg and I haven't been punished for our three-week European jaunt. Our primary reason was to see Europe for ourselves, together, to share Stonehenge and London, Paris and sites I wanted to see again with her—to be my own person in beautiful places with the one person now that I truly want to be with; never to be bored again; never to be put down again, to feel diminished; to be free and to share our women's creativity, unquenchable curiosity, intelligence and passion.

But we'd planned a year in advance for our next Mother and Daughter Weekend at Woodridge in Door County with fourteen of us celebrating our womanhood. So again I left home but with my daughter Jenny and her guest to be with our circle of sisterhood.

This was even better than last year's Door County Mother and Daughter weekend. Bea was happy that her daughter Jill was with her this year. We did the rounds, created beaded necklaces at one craft store and visited Edgewood Orchard Galleries, my favorite art gallery in a refurbished fruit barn with rustic rafters and aged, graying brown hewn logs. I fell in love with an oval-shaped blue, blown-glass vase secretly bought for Bea for $45.

While waiting for the others to finish their browsing, we stood at the gallery's rugged double doors of this restored barn with its slanting farmhouse and pottery barn nearby, all surrounded by gravel and stone paths circling around patches of Queen Anne's lace and cascading colors of summer annuals. Anna Spence's daughter, Elisa, snapped off a branch of one of thousands of the Queen Anne's lace that surrounded us and I heard a song from the past, one of the songs I taught them as children in our church school. Her sister Angie joined Elisa and sang, "When you walk in the forest, let it be. There's a flower in the woods, let it be…" and the others who had been in my worship group years before joined in singing the Malvina Reynold's song. "…and it is innocent and good by the stone where it stood, let it be."

Later, Bea took charge of the Weber cooker and we ate her fabulous hamburgers. Even the hot dogs were extra tasty after being flavored by the heady clean Door County atmosphere. We told stories and jokes around the campfire circle until the embers went out.

On Saturday night by the light of the moon, we all crossed to the center of the forty-four acre field to what I called "Mother's Woods" that was protected from the farmer's plow by limestone outcroppings that made room for wild flowers and several sturdy old birch trees. We sang more songs around the small fire on a rock slab. Someday, I would like my cremaines to be scattered under one of those slabs.

But now I lay back on the soft ground graced by flowers that others may call weeds, and I looked at the crystal-clear night sky with stars gently diffused by the moon's radiance. Bea, who is always at my side, did so too at the end of one of the songs as the others kept on talking until the little fire extinguished itself. The two of us had dozed off and when we woke we were alone. Our company had slipped off to their own sleeping cots in the barn and trailer. The night's breeze blessed us as we slept together and when we woke, the birch tree branches shaded us from the arc of the moon above, making it dark enough to be together, alone, except for Mother Nature.

For breakfast we feasted on a gallon of blueberries, some even in Bea's Sunday's masterpiece omelet breakfast. The other women split in several directions in their cars for another swim or to shop while Bea and I stayed together to work up a luncheon salad and fruit for them to eat before most of them left for home.

While wielding our knives and peeling our veggies, we started feeding each other blueberries, then fingertips. She kissed the palms of my hands before I submitted to her not-so-subtle sensual suggestions, and I placed my palms on her buttocks and clasped her close to me. Empowered and intoxicated with her compliant surrender, I lifted her to sit on the butcher block and slowly and delicately feasted on the gourmet nourishment of her supple body before she moved me to a cot and devoured mine.

Hearing cars returning up the path, we smiled at slipping in another secret encounter in the midst of all these people and returned to the pleasant task of feeding lunch to the others. After they all helped clean up the barn and trailer, our dear Sister/friend Anna, Jill, Bea and I waved goodbye to Jenny and her friends, our other Sister/friend Marge Manley and her mother, Nina, and others to drive off for home.

We left this morning after skinny-dipping one more time before we took our leisurely time driving back. We unloaded our last guests at their houses, and Bea and I ate lunch before we parted again, Bea to her little apartment and I to my husband Alex, son Matt and daughter Jenny.

Hearing Malvina Reynold's "Let It Be" song again and remembering the mid-1960s when I was a volunteer, I'm proud of building institutions that benefited my children. I respect Maria Montessori's concepts that nurture the child's natural creativity, love of learning, sense of order, and independence. And in our Unitarian Universalist liberal church's religious education program, I taught Egyptian Pharaoh Akhenaton's concepts of one Sun God that made this young ruler's brief reign different from the other multi-theistic pharaohs. Bea's son Josh and Anne's son Adam were in my class. It was good to move beyond the Egyptian stories I knew from the Lutheran school of rigid pharaohs and a wrathful Old Testament God, the plagues, and those Ten Commandments with two Thou-Shalts and eight Thou-Shalt-Nots.

I'll always remember the receptive faces of Angie and Elisa, Kate, Sarah and Colleen, Marge's son John, my son Matt and others looking up at me at my little worship services for them in the rented beery bar basement room at the German Brotherhood Hall. We sang relevant songs from The Beatles, Judy Collins, Joan Baez and Malvina's songs, "Let it be…when you walk through the forest, let it be," and we'd talked about peace, self-respect, community and nature.

I remember too when we church school teachers met to share our life experiences and exchanged some of early concepts about religion. Ah yes, that's when Bea and I were just good friends. I was the last volunteer to direct our church's Religious Education program and recruit church school teachers. I persuaded our church board to pay for the next director who was, as I had planned, my dear friend Marge. After being recruited to work where I work, in Lakeshore Med's personnel department, she resigned and Bea took over the job as well as teaching at The Learning Center, a private school for students with learning disability issues.

Marge's dad was a Socialist, she explained. She never went to church and felt like an outsider in mostly Catholic Italian kids in Elmwood's public schools. That's why sending her John and Tim to church school was so important.

Anna said she never was given a middle name because she missed some religious custom, either first communion or confirmation where a saint's name is given. Because Anna's mother died of tuberculosis, she and her sisters only went to church occasionally with their Protestant neighbor. "When I was in college or in the WACs, I don't remember which, someone told me that I'd make a good Unitarian and I wanted to see what that was all about so my kids would have some church, and me too, of course, but I hardly got in the door when Jan greeted me with a hug and swept me off the sanctuary service down to teach the kindergarten kids including your Jenny and my Maria. And here I still am."

Jan gave her another hug. "And I always thought it was you who taught all of us to hug, not like when I was in German Lutheran School. I don't think anyone even touched each other or had fun. And I especially hated Good Fridays when everyone who was Lutheran was supposed to sit for three hours at Memorial Hall while different ministers spoke on the Stations of the Cross or what Jesus spoke while being crucified. All the stores in town were closed from noon until three so there wasn't anything else to do. I'd take those hours and walk along Lake Michigan's shore to our lighthouse and sit and think."

Bea on August 11, 1976

I was truly lonesome already and tired when I dragged my three weeks of luggage into my little apartment. "Alone again, naturally" got into my brain: "To think that only yesterday/I was cheerful, bright and gay/ looking forward to who wouldn't do/ the role I was about to play."

Yes, I'm alone after three weeks with Jan, like a honeymoon, even when our excuse to travel together was to see my Army private son somewhere stationed in Germany. That's over. Back to normal. What's normal? "But as if to knock me down/reality came around/and without so much as a mere touch/cut me into little pieces." I will fix that with some brandy I stashed away just for this time of returning.

After catching up on my sleep, my Jill, Marge, her Timmy and Joel and his girlfriend came to see me to hear about our trip. That cheered me up! Later in the week, Marge and I went to see Charlie again in Indiana with lots of drinks, pub hopping and dancing until about 3 a.m. We all slept late and had Bloody Marys for breakfast and went to a V.F.W. picnic and ate and drank some more at the V.F.W where we danced and finally got to his place at 2:30 a.m. This is quite a different vacation from Europe. We slept late again, and again we had Bloody Marys for breakfast before going to Charlie's Polish tavern for hamburgers. Charlie made dinner after a nap at his place and before he took us to Chicago to see Marge's favorite, Neil Diamond. From seats so far in the rear, Neil looked about three inches tall. We drove home to Lakeshore Bay from there and arrived about 12:30 with my insides a bit rocky, so I loafed today. I have to rest up for my other job, teaching my challenging students at The Learning Center again this year,

Jan came at two and stayed 'til five and we shared the soft feather quilt that we brought home from Europe. What a loving reunion.

Jan on August 16, 1976

Alex left a letter for me to find. It was addressed to him from my mother's sister Leona who came while I was in Europe. My mother's sisters never visit with her and that makes me angry. Leona wrote that a neighbor offered to drive her to Lakeshore Bay to see Ora and to take the two sisters to see my mother at the County hospital. She wrote that Ora cried and said it was too bad only a friend would take them to see my mother, implying "not me."

"While there," she wrote, "Ora asked Mildred if she got a birthday card from Jan. (Why don't we get a card too?) She said no, but we saw one and it read from London. Where are you and the children? Summertime should be with your teenage children. And Ora feels bad that Barney gets all the honors about building the parade floats. That's why Mildred is where she is. Why didn't they mention Ora, Pete, Toots, Norb? Yes, Chas and I even helped make flowers by hand when they started building those floats. They put in many hours. But we are proud that Barney got the honor of Mr.

Goodwill. Saw him on TV at night. How proud Mildred would have been if she could be at his side then. Are there are others in his life, which I can't blame him for. But, I feel sorry for both of them.

"Love to all, Aunt Leona."

My dad and I both caught the fury of Mildred's sisters that both of us ignored after years when they and their children and her friends neglected my mother, especially after she was transferred from Winnebago State Hospital in the center of Wisconsin to Lakeshore Bay's County hospital closer to everyone.

Jan on August 19, 1976

Back in those years, my Sundays belonged to my dad to visit my mother and we wouldn't know until he made his Winnebago phone call to see if we could go to her.

And when we could see her, if you had to walk down the long halls to Mother's room, you knew that she was too confused to visit in the day room where others were around.

So many Sundays in my youth, Dad and I would travel two hours on a train, wait for a taxi and ride out to the state hospital campus which was isolated from the town. In the visitors' room of this multi-storied Gothic brick structure, we'd wait to hear "Anthony" being called and wonder where we'd be taken. Following an aide with a long chain of keys through endless doors, we'd walk up wire-screened, enclosed staircases and through more locked doors and hallways. We'd pass people with hollowed-out faces, without teeth, with vacant eyes, with faces framed by new hair growth reclaiming its rightful space after being removed for sanitary precautions, for shock, and for surgery. We'd pass people with bodies held together by transparent skin over paper-frail bones, bodies perched on hard benches in rows against the wall marking the tragic waste of time and life.

When Mother's door was finally reached and opened, I'd hold my breath, afraid of what I'd hear and see.

Often she'd give no response after our hours of traveling, and we'd sit with her in our own silence, staring through the wire mesh windows listening to the radiator hiss. Many times we'd wish for no response at all if she'd pace and speak unspeakable words or unfathomable statements. Many times she would erupt from silence to shout curses at us for putting her in this place, for letting them give her more electric shock, for not getting her discharged.

Sometimes we'd share the room with a roommate's visitor. For many months of Sunday visits, a gray-haired man with a chiseled nose and steely eyes read aloud from the Bible to his wife who rocked in a straight chair while holding her crossed arms rigidly to her knees folded up against her breasts. Her head would tick and jerk uncontrollably while he droned of New Testament verses in her direction.

One Sunday, a desperate young husband stood through the three-hour visit holding his wife against him. He kept clutching and kissing and rubbing his hard self against her unresponsive frame while his elderly parents looked the other way.

It was somewhat better when we could visit in the day room. She would be more rational then and we would join the others gathered in clusters around the tinseled Christmas trees, Valentine's cupids, potted Easter lilies, or opening Mother's Day gifts in the hot, dry hospital air smelling like ammonia cleaner over vomit.

In warmer weather perhaps we could walk around the grounds, sit on the grass, have a picnic, hear the pleas and obscenities and wire screens rattling from shaking fingers gripped and grasping at the iron grates bolted over the open windows.

Young and old, pregnant and aged, docile and unpredictable women would be led in double files through the yard to get a bit of summer air. Faded flowered dresses were draped on these women who wore baggy brown cotton hose and quilted cotton slippers made by patients in therapy from recycled mattress pads from the hospital linen room. The dresses somehow had endured massive doses of hot water, strong soap and disinfectant, and heat—their buttons melted or lost, their belts taken away, their owner's names tattooed in black letters marking the ward from where they came.

I hated my feelings of anger at her because we both suffered, yet I pretended to be lighthearted so my father wouldn't feel more pain. I loved my mother and tried to remember, with pride, her ability and beauty and joy before all this. I loved her and needed her so much.

When visiting hours were over, she'd often plead and beg and grasp at us as we left. We would tear apart and I'd follow Dad's resigned footsteps to the door marked EXIT where we would stand and wait for an aide to unlock it, let us out to retrace the crazy maze that led us there.

We would have to wait four hours until the train came to take us home. We'd walk Oshkosh's empty, windy downtown streets void of people who had happy places to be on Sunday. The bar and restaurant would be open soon. Maybe we could go bowling? How about a movie? Most of our cash went for transportation, not recreation. Money for fun things went for an endless waiting game. We could miss the once-daily train if it came early. Usually, it would be late and we'd wait in the crowded station that was grubby and filmy with Lucky Strike smoke, cluttered with Hershey bar wrappers and the Sunday comics.

When the train finally came, I'd again follow through the aisles of passengers' faces, more empty faces of people who could not imagine, nor would they care, how awful I felt. Why should they? I'd search for a place on the packed train, hoping to find a seat by the window to rest against, to feel the cold glass and create images of the night lights streaking through the reflections from inside the car full of strangers.

After two more hours, we were at our station and, if the cabs weren't waiting or if we were short of cash after the Sunday was spent, we'd stand in the night waiting for the city bus to make its solitary way along the old State Street buildings, drop us at the seedy shack of the downtown transfer point where we'd wait for another bus to take us to the corner near our home.

Finally, after entering our empty house that we'd left twelve hours earlier, I would say little but "Good night," go to my room, and try to sleep. I waited for school on Monday to be with friends, to horse around, to shoot baskets, to enter rooms where people laugh, work, talk, tease and share, rooms where I could breathe, and be alive again.

A person is either in control of her emotions or ruled by them, and if she becomes dominated by emotion, her friends and family may abandon her. A normal, well-adjusted person controls her emotions, but it's only natural to lose control under stressful conditions. The changes that evolve during emotional stress are dynamic and overpowering until intelligence takes hold and the emotion is repressed. I discovered that if my reactions to situations are extreme enough to lose control, I'd choose sadness and self-pity for a while until I renewed my relentless optimism.

Mildred's undated letter from Winnebago

Please Barney,

Come on and get me. How much longer do I have to stay here? I feel fine and then they give me another electric treatment. Can't you take care of me yourself?

Crying and carrying on isn't going to help me and I don't know what can help me get well so I can leave here. Will you write me a letter anyway and let me know what to expect. I've been sleeping without pills for a week now.

Please come and see me. I'm getting lonesome.

Perhaps I'm getting a lesson in discipline. If that's what you want I can be that way too. I would much prefer you would work with me and not be so quick to send me away. My heart has been broken ever since you have been so quick to send me away. What are you afraid of? Have I hurt someone? Do you think I will?

Jan on August 22, 1976

Mom was discharged from Winnebago State Hospitals in April 1951 and returned home to us. I lived at home, finishing my college sophomore year. My work for the 4th of July and my summer job as a playground leader kept me close where I'd run across the street to see if she was all right, have lunch with her and make supper. I was afraid that when I went away to Madison for my junior and senior years, my mother would get sick again.

She always said, "September is my worst month."

September came and I went to UW-Madison. Alex, who now was a sophomore, came to Madison with me. He could have stayed at home for another year, but he made the decision to follow me and live in a dorm a quarter-mile away.

Seemingly minor life choices make fundamental differences. Though it would cost him more money in dorm fees to transfer to Madison, he was able to qualify for Reserve Officers Training Corps (ROTC), which eventually earned him officer status in the Signal Corps. If he'd chosen to stay home and let me go to Madison alone, he could have ended up being a private in Korea, and who knows where I would have been—or met—without him there to supervise my behavior by being "Alex's girl."

Before leaving for Madison, I told Dad not to let Mom shop because it would be too confusing for her. Groceries cost twice as much as the last time she went shopping.

One day soon after returning to the dorm, the phone rang in my room and I went into the hall to get my call. It was my dad and, while crying, he told me that she quarreled with the butcher at a downtown store. He continued with both of us in tears, "They took her back to Winnebago." I was so struck that I could not speak.

I did not feel as sorry for my mother as much as deep remorse for my father's loneliness. I was one hundred miles away and could do nothing about it.

<<◇>>

CHAPTER 2

Bea on August 27, 1976

Ducky checked himself out of the nursing home yesterday and took a cab to his apartment. My dad hadn't been well for a week and then I got a call from the ER. I went right over. His lungs are full of fluid and he was admitted. On August 18, Dad had a code blue in middle of night but he was stabilized and we decided to place him in an Elmwood nursing home again where he proceeded to get better and they discharged him. They needed beds for more serious patients.

I went to see him today and found him drunk. I made him some soup and stuck around all day, getting his prescriptions organized, etc.

Then Marge and I went to our hangouts, The Docks and the Silver Latrine.

I am someone else, different, rebuilt on the old foundation, now sleek, modern and functional, not traditional. I've been rebuilt anew in the latest design, but why do I see cracks in my plaster?

I haven't written a poem in a long while—nor has Jan.

I am loved and loving,
given over completely to my love—
no longer holding back,
no longer any reserve,
no longer any place within myself
where my love can't find me.
I am always naked with you.

Bea on September 2, 1976

Just last Saturday I slept late and was feeling good so I went to visit
with Ducky and I found my dad drunk again and on the floor. I called
the rescue squad and they got him into bed. I stole his keys and his
money and left him to sober up. The next day he called me and I
gave him his stuff back with warnings about how he was going to
kill himself with all his drinking.

He grumbled at me and I left.

On Monday, Jan and I went to look for a car for her. She wanted
a sports car. "I've wanted one," she declared, "since I fell in love
with a white Mercedes 220 SL with red leather upholstery when we
lived in Germany, but, of course, Alex won and we bought a black
VW bug instead."

But when she drove an MG that she liked, she discovered that
it cost too much and that she'd missed her chance to have a sports
car twenty years ago. She was too old now for a sports car. Her back
ached from the car's body shock and she said she couldn't get out of
it, especially in the winter when she'd slip and slide, squirming to
unfold her body out of the driver's seat.

Last night I went on a dinner date with this artist who wanted to
show me his studio and see his work. Why not? I'm an artist too. He
and his place were interesting but I decided I didn't want to have sex

with him. My terms! He wasn't too happy when I had him take me home.

Jan came for breakfast this morning when my dad's lady friend called me. Janine had tried to phone him, but no one answered. I was scared and Jan came with me but we drove our cars and parked behind his upstairs apartment next to the Sunnyside Liquor Store. The outside wooden steps leading to his porch had blood spots. We followed the blood to his door. I unlocked it and let us in.

"Dad? Dad! Are you all right?" Blood spots led the way past the slightly opened door into the bedroom. No one answered.

"Dad! It's me, Bea!" I entered his kitchen with Jan following me.

"What? Yah. OK. I'm coming," came a slurred grumble from his bedroom at the end of the hallway. And out stepped Clarence "Ducky" Holmes, his head almost touching the low, slanted ceilings under the roof of his tiny apartment. If he'd spread his arms, his fingers would touch each wall. He had on an undershirt, a pair of brown plaid cotton boxer shorts and calf-length socks. "What's wrong? What'da want?"

"Janine called me and told me to come over. You didn't answer the phone and you scared us, Dad. And what's that blood all over the porch?"

"I got a bloody nose, that's all."

"Well if that's the case, why do you have a black eye?"

"I have? Well, what'da know."

On his approach toward us, he seemed even larger as he looked past me and stared at Jan. "You remember Jan, don't you, Dad? She came up with me to see you when you were in the hospital."

Separating his lips and his tongue from the roof of his mouth as if he had cottonmouth, he reached for the half empty water tumbler of brandy that sat on the kitchen counter. "I'll be all right. I must have fallen down somewhere, but I made it home OK."

"Yah, Dad. OK."

I called Janine to tell her he was all right as far as I could tell. I also thanked Jan and sent her back to work as I cleaned up the blood, washed his shirt, pants and bed linens, and remade his bed while he sat at the cold metal kitchen table watching me with his almost empty glass in his hand.

I got him back to bed again and told him to sleep it off and not drive anywhere for a couple of days. "And call me every morning and night." Then I phoned Jan at work to tell her what I'd done and that I'd see her again as soon as I could.

Jan on December 2, 1976

When I answered the phone at my desk today, I reacted with a stupid question. "Does that mean he is dead?"

"I'm sorry, lady, but when you get a call from a coroner, that's usually the situation."

"But how did you get this number?"

"I got his I.D. and his keys and came to his apartment to look for someone to call. I found a telephone bill in his kitchen that listed this number from September 2. Did someone call you from here on that date?"

Bea had called me at work to tell me her dad was all right after we went there and followed blood stains up his outside steps. Today the coroner would find my work number on a telephone bill to tell me that Bea's dad had fallen over with a heart attack next door at the Sunnyside Liquor Store and died.

"Yes. I got that call and I'll go and tell his daughter right now. We'll take it from here." And after giving me some more instructions as to what to do next, I called Bea's Learning Center immediately and arranged for her to meet me at the school entrance right away.

I rushed the two blocks home to get my car out of my back yard and drove the next two blocks to reach her school. She was standing there, shivering, slim, frail. Her long locks, curled at the ends, framed her angular face as she waited for me in her thin fabric coat while the damp, icy air rolled in off Lake Michigan.

"What's wrong!?" she asked as she jumped into the warm car.

"Bea. I'm sorry to have to tell you, but the Elmwood's county coroner called my office from the long distance listing on your dad's phone bill. The coroner told me that your dad has died."

With a slight choking sound that betrayed her feelings, she asked what I thought she should do next and I told her what the man had told me.

"I'll take my car, Jan, and go home and call the kids. We'll be all right. They'll help me through these steps or I'll do it alone. Your mother just died and I don't want you to have to go through this all again. You go back to work. The kids will help me. And I know you'll come when I need you."

"Are you sure? Yes? Well, please then, let me hold you for a while so you can collect your thoughts." And I moved the car away from the door and parked along the lakeshore where no one could see us.

Bea on December 22, 1976

My mother "Oma" for Omaha Holmes, 1899-February 21, 1972, was married for fifty years to Clarence "Ducky" Holmes. She died after surgery to remove polyps. She was fine at first after the surgery, took a turn for the worse later in the week and continued downhill after that.

One night, the nurse sent my dad and me home. "You can't do anything here, now. Go home and rest."

My dad said to me, "Fine. Let's go get a drink!"

Mother died alone during the night on February 21, 1972.

It's good that I always keep my little notebook with reminders of what transpires every day because I'd never remember nor realize how much is going on. One thing I don't need to make reference to is how much more I'm drinking now as my unhappiness over Jake continues to grow.

I spent weeks getting ready for my mother's final rummage sale with her piles of supplies and stacks of cottage cheese and egg cartons, fabrics and sewing remnants, ceramic materials, her kiln and Christmas crap—so much that we rented a trailer and we threw the junk no one would buy out of the attic window, the kitchen window, whatever window—and cleaned her stuff out of the house and off to the dump.

I had help from some of her lady friends and my aunt, who claimed Mom's mink coat and hat. I acquired my mom's gold-trimmed floral china, some crystal, and a few other items I'd fit into my small home.

My brother, Calvin Holmes, died March 19, 1962 at age 42. My father disowned Cal when he told them he was a homosexual; perhaps my mother said one of her favorite expressions, "Go take a jump in the lake." And he did. Now Clarence Holmes, 1898-December 2, 1976, died in the Sunnyside Liquor Store.

I loved my dad, yet I hated what he did to my brother. And what would he have done to me if he found out about us. Well, Dad's gone now. One less worry.

Oma helped my dad build a log cabin in 1946 on Door County property on the Green Bay shore. Their friends, the Normans, Cal and I helped too and spent many weekends working on the cabin.

One Saturday night at their Door County supper club, Mom and the Normans convinced drunken Ducky to let her drive them home after dining out when a teenage boy ran out of the bushes directly in the front of their sedan. His body slammed over the hood and against the windshield and under the visor right in front of Oma at the wheel. The boy was dead but she did not get arrested. "Just an accident," said the officials, an accident that she would always remember.

Bea on May 25, 1977

Another birthday today. I remember when I turned 40 and didn't like what I saw in the mirror—a plump, matronly woman. I've been a professional mother to my now teenage children —and a good wife. My family has been my top priority—that includes my mom and dad, too.

(I've even lost all my teeth, having succumbed to gum disease eleven years ago, but now I have a pleasing artificial smile. Six months after me, Jake had his teeth removed by the same dentist. One would think he was more into dentures than dentistry.)

With my husband, I've participated in building seven boats. We did that well together.

The last boat, a 17-foot cabin cruiser, was mostly designed and crafted by me. I did all the fancy woodworking from scratch: the helmsman station, cabinets, drawers, doors and joinery, and even the mahogany ship's wheel. I designed the cabin top and the flying bridge folding windshield. Boating has been a life-long passion and this one was our seventh boat: a 12-footer after we came back from our honeymoon, a 15-foot cabin cruiser, two 5-foot sailboats for the kids, another 12-foot flat-bottom rowboat, a 17-foot cruiser hull for a friend and finally this one launched it in 1967. It took us two years to build it, not because we were slow but because we ran out of money. It's named *The Dollar Sign* posted as $, the symbol of capitalism and self-expressed freedom as in Ayn Rand's *Atlas Shrugged.*

Something startling changed my love of woodworking and my life! I made the acquaintance of Roy W. Morgan in my senior year of high school. I managed to charm Morgan, a wonderful old violinmaker working on the northwest side of Chicago, into letting me be his apprentice and build my own violin. In exchange, I worked in his shop, made repairs, did varnish matching jobs, and redesigned his shop front.

At the same time, I worked at F.W. Woolworth & Company for almost two years as a sales clerk in the record department while I helped out at Morgan's shop. After my high school graduation, he took me on full time. I finished my violin, a pretty good one at that, and began another. But Mr. Morgan couldn't afford to pay me $36 per week. He didn't earn that much himself and he had to let me go.

Unfortunately, I never went back to Mr. Morgan and wound up trying to survive in the working girl world. I paid room and board at home and my parents declined to send me to The Institute of Design in Chicago where I had been registered before I graduated. "You don't need to go to school. We can't afford to send you." I had to have a job; therefore I became a file clerk at Montgomery Ward.

I hated it and a few months later I took another file clerk job at Marshall Fields in downtown Chicago.

I realized I was wasting my life and decided I must go back to school—to college. Chicago's Wright Jr. College costs only $10 per semester plus books and after much talking, I finally convinced my parents that I could still work part-time at Fields and pay my own way toward my tuition for as long as I could.

I decided to lose weight and became a writer, painter, musician— and a damn good Scout leader for my kids. What's the rest of my life going to be? I will become a new woman for the second half of my life. I need to get my act together.

I went on a diet, learned scuba diving, went roller-skating, bowling—and lost fifty-seven pounds. When my mother acknowledged my weight loss and a new figure, she said, "I thought you were getting too fat."

I wrote my first draft of a novel, started back to college to finish my bachelor's degree and took charge of my life.

Half-heartedly, I've been looking around for a teaching position, but Jake isn't happy about that. He doesn't want me to have a job.

I hadn't been all that healthy. Researching my brief daily diary notes, I found in October 1967 that my heart started bonking, palpitating all night. I thought it was terminal. We called the rescue squad and I wound up in the hospital. My heart kept it up most of the day but came slowly down. In early November I felt more tired and weird. Ha! On November 6 it was another ride in the meat wagon for me; a ruinous day climaxed by complete prostrate exhaustion and I was right back in hospital again with shots, suppositories, and hours of oxygen. Depression hit me the next day. I was down a deep hole.

My period came! I felt tons better and my strength seemed to be returning. I was hospitalized for two more days and the doctor said it was nervous exhaustion. I must think positively. From my notes, I determined that when I got better I also got angrier and determined to find answers to my health questions: what was in those pills and when could I go home? I was out of the hospital by noon.

With my new regimen, I became a new woman. I got back into my writing with my rule: advance the story every day. I want to write what I hear and see with feeling. Some days I'll spend the whole day at the typewriter. One day I managed two complete chapters and wrote my way through one of the biggest scenes of my book, *Paradise Enow*. I mailed my *Paradise Enow* to Doubleday but it was rejected.

But that didn't stop me. I was painting too: lighthouses, surreal images with churches on fire, blue robots with locked doors for mouths, and jail windows for eyes with another robot looking through the bars. I created three-dimensional paintings with self-contained frames, ships, and nautical images on stones made into necklaces.

With my two older boys, we earned scuba diving certificates so we could have more fun with our boat, especially when we'd take the family to Silver Lake or dive on wrecks near Jake's dad's place in Bailey's Harbor where we'd crowd ourselves into his cabin.

When I reached 118 pounds, I looked quite stunning. My hair is mysteriously dark with a long spiral curl framing each side of my face and soft curls rolling at the end on my shoulders and back. I've sewn several one-piece bodysuits for myself with low-rise belts and I wear black heeled boots, not unlike my new feminist heroine, Diana Rigg as Emma Peel in *The Avengers* TV series. What a woman! Emma Peel is the first real feminist heroine who actually took care of herself. The character was brilliant, gorgeous and used karate like a guy. She didn't need John Steed to rescue her. She's truly the kind of woman I'd like to be.

I showed my art at a Lakeshore Bay Artists Fair and Wahoo! What a lovely day. I saw lots of people from my old church that I knew, including Jan Carnigian and Marge Bookerman. There was much ado over my new figure and I lapped it up. I sold everything and enjoyed a successful, fun day.

Jan on July 14, 1977

I went a little crazy at our Mother/Daughter weekend last Sunday, I guess. I feel more peaceful now that it's over. But for a couple of hours, I really lost control of myself, my emotions, and my body. I wasn't afraid though. I was with many people who love me.

It was the last afternoon of our third annual women's weekend in Door County, an altogether whirling experience. I was responsible for it all—organizing, purchasing, transportation, and cooking. I had just tossed a women's party two weeks before to celebrate Marge's birthday. I was the complete hostess again, but I had been left with my home in a mess. Everyone but Bea had left me to do the after-party chores. Some damage happened when cigarette ash burned a hole in the sofa. Alex's image of wrath may have intimated everyone. I didn't care, but I knew I would be accountable to him if he finds out about the party and discovers the burn.

Marge left without even thanking me, at least I can't remember her doing so.

So here I am again, two weeks later with five mothers and eight daughters to take care of. I expected disappointment throughout the weekend. Bea and Betty were wound up tight and higher than kites. They talked and talked and would not be interrupted. Anna encouraged them. Marge and I merely punctuated their endless storytelling and a mixed string of sad and funny conversations. I had heard them all before.

I don't really know what my feelings were that Saturday. I do know I anticipated disaster because Bea and Betty had been talking until dawn the night before. There was plenty of drinking. I was staggeringly drunk when I fell asleep in my cot on Friday night.

I sensed a repeat of last year when Marge kept Bea up all Friday night and then Bea fell asleep. Then I dozed off and Marge let me sleep when our daughters drove off without me. Shit. I can sleep at home! Then Marge told me it was my fault for being grumpy because I was expecting too much.

Well, have I set myself up to repeat last year's disappointments again? Are my expectations too high?

This morning, Bea's voice rang through to me as I worked around our barn, cleaning a terribly thick, greasy Coleman stove from brat spills the night before, separating the burnable trash from recyclable cans, burning the trash, and anticipating the return of our hungry teenagers. Bea explained to me, "Of course, I have to talk now. I don't have anyone to talk to at home—I live alone." My heart was touched by her insight and my sympathetic love grew even deeper. But I wanted her to get some rest now, finally, so she wouldn't crap out on me on Saturday night. She was still going strong.

Everyone said, "Look at Jan. She's working so hard. Sit down. Tell me what I can do." They made me parent them. They could see what needed to be done without my telling them. My inside kid said, "I want to talk. I want to laugh. I want someone to do this shit work. I want to hear good things about myself. I want everyone to love me."

Finally, I gave Bea a task. "Please drive to the corner tavern and buy some ice cubes." She was a bit tipsy, but she could drive a few miles to buy fresh ice. I was sober and really wanted a cool martini before the supper, which I was preparing.

She and Betty Willing disappeared for an hour. I visualized them in the tavern drinking more while we were waiting for them. They finally reappeared and then sat in the car and talked for another length of time while the cubes were melting in the back seat. Finally, I went to get the ice, knocked on the door, and opened it. Betty, with her precocious Eloise eyes, said, "We're not doing anything!"

implying that I was checking on their behavior, making me into a parent or jealous lover—two roles that I hate.

All I wanted was ice for my drink and to prepare supper. When I opened the door, I could see that Bea was holding her brandy flask.

Earlier today, she decided to back out her car to the road on the way for a swim. We were the last two to get there and we missed a skinny dip. Big deal! I love to swim in the nude. We were late because she had to chugalug another glass of brandy after drinking all day. That ticked me off. Then I had to warn her, "Watch out for the trees. Don't back out. You're off the road. Stop. You're going to hit the fence. Stop! And she rear-ended the first section of the low-slung fence and broke several cedar logs that Matt had notched together and created. Now I'll have to explain that to Alex too. Shit!

And she still had no sleep. After our swim, she finally settled down but Betty kept bothering her, and, in my premonition of repeating last year, I went over to Bea and quietly whispered, "I think Betty has a plan. She wants to keep you awake until it's time to go this evening, and when you'd still be asleep, I'd be angry again, leave you behind and Betty would be alone with you."

I could see that Bea loved my being jealous. Her dim eyes lit up some. I don't know if I was truly jealous or only determined not to be desperately disappointed again. Let her think it's jealousy if it makes her feel good.

I had to be in charge of the Weber grill because Bea finally fell asleep. She woke refreshed when it was time to eat. My food was delicious. My "family" seemed happy. We were ready to enjoy Door County's old-fashioned carnival park—and we did. We screamed in the Haunted House, and ate popcorn and candy-fluff stuff. The kids had great times on the unsophisticated rides, and I even had the chance to bang out some aggression toward Bea in our separate bumper cars.

We returned happily to the barn and enjoyed the most beautiful campfire harmonizing ever experienced—and sang and told jokes and stories until 2 a.m.

Everyone went in but Julie who found me to unload on, cry and shake. I held her close, even took her in the hammock in the woods and I rocked her. She said she was so alone and angry with her friends because they disappointed her by not helping her when she needed them. Christ. I could identify with that. I didn't want to stay alone with her too long for fear that my holding her would be misunderstood. We walked together to the outhouse and then said a kindly good night.

Earlier that afternoon, Sue was sitting alone at the fire ring, and I became involved with her unloading her troubles on me too.

They all look at me as being so strong yet I'm as adolescent and weak as they are.I was the last to finally head for bed and I crawled into Bea's sleeping bag with her. She didn't wake up and I fell asleep holding her. It had been a beautiful night. All was well.

Before the others woke, I climbed into my own cold cot, sleeping until Anna, Marge and Bea concocted a noisy omelet breakfast preceded by Bloody Mary drinks. I grilled bacon and we left loads of kettles in the sink for the non-cooks to clean. We playfully walked down the neighbor's cow path, stepped in a cow pie or two, and found good bones in the farmer's dump. Life was fun and warm and beautiful. We returned to the barn and Jill, Jenny and Susan went off shopping on a Door County pilgrimage with Bea's Jill.

The rest of us drove to my favorite Edgewood Orchard Gallery. Before leaving, I had tossed down a second strong Bloody Mary. "I can play too," my "inner child" said, and we enjoyed our trip to the gallery. Bea bought me an artistically designed pillow I had admired to hang on the wall of my study as a reminder of this special weekend.

Somehow I was mixed in with one of the daughter's cars and, on the way home from Edgewood Orchard, I saw Betty get out of Marge's car to buy beer at our single corner tavern. I was thirsty too, but I brought watermelon from home to share. Well, there they go again—out to find more to drink. As if we haven't had enough. We've practically devoured everything in sight already. I started to get angry; three of our adults were off looking for more to drink.

We went to the barn. I sliced the melon, took care of supper preparation details, and made myself a cool martini. I couldn't find a clean glass. The sink still had breakfast shit in it and it was getting close to winding up the weekend with a swim, supper, and then home.

Our daughters were outside sunning themselves. I was inside, in here alone again—and I started to combine leftover food for a creative bean salad. Time went by. Where were they?

I'm feeling sorry for myself again. All I have to do is call for help—but then I'm parenting again. They can be responsible, too. Why did they leave me? Anna's sleeping. The kids are talking. I'm working among this mess of dirty dishes and pots and it reminds me of my kitchen when I get home from work. And I'm drinking the leftover vodka. I don't know how much. So many times before, I've been stranded in this barn for hours waiting for "the fishermen" to come home. I have entertained about a hundred guests up there. Often I've had more help from less intimate guests. Where are they? Why did they desert me?

In the midst of this turmoil inside of me, the trio walked in laughing and chattering. Bea handed me four cans of beer joined by their plastic rings.

"I don't need anything more to drink!" I was chopping the last onion, leftover hamburgers, brats, and tomatoes. It was done. I created a fabulous dish for them all.

In my frustration and drunken anger, I took the chopping knife and plunged it into the watermelon remains. Betty, who's been known for stabbing, jumped sky high, and like a kid, she grabbed a broom and started to make up to me, "her mother," by scurrying around sweeping the debris around the floor.

The rest of the girls all came in to change for a swim and finally saw the mess. Somehow between a swim and my loss of control, all was cleaned up. Marge started to look for fixings to make a salad. Bea said she'd help with the tomatoes.

"I don't need your help now! It's all done!"

We'd go for a final swim before supper. Somehow I twisted myself into my suit, poured myself another martini, and squeezed into the back of a car with Bea and some girls. I was crying a gushing flood of emotion. I spilled a bit of my precious martini but managed to drink it all down before I threw the empty cup into the shoreline rubbish can and walked into the water.

I dove. I churned. I cried. I floated. "The water flows around me" was my mantra. I knew Bea was there to help me. Perhaps I could "exorcise" myself of this tearing, emotional trauma.

I don't want to go home to Alex. I don't want to feel responsible for anybody. I want to be free, yet I want to take care of my responsibilities. I love my children and want to be with them. I love my Bea and want to live with her. I'm confused by all this interplay among my so-called buddies and Bea's irresponsibility. I'm mad at Marge and Betty, even Anna for not helping me. I told them I was shaky three months ago, but I was faulted for "being too good."

I cried all the way back. I must have scared the shit out of those kids.

When we returned to the barn, I took off my wet swimming suit while I was still crying. Tortured. Bea said in my ear, "Jan, you're standing with just your bra on, and I'm standing with just pants on and holding you. This looks pretty cute, Jan. Get your pants on," and then she put me down to cover me up for a nap.

She took care of me while the others finished cleaning up. I shook and shuddered for endless minutes—making the cot tremble. I'd never experienced the electric shock response of real electric emotions as I did then.

Finally, I fell asleep.

Instead of waking me to enjoy with them the supper I had created for them, they let me sleep through the meal and the cleaning up. Bea thought it would be best for me to sleep more than to eat. Yet it was I who prepared this "Last Supper" and I missed the communion of it all. I couldn't believe they would exclude me from my "family," especially when I had labored over it all alone. I might as well be the family dog eating the scraps left for me.

The shock that shook me to my soul before jolted me again, yet I was too exhausted to do much about it. I couldn't eat, but I knew needed nourishment to neutralize the vodka and bolted down some of their leftovers.

I was so angry. They let me sleep through supper, and again I missed something important to me. Childish. Yes. Honest. Yes. Temper. Yes. Hurt. Yes. Yes. Yes.

Bea tried to comfort me but after following me outside trying to explain, I insisted that I was treated unjustly. I muttered, "I don't want any more communes. My dream about that is shattered. I would be the responsible one." I turned to her. "All I want is to live in the woods with you, Bea." I tried to explain that I was so angry at being left out, at being responsible, and at not being able to let my happy kid out. "You and Betty can be bratty ten-year-olds and have your fun, but I don't want to be ten years old again!"

When Bea helped me understand that statement, I realized the impact of it all.

My life and my security fell apart when I was ten years old and, in many ways, I've been responsible for everyone since then. And I didn't want to be responsible then and I don't need it or want it now. My mother died this year. Where has she been on my daughter and mother's weekends with her for all those years? My weekends were spent in sanitariums.

In contrast is the manner of my own daughter and that I want to give her all that I lacked. During this weekend, she stayed as far away from me as possible. I received more love from other people's daughters, and I wanted Jenny to love me—or at least to show me something else but tolerance or indifference. Jenny treated me as if I farted all the time. Where is her sense of humor when I'm around, her caring? She must care for something about me. Why couldn't she sing around the campfire too? Or help me organize the clean-ups. Or give me a hug.

Bea left me alone in the field saying I could not be reasoned with. I was alone as I watched her move away from me. I was ashamed that I had lost control. I was afraid I had spoiled everyone's weekend, especially after working hard to try to make it a success. I was angry and hurt that it had come to this.

And I knew that in a few hours I would have to return home and face that wasteland scene; the disintegration of my dreams for a women's community as I'm left with all the hostess work; the disintegration of my dreams of a happy married life as I am forced to see that I cannot continue hurting my loved ones—both my family and my lover; the loss of support from others under tension; the chaos of it all. I had a small nervous breakdown during the last days of the last time I imagined I was to be on my precious Door County land. My friends there did give me some support but they were afraid my irrationality. They did not know the depth of my feelings and I could not tell them. My daughter was scared. So was I.

Soon a posse of teenagers was marching toward me through the grass. Each of them was focused on me. Had I scared them? My God. What's going to happen next?

"We're going home," they said, "and we want to say goodbye."

What could I say? I apologized for losing control and said something to gloss over this whole mess. "You know that each of you, as you grow out of adolescence, makes decisions affecting your lives. In many ways, I'm an adolescent again and I'm having to make decisions again that affect me and the people I love—and I don't want to go back home."

I realized Jenny was there and I had hurt her feelings—and I stood up and tried to reach her. I said, "Jenny, I love you so much." She didn't come to me but there was a huge hug from the other daughters and Anna with me in the middle. And we all cried together. Why they cried, I don't know. It made me feel bad that they did, yet these feelings rise to the surface when we're in a protective atmosphere—and so close. Each one could cry for her own insecurities and uncertainties. They all were as deeply involved in personal issues as we "grown-up" are. And each one could share the caring for the other.

They all walked me to the barn and I walked them to the cars. They took off for home and reality—and I was sorry that I had acknowledged reality by cracking open my soul in front of them.

They didn't need to see an old lady fall apart just when it was time for them to face the world.

About ten minutes later they all returned!

"We forgot to take our group picture," they hollered.

I was so pleased. It meant so much to them, this tradition of our pictures, together, each year. I hope, in spite of my insecure marital situation, that there will be other years on the land. I always say goodbye to Woodridge as if it is my last time—every time I leave.

I'm so happy they love our Mother/Daughter group pictures.

My treasured real family picture has me at age nine with my arms around cousins as I lean out to celebrate my world. My family was then my mother, father, my mother's parents, her aunts and their husbands and my cousins. After the picture was taken, just before World War II, they all went away—all of them in sequence: to the Army, to the Navy, to work, to be grown up and get pregnant, to the insane asylum.

But I will have a new picture soon. I can't believe how good we all looked together, except for Bea who looked so drawn and tired. She had quickly and ingeniously set up her automatic camera and leaped over us to hug her Jill. I wore dark glasses to hide my eyes and my smile was wide in the midst of the community that we had fostered, that I had helped to build when I asked Alex to build a barn for large numbers of guests.

They care. They'll move away. Each year for as long as it lasts, there'll be changes in our group. Yet each one will remember some details and a lot of care, a free and open and accepting atmosphere, even when all hell breaks loose inside of someone 'cause that's a place where hell can break loose—if it must.

Our daughters returned to their cars and headed out again. The remainder of us packed up, closed the shutters on the windows, locked up the barn, the outhouse, and the trailer. Marge, Betty, and Carla disappeared in a flash down our dusty dirt road.

Bea stayed by my side—finally, holding me, helping me on my journey back home. She folded me into her car and I slept for over four hours—all the way home while Anna, Bea, and Jill talked on and on about their problems.

Bea and Jill took turns driving home. When we drove to Anna's, Jill gave Anna a hug; they had bonded on this trip. When we got to Bea's, Jill gave her a hug and a quick one for me and got into her parked car to drive home.

Then Bea drove me home.

And again I slowly walked the long path to my back door.

Bea on December 23, 1977

Merry Christmas! This is a challenging new year and holiday season with so many changes happening around us: my divorce, Ducky dying, teaching at The Learning Center until it closed, working with Jan at Lakeshore Med and then 'let go' in a traumatic administrative injustice. Plus, Jan's leaving Alex and he's starting divorce proceedings after our four years of some wild adventures and trembling sad times.

But we're on to healing, I hope.

Last Wednesday, we decorated Jan's first Christmas tree on her own with new lights and silver ornaments, half of them decorated with Mickey and Minnie Mouse, Donald Duck, Goofy, and even Winnie the Pooh. We used bountiful white garlands to spiral around the green and it became the most beautiful Christmas tree I've ever seen. That helped me get into the holiday spirit after being depressed about the season, as usual.

Then my son Josh came home wearing his Army uniform. On Friday, I took off a half day to get ready for the party at my family's new house that ex-husband Jake bought a block away from where we used to live—a house almost identical to the one we had, except that this one has the basement we couldn't afford to have when we had our home built. Jan and I were invited to a Christmas party and all the old gang was there. We danced and drank and hugged and laughed. It was a great reunion with those teens, now adults, having a good time again together. We all shared a puff from a couple of joints that appeared and were passed around. After saying goodbye we came home to my apartment at 3:30 a.m. What a great night!

Jan on December 23, 1977

Writing Christmas cards was awkward this year. No family photo graced my greetings, as was my family's custom. Some of my store-bought cards deserved a letter, but rather than making copies, I customized and retyped individual versions, but not as detailed as this letter to Alex's best friend from the three years Alex and I spent with the Army in Frankfurt, Germany in the mid-1950s.

Dear Nick and beautiful Olga—but mostly to Nick because I know him better—even after all these years, and I really haven't had a chance to get to know you, Olga, because of kids and distance and time.

Nick: Back then you gave me a cop-out excuse which I will always remember because it was the first time I had ever heard it: that women didn't need to be creative because they held the ultimate existence, the creative power of the generative forces within them.

At that time, I wanted to have a child and did not argue with you, but I have never forgotten that statement said in Frankfurt, Germany, which said, 'Lay over, woman, and produce and be happy for that is your role in society.'

Nick: Perhaps I may be as good a writer as Kurt Vonnegut. I have the same insights and creative powers and I can try to speak a similar message: "There's only one rule that I know of, babies—God damn it, you've got to be kind." I have even more to say for I am against war and death, inequality and injustice. I am against the power of having someone say to me that I have the ultimate creative power to make life—when making babies is not enough.

"I wish I could have said at the time that you and Alex were victims of your own ethnic standards, your own cultural values. Yet for a man, it's productive to be Greek or Armenian, but it's difficult, after almost twenty-five years to say 'So what!' and 'Goodbye.'

Yet that's what I've done.

So why am I telling you this after sending you brief messages on our Christmas cards for all these years? Because I still feel the soul among us all, but it's so often the suffering soul, like Zorba, "…marriage, children, and the full catastrophe." But Zorba spoke for himself and not for a wife. Women today speak for themselves.

At age 42, I began to become unsettled; at age 43, inspired; age 44, angry; age 45, scared; finally at age 46, free.

I moved into an apartment only one block north of our home, hoping to be close to Jenny who's at home with Alex, and without alienating Matt, who's now college.

Alex and I have begun divorce action.

My apartment is perfect for me and am able to be and to write and to feel like my own person after so many years. There are times in each life when choices are made to take one path or another and, many years ago, I chose to take the safe, conservative path of the respectable, traditional wife and mother.

In reality, I am a successful public relations director for one of two hospitals in Lakeshore Bay and I edit and write and create good hospital literature that is a creative voice that celebrates the work that the hospital does.

I'm also writing (with frustration) a novel using neutral pronouns for six main characters plus unborn children and God. I started it a year and a half ago, then a six-week strike broke out at the hospital and I became the Thomas Paine of the hospital with propaganda and news every day to help win over the rabble-rousers organizers and the picket line walkers, yet I was the biggest rabble-rouser of all. And I learned what communicating with people can do.

We won the strike. I've lost a marriage. And in major ways, my children.

Alex is still the stable one. He has his career under control and can pick and choose what his goals and schedules will be. (If I had been his employee instead of his wife, he would have given me a raise.)

So hang in there, you two, for as long as you can, love and accept and respond to each other. And if you should come our way again, please stop and see the two of us living, really living at separate addresses and benefiting from all that has passed and from all that will be in the future.

So it goes.
Jan

Bea on Christmas Eve, 1977

We dressed up in our holiday clothes and went to our 4 p.m. service
at our most precious Unitarian church.

Jan's soon to be ex- and her Jenny and Matt, home from college,
stayed on the opposite side of the sanctuary.

We celebrate all the season's holidays tonight: Winter Solstice,
Hanukkah and Christmas. Some new gay guys who are florists and
interior decorators have joined and made our little church
overflowing with golden garlands, beribboned angels and tall
evergreens glowing with pure white lights on each side of the church
organ behind the altar platform.

The Rev. Dr. Tony Logan traditionally begins the service with
the room in darkness. He wears a simple white robe and enters
holding a torch and chanting, "Let there be light." We repeat the
chant and he slowly paces his way to the altar while ushers gently
begin lighting hurricane-globed candelabra perched on white iron
pedestals standing about the sanctuary. Then Tony and everyone
sings "Dona Nobis Pacem" as a round.

Jan and I joined the line of folk dancers to do the Hanukkah
Candle Dance. Jenny didn't join us this year. After that music
stopped, the Hanukkah menorah was lit with words read by two
church members in English and Hebrew.

Someone worked hard sewing sheep, angels and shepherds
costumes this year as the children performed a delightful Christmas
pageant. We sang the traditional Christian carols and heard the story
from the Gospel of Luke. Every so often Jan would glance over at
her kids with Alex. That made Jan tense, but we sang out through
the service and I added my single-voice harmony to the
congregation's a cappella singing of "Silent Night." I love doing
that.

As we all stood for the closing words and the last song, we heard the sounds of a banjo plus Tony and his guitar playing the opening chords to a song never heard before at our Christmas program, "The Rainbow Connection." It's a hard song to sing, but we did it. When we got to the line, "All of us under its spell, we knew that it's probably magic—" and a rainbow spectrum beamed out from behind where we stood and was projected on the wall over top of the altar, Christmas trees, the organ pipes and pageant decorations.

The congregation gasped in awe-filled delight and Jan caught her breath in surprise and began to weep on my shoulder as I held her in my arms while I continued to sing, "Someday we'll find it, the rainbow connection: the lovers, the dreamers, and me."

Tony encouraged the group to greet each other in the spirit of the season, and to help them feel comfortable if they wanted to hug, two large mistletoe balls slipped down from the ceiling vent and across the room on fine wires. Bowls of hand-printed greetings of Love, Good Cheer, Good Health, Happiness, Joy, Peace and more were written on labels. Ushers brought them out from under the end of each pew to pass them around and people stuck them on each other in a bubbly rumble of good cheer.

Jenny and Matt came over to us and we decorated each other with sticker greetings before they rejoined Alex for a quick exit.

After church, I was to play Santa with gifts for my kids at their house and went to my apartment to fetch the packages. When I carried out one load to my car, I locked myself out of my apartment. I had to wait for the manager to finish playing Santa to the kids in the apartment complex and then he came to unlock my door. I offered him a drink, which he accepted now that he was finished with his rounds, and I was privileged to share with Santa a brandy rather than cookies and milk.

My Christmas run to their new house turned out all right, especially with Josh and Jim home from the Army for the holidays. My ex-husband is pleasant enough. Actually, Jake's not much different than he was before we were divorced, except perhaps more relaxed, if that's possible. We had a nice dinner, even, and had a few drinks. It was great reminiscing about old times with them when they were kids. We exchanged presents and then I drove to meet Jan.

She had made an agreement with Alex to split the time spent on Christmas Eve at the Kramer's. Honestly. How petty. "You go first and I'll come later," he said, but he was there early and Jan didn't leave. Can't he tolerate being in the same house with her—and me, even on Christmas Eve? Obviously, his plan didn't work because she was still there when I arrived and we stayed with our UU-friendly family, young and old, and had fun with them until we left for Jan's place after midnight.

We celebrated our Christmas morning together and I made an omelet for us in the new omelet pan that Jill gave me. But I got out of there before Jan's kids came and went to Betty's for an open house. Nora Carpenter, our friend who is an alcoholic counselor at St. Paul in Milwaukee, Em Kuiper and Pete Kramer, Carolyn Schafer who, with Betty, was in my "Employing Your Total Self" class, Betty's daughters, Kate and Karla and, of course, Jan. We had a lot of fun sharing our stories together.

Chapter 3

Bea on January 7, 1978

While our first Christmas tree was still up and beautiful at Jan's apartment, we had an impromptu gathering on Friday with friends, straight and gay, coupled and single, including some from work. They seemed to become desensitized to Bea's paintings of me, life-sized nudes hanging about on the walls. They mixed well and stayed for a long time. We hosted a very nice party.

Jan and I woke at 3 a.m. to celebrate Jan's new independence and our love and happiness—then again during the day and another during the evening. We're reading the new book that she gave me for Christmas, *The Joy of Lesbian Sex*. She ordered it from Sistermoon, a woman's bookstore in Milwaukee, because there are no bookstores in town that sell it. And who would be brave enough to buy it? The women in the illustrations are smooth and beautiful, just as in the heterosexual coupling of the first book, *The Joy of Sex*. These books sure beat *The Joy of Cooking*. That book and our gentle, relaxed interludes made me forget my headaches for a while.

Books seem to be the only resource we know for us to find out more about lesbians and their lives, plus one or two movies we've seen like *The Children's Hour,* but most of the fiction and its characters are pretty depressing. Betty Willing had given us a list of books with lesbian themes. It was two letter-size pages printed on both sides. She treasures it and made me sneak a copy at work and return it quickly before it's lost among the piles of reading materials that Jan and I own. That list was compiled by Barbara Grier who, with Donna McBride, own Naiad Press in Florida and publish only lesbian titles. Betty said someone had given her the list and she didn't know where it came from before that. The print was pretty gray and I could imagine it had been copied many times before we made one of our own.

Jan was fascinated when she read about June Arnold who wrote an androgynous book, *The Cook and the Carpenter.* It steals Jan's thunder. She's not the first person to try to write a gender-vague book. Besides, she's too busy now to write much of anything not related to work or about what we're doing as we scribble little notes in our date books and calendars, or as she writes and types long documents with carbon copies to save.

Jan on January 7, 1978

Bea and I nestled together in her or my apartments for this New Year's holiday weekend. Even with her headaches, she read two books on one of our days off; I rested and read some beside her. The snow piles make us struggle to dig the two cars out of the streets or the parking lot at our two apartments so this weekend holiday, for as long as possible, we let the stormy weather happen and stayed where it's warm. We played Monopoly and Scrabble and drank two bottles of champagne for our New Year's Eve party and spent these leisurely days taking two time-outs for making love.

I rest now—in winter hibernation. A cold world, a warm nest, a friend's breath protects me while I sleep away sad memories before springtime's hopes renew me—and the bears and the buds and the birds—to be again.

While she slept, I sorted piles of memos, poems, brittle pages and photos from boxes not yet assimilated into my new life.

I wrote a note to Bea, "Feathers flew from every corner, from every place as I sort out my life in bits and pieces. Old photos bring back memories as white feathers from a cavalier lover's memory fly amid the remains of the past toward the dreams of our future." Then I took my note and a few of the photos and trinkets we've exchanged and stealthily slipped into the bedroom and tucked them among the soft crevices of our quilted haven for her to find when she woke.

She did and slipped out to find a pen and paper to respond to my note:

"It's like Christmas! I dreamed I would wake and find some of your treasures. No—more like Easter and finding hidden eggs everywhere. Such pleasure. Such joy to share memories with you. Love, Bea"

Barefooted and more, she slipped up behind me sorting through my archives, and added her note to the top of the treasury of love poems we've shared over these four years and some months. We returned to our soft haven to share old memories and create new ones.

I'm saving two Christmas card responses to the letters that I wrote with my Christmas card friends. The words were based on many of my previous letters to Jenny and Matt and to Alex, but softened and customized for the individual reader and, of course, I did not indicate any lifestyle changes to anyone.

These responses came after the holiday. Anna Spence's daughter Angie wrote from Chicago, "I want to express to you the deep feelings I have in my heart for you. I understand more now that I'm living on my own. You've always been a friend and a teacher to me—a highly cherished one and I've got to include our Women's weekends. You've enriched my life so much by just being. You're really beautiful, Jan. Be strong and happy."

And Mitzi, my dear college friend, wrote, "Gin, My dear precious friend. Having finally gotten thru the holidays, I found a free moment to reread your letter. I can't tell you how touching it was for me. I'll never throw it away. I will put it in my 'Blues Box' to read when I'm feeling down. Anyway, you know how I feel about you—and always have. I'm delighted you're finding freedom. It's truly a primary need in order to flower, which we must. I'm sorry for Alex and am not sure he'll ever understand what you're striving for. Lots of love, Mitz."

Jan on November 1, 1978

We needed help from a guy to make Bea's dream of owning a bookstore come true. My dad, Carl Barney Anthony, just happened to have an unused store off Lakeshore Bay's Main Street's Downtown and he was happy to have us open a bookstore there—without rent. Bea and I worked our buns off to restore my dad's neglected storefront into our own Mother Courage Bookstore and Art Gallery that opened two weeks ago. What an accomplishment! We are so proud, especially when our destiny depends on being accepted by him, our customers, the general public and by our lesbian selves.

Bea on November 3, 1978

Jan was writing up a storm for our first *Mother Courage Courier* newsletter after her regular hospital work schedule. We did a lot of research and used the article and our bibliography to fill the eight-page, legal-sized paper that we typed out in two columns for our first edition with a mailing list of one thousand. It starts with a poem.

"Beginning"

> We're just beginning after all these centuries,
> and who knows where our dreams will take us?
> That's where many women are today
> looking to be reborn right where they're at
> revitalized and ready (Informed and active)
> to challenge the world. (Stop hunger and War.)
> Well, maybe just the country. (ERA)
> Well, how about state and local government?

(More women as decision-makers.)
Why not the church? (Beyond god the father.)
 Maybe just our working lives. (Equal pay for
equal work.)
Perhaps 'just' our families. (To be valued as a
person.)
Certainly ourselves! (Self-esteem and confidence.)

We're just beginning, too. Mother Courage, that is.
And who knows where our dreams will take us?
Right now, we want to provide
the people in this area with information about any
subject
that interests or entertains them.
But many people, not aware of all there is to
discover,
may not know what to ask for
about women's subjects, and many women
are just beginning to take a new look at their lives
and to wonder what has or is happening to them.
They're looking for choices among alternatives.
They want to grow.
Mother Courage's *Courier* is for your information
on books and art and people.
Write to Mother! Let us know your interests,
your opinions about books and art,
your feeling about who you are.
We're just beginning, and who knows where—
together— our dreams will take us.
Jan and Bea

   We reviewed Rita Mae Brown's new *Six of One* hardcover
novel and printed her striking black and white photo in our first
edition. The second page had three books on sexual blackmail at
home and work including the first book to cover stories of incest,
Kiss Daddy Goodnight by Louise Armstrong. The rest had art

gallery news, best sellers in stock, children's books, a page on how to sell creative work plus The 1979 *Writer's Market*; quick reviews of books and women-made records in the store, and more books about motherhood and mother/daughter relationships and an editorial about the Equal Rights Amendment with a postcard sketch showing four iron-caged floors of women in prison, dressed in long black dresses, aprons and white head caps tied under their chins. The wording around the drawing, set in Charles Dickens-era type, pronounced, "Stone Walls do not a Prison make, Nor iron Bars a jail; But 'til the E.R.A. is Won, We're only Out On Bail."

We reprinted Jan's witch-burning commentary and then described the key points from our research and proudly listed our bibliography—all books are available in our store:

June Sochen's Herstory, *A Woman's View of American History*;

Selma Williams' Demeter's *Daughters, The Women Who Founded America, 1587-1787*;

Andrea Dworkin's *Woman Hating*;

Mary Daly's *Beyond God the Father*;

Ehrenreich and English's *Witches, Midwives and Nurses; A History of Women Healers*;

Seon Manley and Gogo Lewis' *Sisters of Sorcery*;

Penelope Shuttle and Peter Redgrove's T*he Wise Wound, Eve's Curse and Everywoman*;

and Merlin Stone's *When God Was a Woman.*

Our women-made records included Malvina Reynolds, Meg Christian, Holly Near, Cris Williamson, Margie Adams, Kay Gardner, Lilith, Judy Grahn, and Pat Parker plus "The Return of the Great Mother" and "Side by Side: Reenactments of Scenes from Women's History, 1848 to 1920."

These courageous authors, scholars, and independent musicians risking all to rewrite and create women's history and inventing and singing women's lyrics and music, together and with others, are creating a revolution, and I know that we're a part of that same revolution for women's rights—and human rights too.

Bea on November 18, 1978

We've been getting some young women feminists into our Mother Courage Bookstore who attend Methodist College in Elmwood. They're starving for support in this primarily macho campus. Laura Sawyer, editor of *The Arrow*, asked if she could write a story about us and of course I couldn't turn down that opportunity. We photographed our library ladder filled with titles that would attract any woman's ideas of starting a little revolution in their area of influence.

"Mother Courage Dream Fulfilled"
by Laura Sawyer, a Methodist College senior

The doorbell clangs a strong definite clang, not at all the kind of chime one hears in the soft-spoken foyer of those shops with the fragile glassware and calligrapher "Touch at your own expense" placards.

"Welcome. You can hang your coats in back. Looks like you really got drenched in the downpour. Would you like some coffee or tea?" The woman behind the counter is in blue jeans, old sweatshirt, and striped tennis shoes. Hang your coats in the back. No saccharine sales pitch; no "May I help you" to help "my commission."

Just a pleasant kind of mustiness.

We have entered Mother Courage Enterprises, a book store/art gallery/creative services compendia located at 214 2nd Street in Lakeshore Bay. Owned and operated by Bea Lindberg and Jan Anthony, the business offers a full-service bookstore with an emphasis on women, a gallery for local woman artists. And a center for support of the arts. Opening just last October, Mother Courage has already begun to publish a regular newsletter, *The Courier,* and is currently planning discussion groups and poetry readings for the spring. For both of the women, the store provided income and a creative outlet. For Lindberg, the store also awakened a dream she has harbored since the age of eighteen. How did this all begin?

Anthony is the director of communications at Lakeshore Medical Center and a former high school teacher. Lindberg is an artist who formerly worked at Lakeshore Med and taught learning disability students. The two friends met teaching Sunday school.

After twenty-five years of "raising our kids and doing our housewife bit," notes Lindberg, "I didn't seem to have a definite direction."

Then came the flash of insight. Dining at the female-owned and operated Lysistrata restaurant in Madison when Lindberg was exhibiting her paintings, the two envisioned similar opportunities in Lakeshore Bay. They too could own their own business. With the reinvestment of some previously earned funds and a good credit rating, they were already on their way. Obtaining a building on the river in Lakeshore Bay gave the Mother Courage dream brick walls.

"When you open up your life to the living, all thing come spilling in on you/ And you're flowing like a river: the Changer and the Changed. You got to spill some over, spill some over, spill some over, over all."

Now the brick walls reverberate with the quiet folk voice of Cris Williamson, the brick walls splash with rows of books and brightly hued posters.

Lindberg props herself up on a stool behind a stack of "famous women" note cards she recently designed and released for national publication. Anthony sits halfway up the library ladder.

The business has been successful despite the customarily slow January-February customer slump. "People," notes Anthony, "have gone out of their way to come to Mother Courage; the possibilities for growth look optimistic." But Anthony realizes a more tangible return, as well.

"The idea of having the selection of women's titles has really brought loyalty," she says. "There's a positive feeling you get back from your customers when you sell these books."

And besides, adds Lindberg, reflecting somewhat wryly on her past career, "It's all right to be out of the kid business."

"When you have a career choice to make and someone advises you that one is more practical than another," says Anthony, "go with your dream because you've got a lot invested in it already."

Leaving the store, we are clutching Lindberg's prints of Susan B. Anthony and copies of the last three newsletters, but we also have our intangibles.

"Sometimes it takes a rainy day/just to let you know everything's gonna be all right." Cris Williamson's music and lyrics flood out into the street and the door of Mother Courage clangs noisily behind us, but even the rain feels a little bit warmer.

Chapter 4

Jan on January 29, 1979

I hope I made my dad proud because Lakeshore Med's *synergy* magazine and the annual report/calendar insert, "Lakeshore Medical Center Is in the Black" won a Southeastern Ad Club Award for Excellence for Bea's and my work from the previous year when Bea still worked with me at the hospital.

Barney Anthony is our city's premier parade float builder and sign painter who's been a long-time member of the Ad Club. I remember many special events he created with his high-salaried advertising buddies from the big manufacturers. When I entered the contest, I considered our hospital magazine *synergy* to be great enough to compete favorably with other manufacturing and business magazines, so I treated myself to a ticket to the awards banquet where all the exhibits would be on display.

Ironically, the day before I submitted my entry, a sales rep from an Elmwood agency stopped by my office to let me know how his consulting firm could serve my hospital. In his presentation, he showed St. Agnes annual report and told me that a Madison firm wrote the copy "and the St. Agnes PR man did the photos." Big deal!

My printer, Print-Line, also printed St. Agnes publication and is a printer that I've always valued as the most competent short-run printer in the area. The company started in a little house two blocks from my hospital, and a married couple and their staff became close work teammates and friends.

When I walked into the Ad Club's reception, I discovered the entire Print-Line crew hosting my St. Agnes cohort and his wife because Print-Line and the agency had entered St. Agnes annual report, designed and copy-written by outside agencies "…and the St. Agnes PR man did the photos."

This is the second time that my once close relationship with the Print-Line owners shut me out: a major customer but now no longer a friend since my divorce and rumored lifestyle change. I sat at an open space at another table and enjoyed the evening chatting with strangers and making new friends.

Well, Lakeshore Med's *synergy* became the first Ad Club non-member to receive an award and the only hospital entry to win.

JAN ON JANUARY 30, 1979

UW-Oshkosh's photographic intern Bob Haban began working with Carolyn Schafer and me for several hours a week this semester and we really need him to fill Bea's photographic talents.

Bea and I made quite a team before she was "let go" from Lakeshore Med after we bought our home and moved in together. A mystery Personnel rule that was never shown to me in writing that prohibited a supervisor and an employee from living together, but Bea had to leave her hospital job working with me and find other employment.

Now we moved desks around to make more space for Bob in Carolyn's and my little office. For Bob, we'll be getting more ventilation into the little dark room with its photo processing chemicals and where Bea said she almost killed herself once when she farted. He'll learn a lot working with us taking photos for new publications, displays and exhibits, fairs and open houses coming up now and within the year.

Carolyn's warmth, cheerfulness and creativity makes our department whole again after Bea's leaving. In addition to her many responsibilities at the office as my new assistant, Carolyn will be happily creating twenty-five individual department banners over the next year with an appropriate symbol for each unit to have them ready by the dedication and open house of the new hospital building. They will hang majestically in the new cafeteria and herald in grand style our total hospital renovation project. Of course she has to do this at home with a sewing machine, ironing board and whatever, so she can also earn a lot of comp time hours to be with her lover when Roger's in the area. Carolyn's a divorced mother with six teenagers, and she deserves someone special to love her. And I love lovers.

Carolyn and I acquired other new team members to work with, or to work for. One of The Dynamic Duo is the unpredictable and lively Laura Williams, RN, who's initiating community health education programs and support groups. She's a whirlwind go-getter. Her cohort is clever Pat Holmen, RN, a wildly humorous cynic who loves to teach health and wellness, a new hospital marketing trend. Both women are unique characters and enthusiastic buddies since their nursing school days. Pat Holmen's theme song could be from the Gypsy musical, "Let Me Entertain You."

Laura's personality may be captured only by the contrast of two song lyrics.

"Hey, mambo! Mambo Italiano!
Hey, mambo! Mambo Italiano
Go, go, go you mixed up Sicialiano…
Just make-a wid da beat, bambino,
It's a like a vino.
Kid, you good a lookin' but you don't a-know what's cookin' till you—
Hey Mambo, Mambo Italiano . . ."
Rosemary Clooney's "Mambo Italiano"

And/or, depending on the need,

> "Spirit of life, come unto me.
> Sing in my heart all the stirrings of compassion.
> Blow in the wind' rise in the sea;
> Move in the hand, giving life the shape of justice.
> Roots hold me close; wings set me free.
> Spirit of Life, come to me, come to me."
> *by Carolyn McDade*

Laura took charge when she dashed into our office expecting immediate help in promoting their innovative programs. Sorry to report, but no one had told us about these two and their many projects, and Laura's intense enthusiasm caught us by surprise. She's ready to take on pioneering hospital territory in teaching health and wellness rather than merely treating the sick. A few years ago, I took her photo standing tall and erect over a classroom projector with its light reflecting on her face. My first impression of her was that she's too stern in her crisp white uniform with its obligatory gold nursing pin on the collar. Her trim brown haircut was curled at the ends and over her forehead in lieu of wearing the traditional nurses starched cap. She was in command. But in those days she was teaching in-service procedures to other staff nurses, correcting old and teaching new patient care procedures while setting high standards by her example.

She's taken on the physicians, too, to make them aware of the patient's point of view, and when you watch her move among them, her chocolate brown Italian eyes get their attention as she smiles and cajoles, coaxing them to understand and to actually participate in her programs. Most importantly, she's not intimidated to make physicians laugh with her while earning their respect for her enthusiastic goals and her intelligence.

Her best friend and sidekick Pat Holmen, as quick-witted and perceptive as a late night TV talk show host, is smart enough to be a physician—and she should be. Pat's educational philosophy is "If you entertain them, you can educate them." Together, they overwhelm everyone with energy that forces us to rethink, reprioritize and expand our department projects so that we all work together to benefit the patient, the hospital and the community.

Another critical factor in our working relationship among us four women is our growing camaraderie through our expanding feminist awareness. Bea and I censor ourselves about our relationship. Except for that, we four would speak freely. Along with a few other nurses, including their boss, Nursing Director Donna Durand, we could discuss women's issues. Except for Pat Holmen, we've all either been divorced or are close to it. Laura has two daughters and was divorced in 1975. She's dating someone and he has three daughters of his own.

Laura is studying for her master's degree in adult education so she's working hard starting her new wellness programs and support groups like Parents Caring and Sharing for people who have lost a child.

With their proactive community programs and our promotional skills, we will help regain our competitive edge over our constant rival, St. Agnes Hospital. Soon its new hospital will be built in its spacious "medical center" location with acres of parking spaces, and join our other competition with other hospitals and clinics near and beyond.

Jan on January 31, 1979

Through the grapevine, I found out that my exasperating boss Randy would be away for three weeks. That relieves me of undue stress from his administration and gives me easier access to our top administrator Clark Young, a true gentleman but one who can and has blown his cool on occasion. Mr. Young, however, has always credited our office for doing exceptionally fine work and he lets us know it.

I also had a long talk with Wisconsin Hospital Association's PR and marketing friend Al Carter about story ideas for the HPRW newsletter. I suggested a salary comparison for hospital PR people with other hospitals in and out of the state, their relative number of beds, PR experience and also overall comparisons of PR salaries in the healthcare industry. He knew that college grads with two years' experience might earn about $12,000 with the top range at about $30,000.

Of course, I'm especially interested in this because I feel that my "exempt from overtime" salary at $15,000 is grossly unfair, especially when they put me on a 35-hour week as a part time employee who works much longer and always has. When I became a single person after my divorce, my entire tax structure changed and I made less money doing more work while supporting my partner and myself.

Al said he would find out what he could.

I thanked him for the note he wrote "to compliment you on the winter issue of *synergy*. Good, interesting stories, especially like the insert calendar and nutritional chart. Nice cartoons by your ex-colleague, too."

"That was Bea's work, of course," I told him.

My St. Agnes PR peer Ben Tolken called to acknowledge our award and we bantered a bit about Lakeshore Med "being in the Black." I'd heard about St. Agnes administrators joking about our hospital as being in the Black—the inner city, that is. Even when I do well, I am a threat to many of them. Maybe it's because I'm a woman, and one who's become a lesbian. I'll bet Bea and I are the only woman-loving-women they know, and divorcing Alex only proves that lesbians hate men and are "ball busters."

The trips to my state hospital organization, HPRW, and then to the PR Chapter of Greater Milwaukee now frustrate me with all the tasks I'm leaving undone in the office. I hate the time it takes me to drive to other cities, especially when the meetings are routine. The president of the Milwaukee PR Chapter is a flakey elder, seems like he's eighty. I guess he's from some Milwaukee County hospital.

Also, Ben has established himself with the Milwaukee guys network because he never misses a meeting, could probably even take time off to play golf with them and network even more. While his consultants and design people are doing St. Agnes work, he's busy selling himself. There's a lot of Boy Scout buffoonery that I find disconcerting, but I have three or four hospital PR women friends to ventilate these issues.

Ben is really doing what he has to do in our political and competitive environment, and he's been pleasant and helpful to me despite the ruthless competition between our two hospitals. During some of our car-pooling together to meetings across the state, he's always seemed to treat me fairly. When Ben told me of the new St. Agnes scheduling of a Wellness Day Fair for a weekend in May or June, I told him we would need a large room, not just a booth, to demonstrate Lakeshore Med wellness programs. He wasn't exactly ready for that, but neither was I. We can't go into our major competitor hospital and have just one booth! I didn't let him know, but with Laura Williams, Pat Holmen, Carolyn, Bob and I, we'd take over their entire new hospital, or "medical center" as they now call it.

I was told that very quickly and quietly, St. Agnes had worked out a deal with the City to offer St. Agnes acres of land next to the cemetery on the western edge of town with fields of grassy space to add more buildings and parking lots in the future. In the process, St. Agnes neighbor, Jefferson Medical's manufacturing site, paid St. Agnes (I've heard about four million dollars.) for Jefferson Medical to renovate the antiquated hospital and expand its offices next to its manufacturing site. The money gave St. Agnes a hefty start to fund its new hospital in the expanding west side of town. It also gave Jefferson Medical space to stay in Lakeshore Bay and build up its facilities. What a political coup d'état!

During one of our many informal breakfast gatherings with Mr. Young in the Auxiliary Coffee Shop, he would joke about St. Agnes patients having a good view of the cemetery. We laughed with him, but some of it echoed the nervous laughter that a person could have, standing on the gallows waiting for the floor to open beneath him.

Laura and Pat frequently come bubbling into our office with grand new ideas to rally support and advance their new wellness programs to save the health of all people—and we'll have to put on our "dog and pony" show again. The School of Nursing needs promotional help to keep up recruitment, and somehow we became caught up in creating a heart sun catcher as an invitation for a physicians' Valentine's party. The OB department needs a regular newsletter to help unwed teenage mothers during their pre- and post-natal months. And, of course, it has to be cute.

And projects keep being added. Now we've created a promotion concept by constructing a fake telephone booth to go with "Supersaver," a "Superman" cost-containment campaign including Daily Planet newsletters featuring winners of cost-cutting ideas. Money was spent for coordinated t-shirts for employees who submit cost-saving ideas.

In looking back on old reports, I laughed at the long list of A, B, and C-labeled responsibilities. An "A" designated vital information, including immediate deadlines like "Get Santa for Christmas party" and a "C" was "Meet with Rollo's International Flea Circus."

With so many crucial hospital issues to be solved and communicated, including helping to save the hospital's School of Nursing's diploma program, I often moaned that I was being nibbled to death by ducks.

Yes. We have an over-all departmental plan that gets screwed up with all this extra stuff coming in and without any support or positive direction from Randy. Yet we'll do all this, and our publications, and more. We'll prove to Nick and Randy, the two male administrators just beneath Clark Young, that I am a worthy and respected member of this hospital staff, just as I was when I was a respectable married woman with children.

Jan on February 2, 1979

Matt is twenty years old today, yes, Groundhog Day. He's transferred to the UW-Madison and lives in a vegetarian co-op. He's learned to make tofu. I never heard of the stuff. That's quite a change from the bloody footsteps in the hallways of his former South Dakota men's college dorm during hunting seasons. Matt must have seen his shadow somewhere and returned to his groundhog den of his UW Badger's home state. It makes me happy to have him closer.

To finish Mother Courage's February's *Courier,* I hope to create positive energy, and more customers with a headline, "Awareness Raising." I wonder who and how many people actually read our rabble-rousing little newsletter created and mailed from our storefront feminist missionary.

"Being Rising"

In 1968 I wanted to read Simone de Beauvoir's *The Second Sex* but couldn't find it in our local bookstore, and the library owned a reference-only volume that couldn't be checked out. I had to read it there. So, for six afternoons in a row, I spent hours in the library devouring her writing. Finally, the hardcover edition that I ordered for myself arrived at Martha's Bookstore, owned by a former library lady who resides with a librarian at our public library, what you historically call, "a Boston Marriage."

The Second Sex quickly generated new energy in me. It helped me understand my discontent and I realized I was not alone. Its scholarship and intelligence gave me a proud confirmation. It gave me the courage to be an independent and self-reliant woman who could grow, hopefully, in a society where equality among men and women, once achieved, would free both sexes from the restraints placed on them by their gender roles.

Though published in the U.S. in 1952, I found the book in 1968, and now, in 1979, I look into its pages and find significant messages underlined.

"Let them [women] be provided with a living strength of their own, let them have the means to attack the world and wrest from it their own existence, and their dependency will be abolished—that of a man also…both will profit greatly from the new situation." This is but one challenge written by this French woman scholar.

Many books have been written since 1968 when women started working their way out from being the second sex. Some women realized their second-class status as envelope-stuffers and coffee makers in the Vietnam protest movement. They became angry, recognized their own strengths and began to write. De Beauvoir predicted it. "As long as she still has to struggle to become a human being, she cannot become a creator…"

"She" became Betty Friedan writing *The Feminine Mystique* that dared to suggest that middle class suburban wives aspire to more than reigning over an immaculate house.

De Beauvoir quoted Balzac who wrote, "treat her as a slave while persuading her that she is a queen."

"She" became Kate Millett writing *Sexual Politics*, a contemporary American counterpart of de Beauvoir's work. Both challenged patriarchy— revealing its purposeful control on women that causes them to fail as free and independent equals.

The energy accelerated.

"She" became the angry writers of the Second Wave of Feminism. The First Wave were feminists like Margaret Fuller, Susan B. Anthony, Olympia Brown and Elizabeth Cady Stanton. Now Mary Daly, Robin Morgan, Gloria Steinem, Adrienne Rich, Andrea Dworkin, Susan Brownmiller and more researched new information from hidden history and from new awareness of women's lives and women's histories.

Some say now that anger is definitely out and assertiveness is in. The mood is changing to "get" books for women on how to get power, muscles, and control of their lives. Whether or not the anger is "out" depends on each woman and specific issues, almost like

Kubler-Ross and her five stages of grief. Many women will always be in different states of awareness and levels of consciousness in dealing with personal angers and frustrations. Anger turned inward can become helpless depression while healthy anger can result in action and change.

The *Second Sex* was also the first thorough and rare explanation of being lesbian, a Chapter that I read with intense interest.

Simone de Beauvoir wrote about the particular frustration of the independent woman "because she has chosen battle rather than resignation." Perhaps less strident anger, the kind that does not sap energy from our lives and specific battles, will make us more understanding and supportive of each other's goals toward independence and equality.

Chapter 5

Bea on May 16, 1979

I haven't kept my little diary notes since the first of this year. I got tired of doing it every day. Betty Willing gave me this bigger book a couple of birthdays go. Now's the time to start writing about our trip.

Next Monday we are flying to California starting in San Francisco where we hope to see the city and Judy Chicago's Dinner Party exhibit together. We're also going to see my dear high school friend Liv. Then we're driving to Los Angeles to our first American Booksellers Association tradeshow and convention. I bought a new carry-on bag and lots of film to have photo memories of our adventures. It is all very exciting and I want to record as much as possible.

Bea on May 22, 1979

The Motel Marina is our San Francisco home base and Jan is studying today's newspaper, her maps and guidebooks while I begin our travel journal starting our pleasant three-and-a-half hour S.F. flight. Lunch was steak with a good cheesecake desert. I had a boilermaker before lunch served with wine and champagne—and this was a Super Saver luncheon flight.

We picked up our yellow Ford Fairmont and I navigated to the sites Jan had circled on the map while she drove us up and about. She had been here at age five because her mother's parents lived in Berkeley and again in '72 when she took Alex on her business conference trip and in '74 when he took her on his business trip.

I was in my early twenties when I drove to San Francisco in my black '49 Studebaker. Hope Smith was my passenger for the sixteen-day, 6,141-mile trip from Chicago through the great American West: Carlsbad Caverns; Juarez, Mexico; the Grand Canyon; Los Angeles and San Francisco; Lake Tahoe; Salt Lake; Yellowstone and the Black Hills. I let Hope drive for fifty miles, but when she almost drove into the back of a bus, I took over and drove all the rest of the way.

Jan's itinerary for our first San Francisco stop took me to the Embarcadero Center's pyramid-like Hyatt Regency and up the slanted elevator inside the seventeen-story Atrium. If you survived the feeling of having the building close in on you, you savored a drink at the revolving bar at the top. What a treat to view the city and plan our strategy. Then she took me to the Sherlock Holmes bar on the top of another building to have a drink in an English atmosphere. (My nickname was Sherlock because I was a Holmes before I was married.)

We parked the car and hopped a cable car down to Fisherman's Wharf, boarded *The Star of Alaska* and a great three-masted, square-rigged iron clipper ship, *The Balclutha*, a maritime museum in itself. It's great to experience those old ships and explain to Jan the functions of various parts, compartments, decks, spars and sails, ropes and riggings. I love to impress her by calling them all by name. She accused me of making up names, but I knew she was impressed with my knowledge of ships, especially when I called out the names of all the sails as briskly as I can list all the books of the Bible. I've always claimed to be a sea captain in a previous life.

We walked the wharf, shot some pictures that I may paint someday, strolled on to the causeway and through a few shops and Cost Plus, a giant Pier One store. I bought a boson's whistle as my souvenir in an authentic, not touristy, marine supply store.

Passengers helped turn the cable car around and we hopped on, back to the car and to our Motel Marina that Jan had reserved in advance. There's a garage on the ground floor and we sleep in an airy, open-windowed room above.

After our martinis in our room, Jan drove us for supper at the Marrakech, a romantic Moroccan restaurant that she found in her guidebook research. Thick Oriental carpets embellished the walls and layers on the floor the large but intimate room. Brass lampshades set with colored stones hung low enough to center each area on patrons sitting on low benches and hammered, copper tray-top tables. Each cozy area with pillows around us created an intimate spot in the larger room.

We ate practically sitting on the floor and—without utensils. Before the meal, a woman Jan described as wearing a bathrobe came to help us wash our hands and gave us a bath towel for a napkin. We'd need it. We used our fingers or scooped up the exotic food with flat bread that came from a coolie-hatted basket. Would there'd be a cobra in the basket. The aromatic atmosphere of saffron, cinnamon and paprika blended with honey and lemon to fill our senses with heady expectation. We practiced eating with our fingers on a salad with a relish texture and mildly spicy, warm and flaky pastry filled with rice and chickpeas, chicken and almonds. The main course was tender honey lamb with divine juices.

Everything had been sensually marinated with careful attentions to sweet and spicy flavors, "Musky and lusty," Jan whispered as she put bits of food into my mouth and I could lick the juices from her fingertips.

Everyone in the room hit it off as we sprawled on the giant pillows and exchanged banter among those of us who immersed themselves into the exotic experience. It didn't matter, it seemed, that we were two women, a couple perhaps. This is San Francisco.

Then our waiter, wearing a traditional Moroccan droopy-drawers outfit, brought us an artfully arranged fruit platter and surprised us by pouring steaming mint tea in a spectacular flourish, creating a slender hot waterfall from three feet above poured into the tiny cups below without missing a drop and bringing appreciative applause from the others in the room.

We hated to lift up our satiated bodies from the cushions where we felt like we could have spent the night, but we were on a quest to find the famous women-only bars listed in the gay and/or hippie-based *Gaia's Guide*. Ho! Ho! The first one fit the dive-firetrap category, and luckily it was closed. Jan would have wanted to go in and we could have had an argument about that.

Castro Street had absolutely nothing going on with hardly a soul on the street, a few cars stopping at traffic lights—nothing like we'd heard or imagined it to be. We finally found the second bar we were looking for after going further to see the Cliff House on the Pacific Ocean near Seal Rock. We had to stop there for a drink because Jan remembered being there as a child excited by the seals that are still on the rocks below.

Finally we found Peg's Place-A Woman's Club, the famous lesbian bar, but only a star or two above our Milwaukee's Sugar Stop's women's bar ambience, less seedy and larger with side rooms. As we walked in, two women sitting at the massive bar stared at the TV showing some cars on fire. We had no idea why they had that news on the TV. And the woman bartender was preoccupied and not the least bit friendly. A couple more dykes were playing pool in one of the other rooms. After our shot and a beer we went home for a nightcap and to bed after an extremely long day. But what a dead town for the gay crowd! It was nothing we had dreamed it to be!

The TV morning news was stunning.

Last night we had driven on Castro Street *after* hundreds of people finished their demonstration and started their protest march. We missed the typical Castro Street atmosphere because gays, lesbians and their friends had marched down Market Street to City

Hall where their frustration and anger exploded over the news that Dan White was given a lenient jail sentence for his blatant shooting of openly gay Supervisor Harvey Milk and San Francisco Mayor George Moscone on November 27, 1978. The murderer only got a second-degree manslaughter sentence with a maximum length of seven years—for killing two people, the mayor and a city supervisor—a gay supervisor. White's defense claimed that he was so depressed before he shot them and had pigged out on junk food that caused a mental condition that made him crazed. The media said, "Twinkies made him do it."

Except for glancing at last night's TV at Peg's Place, we were deaf and mute strangers standing on the edge, completely unaware of the chaos going on in the city we were visiting.

Shock! Twelve police cars were set afire, gays had rioted and police had clubbed them. The motel TV showed last night's torched police cars, sirens screeching and lights swirling around the civilians and uniformed police beating on each other—turning this beautiful city into an urban battleground. We looked at each other in disbelief—and in gratitude that we didn't get caught up in the bedlam that the immediately appointed Mayor Dianne Feinstein was trying to subdue.

Not intimidated about how closely we came to this rioting, we followed our plan to go north from the city. Mentally we were still on Central Time so it was early in the morning when we started off across the Golden Gate Bridge for Tiburon and Sausalito. Again there was hardly any traffic. We stopped briefly at the bridge's base below the Presidio to take some artsy pictures. I drove across it so Jan could enjoy her customary "bridge euphoria"—a big rush for her crossing the grandest bridge over a most magnificent land and seascape.

We stopped at Muir Woods and walked peacefully through the redwood forest with awe-inspiring appreciation for Mother Nature. Then in a little cafe overlooking the bay in Sausalito, we stopped for espresso and a croissant, looked in a few shops, bought a rooted baby redwood tree in a plastic envelope and California poppy seeds

to take home. We went on to a salvage marine warehouse in Tiburon
to look for a hatch cover that we could use as our bed headboard.
The place was closed but a young man let us in. He didn't have any
thing for us but I got some creative ideas seeing the seafaring gear
and hardware that I could name and remember from all the nautical
books I've read in my life.

We headed for Sam's Anchor Cafe in Tiburon, opened the
narrow front doorway, walked toward the light at the back of the
room and stepped out onto the broad deck and bright sunshine with
a knock-out view of San Francisco, Oakland and Berkeley, the
bridges, low-flying sea gulls, sailboats and rusty old Alcatraz in the
center of the bay with its fresh water smells mixed with the saltwater
air of the Pacific Ocean. Sam's deck was ours alone. We ordered a
bottle of champagne that came in an ice bucket and we drank it with
many toasts to our good fortune. When our luncheon arrived, Jan's
eye glasses fogged up as she leaned her chin over her silly lobster
bib to peer into a cauldron of steamy pink clams and various
crustaceans with heads and eyeballs, spindly feelers, dozens of legs,
tails and all. She tore them apart with passionate fingers, sucking on
the shells to consume every morsel between sips of our champagne.
I used a fork and enjoyed my delicious American red snapper.

After this bodacious lunch, we drove back to San Francisco
stopping at the first gas oasis. A gas shortage recently caused long
lines and angry customers. It was no problem for us because we had
a receipt for our rented car and a green flag to fill up our tank.

Somehow Jan maneuvered the car through the city streets to the
spot where so many tourists flock. She surprised me! "Jeez, Jan!"
She shot the car right over the edge and down the crooked, sharp,
hairpin turns of Lombard Street.

When we headed to the Civic Center area for Judy Chicago's
The Dinner Party exhibit at the San Francisco Museum of Art, we
realized the extent of last night's rioting but the area was calm and
orderly now. The civil defense alert brought more police and, except
for some boarded-up windows on City Hall, the area was quiet, yet
you could still smell metallic smoke. We parked right in front of the
museum, probably because most normal people stayed away.

"Look over there," and Jan pointed to a helmeted and fully armed National Guardsmen with rifles standing at attention around the City Hall. We passed through four policemen wearing riot gear and holding long billy clubs who seemed casual about their assignment to guard Judy Chicago's work and the art museum.

The Dinner Party was more than we imagined. An awesome pilgrimage. Phenomenal. We knew many of the details of her work because we'd heard Judy Chicago speak and show slides of the project at a Wisconsin Women in the Arts conference in Green Bay and we had studied Chicago's book, *The Dinner Party, A Symbol of Our Heritage*, with its ingenious formatting and dramatic photographs. But the experience of entering the satiny, colorful, banner-lined narrow corridor made this a sacred journey of being reborn into the newly acknowledged history of womankind. As we waited to enter, we could read Chicago's words and I can remember some of it that especially struck home to me. "…And then all will cherish life's creatures/ And then all will live in harmony with each other and the Earth/ And then everywhere will be called Eden once again."

We turned the corner to enter a dark, enormous room free of pillars to support the ceiling. The illuminated white triangle, each of the sides perhaps fifty feet long held thirteen table settings totaling thirty-nine majestic places set for dinner guests. It seemed suspended from its base and rose to infinity from the black museum floor. It did feel, as others described it to be, like the Sistine Chapel of the Women's Movement. More than a tribute to 1,038 women who have been lost in Western culture's male-dominated history, it is a monumental honor to the achievements and contributions of all women.

It took Chicago five years and four-hundred co-workers and volunteers to complete the research, the sacred, singularly created symbolic vaginal dinner plates, glittering pure white table utensils and goblets rising from individually designed and exceptionally matched embroidered table linens for each woman's hallowed place of honor.

What an enormous research responsibility it must have been to decide which women to choose as guests at the table or to be honored as the 999 golden names of women of achievement written on the triangular white, shiny Heritage Floor that held the tables. Plus, Chicago wrote books to capture the grand scale of her art so huge that curators say it can't be shown in most museums, but Chicago's books will continue to tell the story.

Moving reverently in line, we began with the Primordial Goddess with her foxy-colored flat plate and animal fur table runner decorated with shells. She's followed by the Fertile Goddess and fertility goddess figures like the *Goddess of Willendorf,* an icon of prehistoric art, a symbol of the sacredness and power of fertility. These initial plates grow and evolve around the triangle table as well as with each plates' vulva symbols and end with Georgia O'Keeffe's subdued pink ochre's earthly muted shades of the ceramic plate swirling and swelling from its creative center—and each with its own unique design and finite needlepoint table runner.

Awestruck and inspired, Jan whispered, "I sense a spiritual humming as if a choir was chanting from the wings of an ancient cathedral."

We didn't want to leave. There was so much to absorb, to experience and to learn, but the line kept us moving slowly, as in a processional that eventually pulled us away from the sanctuary and out the door. We spoke quietly about *The Dinner Party.* It gave us a powerful sense of self and a stronger dedication to advancing ourselves with a dedication to correcting the injustices embedded in women's history and today's issues and in our personal lives.

When Jan was browsing through the morning newspaper, she saw a small notice about the presence of the original Venus of

Willendorf. "Bea!" Jan exclaimed, "*The Goddess of Willendorf* is at the California Academy of Sciences in the Golden Gate Park and we can see her and *The Dinner Party* on the same day!"

Our feminist scholars call her "Goddess," but her archeologist discoverer and male scholars classified her only as "Venus." She is one of the oldest statues of The Great Mother, found in Willendorf, Austria, and dated from 30,000 to 5000 BCE.

Arriving just before the science museum closed, we ran up the broad marble stairway under huge billowing banners and tumbled immediately into a stately hall exhibiting these sacred ancient artifacts, a traveling display that would grace this area for only a few more weeks. And there, in the center stood *The Goddess of Willendorf*, almost five inches tall with huge breasts and buttocks. She was balanced on a thin silver rod in the midst of a rectangular marble base within a six-foot glass case for all to witness every nuance of her ancient sacred image. Small enough to carry in the palm your hand, her featureless face, covered by several braided clay rings, make her look almost humble yet its image is one that we can relate to as ourselves rather than seeing another's face. As her naked body stands under the lights, she glorifies a uniquely bountiful, fertile woman covered in red ochre pigment—like aged menstrual blood.

While taking many photos, I bent down to view her from below. Her fertile crescent beneath her belly was clearly marked. She is so small, yet she projects a huge presence. Her tender little arms rest across her huge, nurturing breasts that cover her bulbous hips and buttocks that smoothly taper down her joined legs to what remains of primitive feet as if someone ages ago could plant her in the soft earth of an ancient ritual circle.

What a gift to see her original Mother Earth self. She is Earth and the Earth's capacity to create and recreate life. Her curves remind me of my "Mother Earth song, "…Lake and hill, can't get my fill of your Sweet land, your sea and sand, your trees and sky, your mountains high."

<<◇>>

Jan took me to the Mission Dolores where her parents took her as a child and where her mother told her that her middle name was chosen from this mission as the Lady of Sorrow. While still in elementary school, Jan altered that. Her mother's spelling always bothered her, she said, because she was born just months after of her parents' great sorrow at the loss of her mother's eight-year-old son who was hit by a car and died—and she had seen it happen. Later when Jan found her birth certificate with her middle name spelled "Delores," she felt better about it. I told her "Delores" means "Lady of Delight," but I don't think it has any different meaning. We'll look it up sometime.

We visited the Old Wives Tales bookstore nearby. We browsed, talked a bit and were surprised when we weren't greeted with a big welcome for a rare couple of lesbian booksellers from Wisconsin who had actually read about this store and came out of their way to come here. The clerk was definitely unimpressed—even a little unfriendly. We brought a couple items and left uninspired by our colleague among our growing women's bookstores network.

We checked out of Motel Marina and made our way to my old friend Liv's home in Hillsbourgh. I hadn't seen her in years. We'd planned to stop in a gas station to change our clothes from our zippered jackets, t-shirts and jeans to something dressier, but there are no gas stations in her elite suburb, so we rang her doorbell, scruffy and too early, but Voila! our reunion was welcoming and warm. We stood in the kitchen and I could sense Liv's tension, not knowing exactly what to say while she prepared dinner. Could she have felt awkward about my relationship with Jan who politely stood about the kitchen waiting until she was offered a seat? Liv and I finally started to laugh, especially when we opened one of our gift bottles of wine and after her psychiatrist husband got home and served us Bloody Marys.

They collect elaborate porcelain figurines of all sizes, even as tall as four feet. The priceless art pieces stood in freestanding glass display cases as well as on the grand piano and in cabinets. And what about earthquake tremors? It wouldn't take much to knock these over. Jan said she was almost afraid to move for fear she'd trip and knock one down. But their big dogs weren't nervous. Liv always loved her dogs. They had no children.

What a great surprise for me! Liv's parents were visiting from Norway and when they joined us, we all had fun sitting around a great dining room table near a vast window with a view across the bay toward San Francisco. They almost cried with laughter remembering times when Liv and I were teens, and when I would hang around and pretend to read the Norwegian paper. My mimic skills came back and I could still make the sounds of reading that Norwegian newspaper to them.

Wine was served again with a delicious dinner and after being swept back in time to our teens, we all realized why we had been such good friends. Jan told me later that our visit gave her insight to my youth. She felt like she was a teenager with me that night and during the years of that wonderful relationship that Liv, her parents and I shared.

It was getting late and Jan called her friend to see if we would still be welcome to stay at Maria Grassi's ranch near La Honda. She is Jan's artist friend from college and they've kept in touch, including a couple visits while Jan was still married to Alex. After college Maria earned a Fulbright scholarship to study art in Italy, married an Italian and got pregnant. She's divorced now and her ex-husband married her sister. Her son is exceptionally bright and attends the best schools. Maria teaches art in Redwood City and she and her guy Paul renovated and sold a Victorian house in San Francisco and bought this octagon home in the country with three dogs, ten cats and a coop full of chickens. We talked for a while but I dozed off so we went to bed at last in a nice room to ourselves, except for a flea or two that Jan didn't tell me about until we left. Maria wasn't surprised that I was there with Jan because Jan hinted to her at their last meeting a couple years back that Jan had a new appreciation of women. Of course, she also knew via mail that Jan was now divorced and about of our Mother Courage Bookstore and our business partnership—and she can guess about the rest.

In the morning, we talked more, ate breakfast and met all Maria's animals, including the chickens. She and her Paul had to go to work and we were off to Carmel by the Sea. What a drive. We stopped at Pigeon Point lighthouse that I had painted twice from a photograph but had never actually seen. The coastal drive south to Los Angeles on Highway 1 along Big Sur and the Pacific Ocean was perfection, especially driving south on the ocean side of the road with grand views and occasional homes build on stilts hanging off the cliffs with the surf below.

We stopped in Monterey for a late lunch of squid for me and cod for Jan and we found a cushy motel room in Carmel, our special destination where Jan has always wanted to visit. We took a stroll on the beach with its incredible white sand and, as touted in travel magazines, couples riding horses as the sun set across the Pacific. We went to a shopping center to visit the huge Thunderbird Bookstore and stopped at a "watering hole" where we could sit on antique couches and sofas and get the feel of a classy old California saloon. We had a beer and home to bed.

Jan really got turned on after the delightfully romantic sites and scenery, and the fresh, salty ocean air surrounding us in our bed among piles of soft pillows and downy bedding. Carmel-By-The-Sea will always be another orgasmic night to remember.

This Thursday we stopped in Point Lobos after we did more Western-styled shops in Carmel and found pewter wine goblets to buy and a box lunch to eat along the shore through Big Sur country! We stopped near a cliffside edge with our wine in our goblets and our box lunch of cheese, ham, bread, even a crispy pickle and an unobstructed ocean view beneath us watching the sand being caressed by the gentle rhythm of foaming waves flowing across and soothing the beaches and gently splashing and playing against the rocks and cliffs. Wow!

On the road again to San Simeon, we settled into our motel after beach combing and a fresh seafood dinner nearby where I ate abalone and Jan had clam stuffed sole. We swam in the motel's warm pool along the Pacific Ocean and relaxed before bed.

After breakfast we experienced the Hearst estate. It boggles the mind. Any description of the vastness of the grounds with originally fifty miles of shoreline, or the opulence of the mansion and the guesthouses and the indoor and outdoor swimming pools challenges my vocabulary. The pictures we've taken should do that job. Jan imagined being among the movie stars who visited there, and she said I had to be Errol Flynn or someone else with a moustache. We wondered how many of these famous actors and actresses were gay in more than the gleeful sense of the word.

After the tour we headed down the coast to Santa Barbara to make my birthday pilgrimage by touring through the mission to Saint Barbara where a giant fig tree has grown for centuries. We chose a charming Mexican restaurant for lunch in nearby Montecito and ate in the garden. Jan learned a new Spanish word when she ordered a diablo sandwich—Hot! She was almost in tears but ate it all. I had delicious stuffed not-too-hot jalapenos. Of course, we needed margaritas and Mexican beer.

Finally reaching L.A., we checked in at our pre-registered and least expensive ABA-recommended motel near the convention site. The clerk asked us what kind of bed we wanted: twins, single, doubles, queen, king or a waterbed? A waterbed! Jan insisted that we try it. She's always wanted to sleep in one, she pleaded, so I reluctantly went along. When we entered the room with our bags, we collapsed after our long drive and undulated with the warm waves beneath us. "Oh, my God! There's a mirror on the ceiling."

"Hey. I've always wanted to sleep in a bed with a mirror on the ceiling," laughed Jan, and she surged over to me, cresting right on top of my weary bones.

"Not now, Jan!" and I got up to find the cocktail fixings. "It's been a long drive and I want to relax before I collapse like a body washed up on the beach."

Of course, Jan is always enthusiastic, seldom tires and has plans to make my birthday supper memorable, so after a few drinks we headed to New Chinatown for dinner. We parked and walked to look for a restaurant where we had to have a hot sake and ate another delicious meal served at a table overlooking an oriental plaza and pagoda roofs. All was fine, but I had had it. Jan said something about going someplace else and I had to stop. I guess I was too loud or too sharp with her and hurt her feelings again. Gads. Doesn't she know when to let up on me? She'll blame me again for being moody. It's always my fault!

Well, I paid the bill and Jan quietly drove us to our flamingo-pink, lurid and mirrored waterbed motel room. What a birthday! "Home" to sleep at last. Well for a while at least.

We both bounced about fretfully in our halves of the bed. I was so hot I assumed I was having hot flashes and I didn't want anyone to touch me. Jan said the waterbed was too cold and sucking the warmth from her body and she needed to snuggle. I suppose I was rude in pushing her off of me, so when she surged off the bed to stomp and search for a blanket, she discovered I had a temperature control on my side which I continually turned down because I was so hot and that each of us had separate controls that she turned up because she was so cold. What a fiasco!

After sprawling naked on the floor on each side to swap controls under the bed, we saw ourselves in the mirror. Well, there's no use wasting a perfectly good (and rare) ceiling mirror opportunity, so we kissed and made up and had a little undulating 2 a.m. respite. But it was hard to concentrate on what our bodies were feeling because of how beautifully distracting our images appeared and entertained us. We finally dropped off to sleep again, but in the morning, we changed our room to one with a king-sized bed—with nothing out of the ordinary on the ceiling.

Saturday, our first day at the ABA, started with the Book and Author breakfast at the Bonaventure Hotel several blocks away from the Convention Center. I had made and paid for all the reservations weeks ago. The shuttle busses were crowded so we walked to the expensive high-rise, glass-enclosed hotel where we found the vast banquet hall filled with hundreds of book people. We picked out a table and chatted a bit with our friendly tablemates among the clatter of dozens of penguin-dressed waiters serving hot breakfasts to hundreds of people.

An undercurrent of mumbling surrounded us, but we didn't know what they were talking about until the ABA chairman announced that there would be a minute of silence for those persons lost in yesterday's airplane accident.

Jan nudged me and pointed to someone's newspaper on the floor under his chair. Its headline read, "273 killed in O'Hare crash."

The silence was broken with the announcement that 21 persons who were to attend the ABA were among those killed when DC 10, #191 from Chicago to Los Angeles crashed killing all 273 aboard immediately after taking off from O'Hare. We looked at each other with a shared gratitude, sensing that if we hadn't taken off for a vacation trip to San Francisco a week earlier and opted for an efficient business trip to the ABA, we could have actually been on that plane.

Ironically, after breakfast was cleared the speakers started to entertain us. I'm sure entertainment was irrelevant to ABA people who knew those who were lost in the crash, yet speakers from the industry brought our minds back to business. Steve Martin, a new comedian, had a tough job after that fateful announcement, but his crazy body moves and wild wit made everyone laugh so hard we were reenergized to take on the ABA.

What a crush to get on a convention shuttle bus and we just made it to the "first timers'" orientation. Then we went to a session for recently opened bookstores and we almost led the discussion with our experiences and accomplishments. We met an Australian author, feminist and magazine editor and her friend, another Australian woman. A couple from California completed our table and we had a productive discussion learning from each other.

Finally we hit the convention floor for the first time. Wow! It's so huge! Books. Books. Books everywhere. Colors! Banners! Elaborate displays! Freebies galore!

We searched our ABA program index and floor map for our top priorities including WIND and the women publishers like Daughters, Inc., Diana Press, Naiad and The Feminist Press at The City University of New York (CUNY), a flagship of the U.S. women's movement founded by Florence Howe. Those were among the few exhibits we could readily find. Diana Press also operates a commercial print shop so East Coast women's publishers need not depend on male-owned printers. Many of the male-owned presses are reluctant to reveal their skills or they put their women's book projects on a low priority, especially since the jobs are usually low-volume short runs—and the owners of banks are unwilling to extend credit to the women's publishing projects.

We met several authors at their publishers' booths whose books we have been reading and selling at Mother Courage. Jan gazed down upon a small woman in the Daughters, Inc. booth and when her eyes focused on the woman's nametag, Jan almost visibly jumped up with excitement. It was June Arnold who had written *The Cook and the Carpenter*, the book with the same goal as Jan's attempt at a gender-free novel using, for example, new pronouns: tey, ter and tem.

"June Arnold!" she sputtered. "Bea," she pulled on me, "This is June Arnold who wrote the other androgynous novel." Arnold was a bit overwhelmed by Jan's enthusiasm until Jan explained that both of them tried to solve the problems of gender inequity by experimenting with pronouns and gender-free language. "But you," said Jan grabbing her counterpart's hand and shaking it, "you actually wrote and published your book."

Experimenting with an un-sex-differentiated third person pronoun: na, nan, naself, Arnold, as the Carpenter character, said she felt that her project might not have worked, "…the differences between men and women are so obvious to all," she laughed.

June Arnold's friendly reaction kept them talking at length. Both of them married their college boyfriends and had children: June, four and Jan, two. But after June was divorced, she went to live in Greenwich Village with her children and made important connections in the feminist/lesbian movement. Based on the movies and novels she'd read years ago, Jan's dreamed that she'd live in Greenwich Village, but how would that have changed all of our lives if she had?

Daughters, Inc. started in 1973, publishing Arnold's books and Bertha Harris and other lesbian authors and poets, but especially 70,000 copies of Rita Mae Brown's *Rubyfruit Jungle* during its first years of publishing. Unlike lesbian novels of the past, Brown told no tragic tales. No suicides. What an important book! As a lesbian, Brown's Molly Bolt is proud and out—undaunted and uncompromising.

Altogether, Daughters, Inc. displayed some thirty titles since they started in 1973 including *Sister Gin*, Arnold's best-known work. Some say it's difficult to read with its experimental format that includes controversial subjects for lesbians: alcoholism, weight problems, infidelity; and she makes her complex characters totally human without glossing over their flaws. We stocked several of Daughters, Inc. books in our store. Jan found out later from another bookseller that Daughters, Inc. had declared bankruptcy last year but they're working hard to survive. Sometimes it's dangerous for a small company to stretch its finances for a winning project like *Rubyfruit Jungle* or to publish too many titles that put it into debt.

I moved on to WIND—Women In Distribution, a new feminist book distributor for feminist booksellers to unify and simplify the efforts of feminist writers and publishers from the U.S., Canada and all over the world so that booksellers like us can find women's resources from a single source. I hope it works. It's difficult to keep up with the tidal wave of feminist and lesbian writing and publishing.

WIND gave us an invitation to a cocktail party tonight at Arlene Raven's home that she shared with another *Chrysalis* editor whose name I forgot. Raven! What a name. I wonder if she renamed herself like many women are doing. But Raven is so much more meaningful than Beardwomon, Dykewomon, Sequoia, Seabreeze and what have you. Judy Chicago changed her name. Jan should be happy I didn't change my name to Bea Bay.

We did our best to find and visit the small presses to meet the women in print that we read about in our little bookstore in Lakeshore Bay. We met Barbara Grier and Donna McBride of Naiad Press who'd phone me on a regular basis about their new books. We met women from Shameless Hussey Press, the first feminist press started by Alta in her garage in 1969. Jan liked the name of Down There Press founded by Joni Blank with her *Playbook for Women about Sex*. Blank's store in San Francisco sells vibrators, sex toys and books. We read of her Good Vibrations store and wanted to check out the store in San Francisco but we ran out of time. Some presses shared display tables staffed to promote only one or two books.

One basic table was staffed with casually dressed women with short-cropped hair, butch-style or bald dykes from *The Lesbian Connection* who started a bi-monthly magazine in 1974 for, by and about lesbians. They sent us copies to hand out as soon as we opened the store and never sent us a bill. Most of them are volunteers dedicated to connect lesbians from around the world with their simple, stapled typewriter and mimeographed format. Their basic costs are low, but postage costs and general organization skills are critical to keep them going at their headquarters in East Lansing, Michigan. Their issues come in plain brown envelopes with the return address as Elsie Publishing. No mention of the publication's real title. Their energy and dedication seems to be working and benefiting all of us. Jan nudged me and nodded toward the green spike-haired dyke wearing a matching dog collar, a man's tank top undershirt without sleeves that helped to display her tattoos.

In contrast to *The Lesbian Connection's* format are the gay guys' slick display booths and stylishly formatted magazines that have been established for years. Their bigger-than-life male model displays of graphic and larger-than-life genitalia challenged our sensibilities—and we're no prudes, yet they have the right to free speech that we all expect to have. It was strange to have pictures of male genitalia hanging out and about when across the aisle were publishers like Ruth Goldstein's Volcano Press who published Del Martin's *Battered Wives*, the first book written in the U.S. about domestic violence. Of course, many of the gay and women-owned presses offered serious, important books too, as do several university presses that publish gay and lesbian academic books and journals.

All these resources affirmed our decision to distribute this important feminist and some lesbian information through our Mother Courage Bookstore, even though I like to describe it as an all-purpose general bookstore.

We allowed the vast ocean of giant publishers' aisles of displays, books and freebies on the convention's main floors to consume us. By the time we were through, mentally and physically, and had collected bags of free books, some autographed, it was 5 p.m. and closing time.

After dragging our loot on the shuttle back to our motel stop, had our martinis, cheese and bread, we rested a bit to get ready for our L.A. drive to the *Chrysalis* party at Arlene Raven's home. We found it right away in a rather run-down but clean neighborhood. Her house sat back from the street with a somewhat haphazard garden filling the space of the wrought-iron fence surrounding it. Opening the garden gate under a vine-covered trellis, we passed the arid garden with large succulent plants flourishing among ornamental grasses growing in a gravely groundcover. It wasn't haphazard; it was perfect for this climate. We walked up the wooden porch steps of the large, square, two-story frame Victorian-style house in need of some fresh paint. Colorful freshly cut flowers burst from vases on porch tables. The door was open but we knocked hesitantly with our WIND invitation in hand.

Were we too early? Too eager? I suppose, but a friendly woman greeted us, introduced herself, escorted us to the hors d'oeuvre and wine table and invited us to make ourselves comfortable. She asked to be excused so she could help in the kitchen. Jan whispered that she was probably Raven's lover. Honestly. Jan now thinks everyone's a lesbian.

We weren't the first to arrive. Others milled about, but right after getting a glass of wine, the room attracted our attention more than the people.

Brightly colored walls, different in each room filled with creatively painted furniture could still not compete with the illuminated paintings hanging on the walls and ceramic and sculpture on display with the artist's name posted next to each piece. Women's art. A woman's own art museum. Jan stared in disbelief and collected me from the wine carafe to come with her to see genuine Judy Chicago paintings hanging in someone's home. Together we toured the downstairs rooms and studied the personal collection of our host Raven, the dynamic feminist art historian and educator who co-founded and edits *Chrysalis*, the most graphically beautiful and readable intellectual and artistic feminist magazine.

It was her *Chrysalis* journal that had inspired us to do programs at church and for our own edification with articles by Adrienne Rich, Mary Daly and more profound women writers, scholars and artists, many who invoked the Goddess in their work. Of all the exhibitors at the ABA, we had gone to the WIND booth today and they invited us to this place. We are blessed to be here.

The room was filling up with artists and book people from the feminist network. Jan turned and saw two older women sitting together and dressed in conservative pantsuits like we wear. "Gads, Bea, that's Del Martin and her life-partner, the one with the glasses—ah, Lyon—Phyllis Lyon. They're the two that started Daughters of Bilitis in the 1950s."

"I don't keep up with all that stuff."

"You know. It started as a social group, named after one of Sappho's lovers, organized for women who were tired of hanging around in bars, especially because the bars would get raided by the police and their names would be printed in the newspapers and then they could lose their jobs. And those two women wrote *The Ladder*, the leading lesbian newsletter of all time. They work together to write books and are struggling with NOW to initiate political action for all women, including lesbians. They're probably the most famous lesbian couple in the world."

"Beside us, that is."

"But they've been together since the early 1950s and have set an example of positive and respected lesbian coupleness."

Jan dragged me over to meet them. We told them about us and they encouraged us to keep up our good work in the Midwest. Of course, like an avid fan, Jan told them we have their books in our store.

Every head turned when Z (for Zsuzanna) Budapest, the High Priestess of the Susan B. Anthony Coven No.1, entered the room dressed in a softly flowing white, floor-length Grecian Goddess gown with a golden rope coiling from her neck, crossing between her breasts, wrapping around her waist and trailing on her gown flowing to the floor. Her short hair was curled above another golden cord around her head to emphasize her up-turned, challenging eyebrows. Her gypsy eyes, shimmering with blue eye shadow highlighted with black mascara, lit her mischievous smile and her crafty, vibrant, youthful face as she nodded to friends about the room. One huge golden amber ring rode on her left hand and a similarly dressed young woman in a lavender pastel gown held her right hand. Z's disciple maidens in varied attire, including a couple of teens in torn jeans, came behind them and when she sat down, the maidens sat in a circle beneath her or stood behind her.

What an entrance. What a ritual presentation of this daring person who escaped from Communist Hungary in the mid-1950s to make her way to the U.S. and, infused with her mother's witchy Hungarian legacy, started the Dianic Goddess movement in L.A. with her goal—to spread the Goddess movement around the world via women-only ritual covens.

Her friends brought her food and wine as if she were a high priestess. I tried not to drop my jaw at this remarkable sight. Her *Themis* newsletter comes to our store so we know who she is. We are waiting for her first book, Holy Book of Women's Mysteries, to be printed so we can learn more about pagan holidays, women-centered basic witchy rituals and ceremonies from her scholarship and her European legacy.

Maybe we will see her and talk with her when we go to her Feminist Wicca store in Venice tomorrow.

The high-pitched volume of determined women's voices stopped when Raven was introduced to speak to her guests. We learned that she co-founded L.A.'s Woman's Building in 1973 with Judy Chicago and another woman who had started the Feminist Studio Workshop earlier to give a voice to women artists. The Women's Building is a place women work within a woman's image of the world. Raven taught art history there and founded the Lesbian Art Project to promote work by and about lesbian artists.

"Arlene is one of the earliest women to begin to write women back into art history," said the speaker, "and her primary voice is through *Chrysalis*, the most influential magazine of women's culture."

And the beautiful Arlene Raven entered the room, her long, flowing black hair gave more meaning to her name. She spoke to us as significantly important women in this revolutionary era and how we are going to change the world, to transform it into a utopia of justice and equality.

I can't quote her directly but I remember her challenging us to work with our brains and our guts. Their new school and the Woman's Building started with nothing, no money or equipment but somehow they did it. And now the first issues of *Chrysalis* are circulating and she asked for support to make it a long-lasting influence for women's culture.

She was stunningly beautiful and dynamic. And she needed funds to make all this work. So do we. So does everyone in the Women's Movement.

Somehow these women like Judy Chicago and their co-conspirators find the support and the power to fight the male-dominated art world and have the energy to organize women volunteers to help. Judy Chicago created Womanhouse where women completely renovated a filthy old house as a work of women's art with rooms representing the woman's condition like the pink "Nurturant Kitchen" with boobs like fried eggs decorating the walls and ceiling that Chicago used to illustrate in her autobiography, *Through the Flower, My Struggle as a Woman Artist*.

Raven told how somehow they also pulled together enough funding and women's energy to create space where painters, poets and performance artists and others rehabbed an old factory into place for women living and working with another vision of the world.

She invited us to visit the building and attend the next program tomorrow night with two women speakers, one a scholar speaking on the Goddess.

Then came the main purpose of the evening—the support of *Chrysalis* as national feminist magazine. We have the first issues at the store and Jan and I devour the articles that interest each of us. Just the name was inspiring, as well as the covers, the art, the format and photos, but most of all, the quality of its articles from leading feminists creative women, their interviews, reviews and news as from the cocoon of a butterfly ready to emerge, to fill its wings with its life force and to fly.

Along with the others, we extended our subscription, made a conservative donation toward its support and promised ourselves to promote more subscriptions through the store.

Every move comes down to money. You have to earn it and/or get it from those who have it and want to give it to you. Without it, you have a lot of trouble.

After Raven finished answering questions, she invited us to stay for more wine and food. The guacamole! It was out of this world! We talked and talked and finally drove home happy somewhere about midnight. And this was only the first day of our ABA adventure.

After our morning's Book & Author Breakfast and entertainment, we started on one side of the convention floor today, scooping up autographed copies, pins, snacks, and almost anything publishers use to get booksellers to stop and talk to an author or a salesperson. Oh yes. We did attend a seminar on publishing and selling gay books. No one is in the closet here.

We dropped our load of freebies at our motel, freshen up and attend the First Timer's cocktail party at the Hilton. Jan invited two women we ate with to ride with us to the Woman's Building. We found the massive old factory at 1727 North Spring Street. Jan was sure it was the one because on the roof right above the entrance loomed Kate Millet's giant metal sculpture of a powerful woman. We missed the first speaker but enjoyed the inspiring speaker we wanted to hear Charlene Spretnak, author of *Lost Goddesses of Early Greece.* Later we talked to many women and moseyed around the building with its raw, unfinished look. Some of the art on display was raw, too, haphazardly displayed, and there wasn't much of it. Naturally, Jan began to imagine her dad's building to be a women's center, the whole lower level, more than the bookstore, having a building to help women work and play together rather than living in lonely, frustrating and uninspiring isolation.

Back to our motel in our new room with a solid mattress on a king-sized bed, we collapsed in a sound sleep to prepare for tomorrow.

Yesterday's ABA breakfast featured Sherry Lewis with her hand-puppet Lambchop and one of my favorite sci-fi authors, Ray Bradbury. This morning starred the amazingly awesome Maya Angelou, Michael Korda and President Gerald Ford. Quite a contrast. All had books and an agenda to promote to this appropriate audience.

Maya read from her extremely moving Joe Louis account. We quickly became bored when Gerald Ford droned on and because we were sitting near the back of the room, we left while Ford was talking and caught the Convention Center shuttle bus and worked the floor this time, up, down, all around, and standing in line at the autograph tables. I took pictures of several authors and some of Shari Lewis who was casually staffing her publisher's booth. Good Luck. We found a booth that served free Coors beer.

Finding *The Feminist Bookstore News* and its founder and editor Carol Seajay was the most important contact of the day. This magazine shares information among feminist bookstores with the goal of cooperation rather than competition. It began as a mimeographed and stapled six-page newsletter when Carol was co-owner of Old Wives' Tale Bookstore in San Francisco. It now has expanded to a bi-monthly magazine that reaches feminist booksellers, publishers, distributors, writers, librarians, sending information and encouragement as it unites these women into a networking community. Carol welcomed us as if we were old friends and we feel that we will be just that.

In this huge hall, we found pockets of feminist and lesbian activists who are using books and printing as their weapons. If some of the women didn't have presses and books of their own to sell, many of them worked for alternative and even some mainstream publishing houses and promoted women-oriented books and alternative publications. New women, new feminists, loaded with ideas of their own, now have the process to share those ideas. They now can express their uncensored experiences because a growing movement and a feminist audience 'round the world—even in Lakeshore Bay, supports them.

We worked the floor until 5:30 and we were about ready to drop and also to drop off the heavy bags of books we've collected. We shopped at our motel's corner store for beer, brandy and wine and settled in our motel with our bread, cheese and our boilermakers too. In need of a quiet respite, Jan watched TV. I fell asleep.

At last, I am caught up with my journal while Jan napped. There's so much to write, to look at and read. We have one shopping bag full of catalogs and a case of books on the counter. Before boxing them last night, we spread them all out on the bed and played with them like the greedy booksellers that we are. We unfurled the colorful collection of posters and spilled out the buttons, pens, pencils and silly stuff. This is truly a book lover's dream convention.

I finally rousted Jan and we went down the block to The Pantry that looked like a crummy truck stop, but Frommer recommended it. It was crowded so we shared a table with some husky truck driver types and I ordered bacon and sausages and eggs. The waiter seemed surprised and asked me again if I was sure that's what I wanted. I said yes, absolutely, and so were we surprised when my order was set in front of me. Huge portions of everything! But I was famished since we hadn't eaten supper last night and I ate the whole thing. The waiter had fun with me and brought me a free plate of ham too.

Happily fed and ready, we plunged into the convention's last day collected more books, autographs and catalogs and placed some orders. We stayed, scooping up goodies until workers started rolling up carpets. Whew! What a grand time.

We drove and parked the car in the convention hall's huge garage for this last big load back to the motel where Jan totaled up our goodies and figured a conservative $500 retail in giveaways for us and for our customers. It was Christmas in California. Good thing we got boxes from display staff and the corner liquor store, and we lucked out finding a UPS close by to ship the boxes home.

Showered and dressed up in our travelers' best, we hopped the shuttle and went off to the Bonaventure for The Big ABA Dinner riding up the outside glass elevator. WOW! Spectacular! The free cocktails were difficult to get to but we managed to down a couple drinks and found a side table near the stage. A lady with a Jamaican guy and two other conventioneers completed our table. Dinner was prime rib. We had bottles of wine on the table while enjoying Les Brown and His Band of Renown with Dick Haymes singing his old hits in a reunion performance.

The Jamaican asked Jan to dance. She hadn't danced with a man in years. They disappeared in the crowd for quite a while. I turned down a dance with one guy. Then Jan came back. The guy made a pass at her on the dance floor—French kissing her—and she gagged when she told me. Then he asked me to dance. He seemed determined to get laid by someone that night. I just played dumb. It was after 11 so we decided to wing out after a trip to the Bonaventure's classy john, and we made it "home" to bed to shift gears for tomorrow's next adventure.

Bea on May 30, 1979

We headed for Anaheim and The Magic Kingdom of Disneyland. We arrived at 9:45, a perfect timing for the park opening. The jungle trip was our first adventure but we timed our way to New Orleans by 11:30 to eat lunch with no waiting at the Blue Bayou Restaurant where delicate fireflies and bird sounds seemed to flutter in the damp atmosphere among the tropical foliage surrounding us. Creole seafood and pecan pie nourished us before we launched off on The Pirates of the Caribbean ride. After years of building parade floats, Jan was in awe of what the Disney artists do, especially when they plus the atmosphere with fireflies.

The rest of the day was to explore everything else including a trip to Mars, the entertaining Country Bear Jamboree, the People Mover, Inner Space, Music American, Small World, The Haunted Mansion, Storybook Land and the Captain Nemo's Submarine, but I wouldn't ride on any rollercoaster rides. Our favorite was Peter Pan where we both gasped for breath when the sky ride chairs swooped us over nighttime Victorian London with its lights blinking and Nana, the dog, barking after us. Jan actually choked up in tears. I always said she never wanted to grow up, I guess because she had to grow up so early in her life.

We stopped and bought Mickey Mouse sea captain caps and sweatshirts; Jan had to have Minnie Mouse on her shirt. What a marvelous day celebrating a grand time together—exciting and fun, and we stayed until the park closed.

Finding our way back to our L.A. motel was easy. We're doing these freeways like Angelinos—including eating at The Pantry for a fabulous T-bone steak dinner.

Bea on May 31, 1979

We intrepid travelers drove off to find Universal Studios Hollywood for more playtime and rode on all the animated attractions—a collapsing bridge, roaring fires, flash floods, the shark from "Jaws" leaping out of the water at us, the collapsing pier, bionic women and men, the "Psycho" house on the hill and the simulated avalanche. I took loads of pictures until we decided we had enough and went to a late lunch at the beautiful Victoria Station, drove into Beverly Hills and walked past Grauman's Chinese Theater and the fancy shops on Rodeo Drive.

But a higher priority for us to find was the famous Sisterhood Bookstore where we were surprised to find it a tiny place about the size of our store but with a bigger inventory. From there we drove on to find Feminist Horizons, another tiny store! We enjoyed a pleasant chat with the owner. I gave her two sets of the Mother Courage Women of Courage note card packets that I had drawn and given to ABA booksellers. I'd been leaving with ABA people. She bought four more for her store so they're all gone now.

Ha! Good Vibrations was an even friendlier store nearby with a most helpful woman clerk who helped while we enjoyed checking out all the options for sex toys and books. At home, the only place we could shop for something similar would be in a porno store—probably penis oriented with some sleazy guy manning the counter—or in some drugstore where you pretend to have a sore back or a muscle that you have to massage. Some of the toys were cute and funny, but we picked out a utilitarian Magic Wand at $29.95, the best seller of the store, said the clerk, "And it's delightful and easy for two people to enjoy at the same time." Jan said that besides the California poppy seeds from Muir Woods, this purchase was the souvenir she wanted.

From there we went on to find Z Budapest's store, The Feminist Wicca, at 442 Lincoln Blvd. in Venice. We asked if Z was in the store so we could talk with her but a woman named Annu explained, probably to many customers for hundreds of times, "Z doesn't work here anymore because in 1975 she was arrested by the LAPD for being paid for reading Tarot cards, and she was dragged through a painful and costly trial."

We said we'd heard about that and thought she'd been cleared. We had seen her at Arlene Raven's, we said smugly, as if we were big shots in the feminist and Wiccan movement.

"Perhaps her name will be cleared from the negative publicity and all," explained Annu, "but instead of being defeated, this gave her another way to serve the Goddess. It's forced her to write *The Feminist Book of Lights and Shadows*, and she travels now and teaches Goddess messages."

"Your store is like a Wiccan mission," I said.

"It's true, isn't it? Our goals include training witches and starting as many Dianic covens as we can. We see ourselves not only as businesswomen here at the store but as teachers and priestesses of the Goddess. Here, take some of our free literature."

The tiny store with shelves built along the earth-colored walls was filled with magic women-made supplies, candles for rituals and hexing, oils, incense, herbs, Tarot cards and other occult supplies. Not being into hexing, we bought a couple books and wished them well.

In sympathy, I said, "I hope you can support yourselves and be successful in what you hope to accomplish."

"As long as Z keeps her energy to travel around the country giving speeches with her slide show and fundraising to publish her next book, *The Holy Book of Women's Mysteries*, we'll start more circles and make it."

We left a donation. "Here's to the power of the Goddess," Jan said as if she proclaimed, "May the Force be with you" from the new *Star Wars* movie, and we both giggled quietly but reverently at her blessing as we closed the door behind us.

Early this spring, I spied an ad in *The Lesbian Connection* promoting Seaworthy Women, a women-owned company that offered sailing trips for other women. What an opportunity to sail off the coast of California—and with women at the helm. I made reservations for an extended weekend stay beyond the ABA.

After checking out the beach and boardwalks in Venice, we drove to Marina del Ray to scout out where Seaworthy Women's boat was docked. We never saw so many boats in one place in our lives and decided to have dinner at The Warehouse rather than attempt to find our mooring for tomorrow. We ate a filling soup and salad in the midst of tropical seafaring decor with window views surrounded by boats and docks. It was almost sunset and we wanted to find our way out of there and back home where we settled up our motel bill and left a call for 5:30 a.m. We watched some TV, organized our stuff and, of course, tried out the new vibrator. After sharing its earth-shaking delights, we fell dead asleep.

Bea on June l, 1979

The wake-up call came but I was awake. We packed up and went across the street to The Pantry for breakfast again but a lighter one than the breakfast feast I devoured before.

Not knowing how long we had to drive to find them, we arrived at Jeannine Talley and Ellen Power's Seaworthy Women's home nearly thirty minutes early. The other passenger, Diane, came soon after and our crew was complete. We loaded our stuff in a camper-bodied pick-up Datsun, drove to the marina, and loaded gear on the 31-foot wooden ketch—*The Esperanza*. We uncovered sails and after everything was stowed, we motored through the sheltered marina waters and out to the Pacific with all sails set. The seas were calm with a good wind. When the motor was turned off and the wind filled the sails with power, I felt elated, lifted on the sea as if Mother Nature gifted me with the salty air in my soul and the strength of moving forward under Her power.

Jan stood to get the feel of the boat, the wind and the ocean, holding one line for stability, but she had taken Dramamine and looked half asleep already. She was sniffling too. Gods, I hope she doesn't have to take an allergy pill too. She'll sleep through the entire trip. About half way, I noticed Jan became awfully quiet but she continued to sit outside with her back against the cabin wall and she did fall asleep. Good thing. She looked a little green.

We sailed the whole distance on a broad reach—Course 171 degrees. On my 8mm sound movie camera, I captured Jeannine's love of her beautiful mahogany-trimmed wooden boat. It was built in l966 in Japan, a Mariner 31, hull #2, ketch rigged. She had everything from autopilot to self-steering vane, radio, etc. The previous owner had really fitted her out. I planned to make our trip into a documentary, and this information is valuable.

After a few hours of cruising, I got to steer and brought her nearly up to Bluebird Cove on Catalina Island. Jeannine asked if I would like to help get the sails down and I went forward with Ellen when she dropped the jenny. I gathered it in but my Mickey Mouse captain's hat flew off and out to sea.

"Let it go," I shouted, but they called out that this would be good practice for a "man overboard" drill. After two circles around Mickey, Jeannine caught my cap with the boat hook. We got the main down and the mizzen. Then as Ellen tried to lower the anchor, the chain jammed in the chain locker causing a few hairy moments drifting toward shore while they tried to get it loose. Finally Diane leveraged up the chain with an iron tool and we anchored without more challenges.

The trip had taken about seven hours and we ate a good dinner in the cabin. Ellen said, "You better eat it all or you get it in your omelet tomorrow morning." We talked and enjoyed rocking at anchor and then settled in for the night. Jan and I each had the forward berths together in the bow—comfortable for me but Jan didn't sleep too well. She felt claustrophobic on a narrow mat stacked on a side-boarded shelf close to the ceiling. She had hoped to sleep on deck under the stars, but Ellen and Jeannine had that spot in case of bad weather, and the rest of the top deck over the cabin was filled with barrels and other equipment. If she tried to sleep out there, she'd have to curl herself around all that. She told me she considered that alternative in the middle of the night but didn't want to disturb anyone. She needs a lot of fresh air when she's on a boat.

Bea on June 2, 1979

I woke up early before the others and sat at the table reading the chart of Catalina. The others finally woke up and Ellen cooked an excellent breakfast on a gimbaled four-burner stove with an oven. After our captains pumped up the two dinghies, Jan and I rowed out to take pictures and then land on the island. We did a little beach combing and climbed up the hill and saw a Boy Scout camp. When we got back to the boat, I put on my swimsuit and a sweatshirt.

Diane dressed in her rig. She has a 1/4" wet suit, hood, boots and glasses, an inflatable swim vest, thirty pounds of weights, plus mask and snorkel. We took her in the dingy to a cave beyond the beach where she swam for twenty minutes and proudly reported seeing a small octopus and a crayfish. It was only her second open-water dive since certification.

Jeannine and Ellen joined us in the other dingy and that's when I went in wearing only my swimsuit and a sweatshirt with my mask and snorkel. After the first frozen shock, I found the water bearable and not as cold as they had indicated. I adjusted well after years of snorkeling in the old days with my family on our boat off Lake Michigan's shorelines. Here I discovered an interesting bottom of white sand and pebbles with long fronds of waving kelp that would roll in with the surge, then, all would gracefully change its dance to the opposite direction as the swell went down. It continually covered and uncovered the bottom. I found empty abalone shells and brought up two. I saw beautiful golden orange garibaldi fish swimming among less colorful fish.It was fifteen minutes before I came out of the water, took off my sweatshirt and switched to a dry jacket. We followed Diane around in the dingy for a bit more before she decided she was through. We pulled her and all her gear aboard the dinghy and headed for *The Esperanza* where we snorkelers enjoyed a well-deserved beer.

Our hosts came back to their boat and made a light lunch of crackers, salami and fruit. The waves and wind turned a bit stronger and the sun stayed behind the clouds so we only fiddled about the boat. In the evening Ellen set out the portable stainless steel barbecue cooker and fastened it to the rail. She lit a charcoal fire and barbecued delicious chicken and vegetables.

We sat in the cabin telling stories like how to get a three-hundred-pound-plus woman passenger into their boat and worry about saving her if she would fall overboard. Eventually we told tales that lesbian women exchange about their lives, their work and their loves. Ellen had lots of stories to tell about being an L.A. social worker helping gay and lesbian, transgendered and transsexual people. One story was about a man and a woman and each was unhappy until each had surgically changed their sex. Then they fell in love with each other as a woman and a man. And the agency she works for helped them with counseling and with most of the funding they needed to complete their changes.

Of course, we each told our own stories, which is part of the healing process from discovering you are not one of society's "normal" human beings and all the chaos that follows even if you've come to accept your true self.

Bea on June 3, 1979

This morning, we saw seals and heard them bark. Took photos, too. We had seen dolphins and a flying fish on the way out, the first one Jeannine had seen this season. About 10 a.m. we were ready to up anchor. I was helping Ellen because a great gob of kelp had climbed aboard the plow anchor and it was terribly heavy. We hauled in the line and had to winch in the chain. At last, the anchor came up and Ellen cut away the kelp.

The sea was up and so was the wind. I took part of Ellen's watch for two hours and the winds were gusting up to twenty-five knots. Jan became greener sooner than on the way to Catalina and tried to stay out of the way while dozing on the deck's padded bench close to the cabin hatchway in case she needed to dash to the head. Our speed averaged five knots with occasional spurts up to six and seven. It was a fun ride; reading again on course 350 degrees, but I was glad to give up the helm to Jeannine at about 4 p.m. Boat traffic was getting thicker through several oil tankers at anchor. Finally, we made Marina del Rey. We had one slow-down when Jeannine took the mainsail down to repair batten pockets. We entered the harbor with the sails at wing-on-wing and then motored into the busy channel. It was almost 6 p.m. when Jeannine put *The Esperanza* neatly into her berth.

Jan wanted to accept Ellen's invitation to sleep aboard. I didn't because it meant camping out another night. But I acquiesced. We drove back with them to our car, said our farewells, and returned to the marina, stopping to pick up some booze. Jan stuck to the directions I navigated back to the marina, found the keyed entrance to where *The Esperanza* was docked, parked the car, carried our belongings to the boat, went to the marina locker area and thoroughly enjoyed a cleansing warm shower and a change of clothing.

With clean bodies in fresh clothes, we returned to celebrate a well-deserved sit-down dinner at the Warehouse. This time we started with a house-drink called a Rum Barrel—so delicious that we ordered our fish dinner and a second Barrel even though the waiter warned us of its potency. Feeling relaxed and safe, Jan said her expectations of the trip to Catalina were quite different than she expected. As a kid watching newsreels and movies and avidly reading movie magazines, she expected that we'd dock at Avalon, a magic place where movie stars and moguls danced at a white pavilion overlooking a bay —like Monte Carlo, a peaceful place for the rich and famous to play and relax. "You know the song," and she sang, "I Left My Heart in Avalon, besides the bay…" with a Rudy Valley or Guy Lombardo impersonation. I couldn't tell which one it was.

I ordered another round of those good rum barrels to enjoy because we didn't have far to drive.

"Well, Jan, you did find a peaceful relaxing spot in Catalina."

"Yah. And we saw a whole Boy Scout camp."

"Oh well. Maybe we'll be back sometime and take the ferry from L.A."

She sipped on her drink and said, "You could write a song about that."

It was a miracle that we found our marina gate to get us to the docked boat for our night alone on *The Esperanza*. Somehow, Jan found it right away through the maze of locked piers of the world's largest man-made marina with room for more than 5000 boats. I don't know how she did it. And we had to find it because all of our suitcases and souvenirs were on board. You'd think after three Rum

Barrels and gourmet seafood sampler suppers, we'd pass out as soon as we hit the deck. Yet all night long we could hear a crunch, crunch, crunch noise echoing from the hull. The chewing din may be from barnacles, I guess. Jan said she knows now what it's like to be a Snap, Crackle or Pop in a Rice Krispie cereal bowl. What a unique and noisy memory for the last night of our trip.

Bea on June 4, 1979

Waking early after our restless night, we packed up everything, drove off to Captain Bly's for breakfast and on to LAX. We were early but we checked in the car, took a shuttle to the terminal and checked our bags, including the new backpack I hesitated to send with the other cases. But we were already carrying our posters, a shopping bag full of souvenirs, two camera cases, and Jan's huge leather camera bag, so I let my precious backpack go with the rest of our suitcases. We boarded about 10:45 a.m. on a DC 10 and I was a little apprehensive thinking of the DC 10 Flight 191 that had crashed in Chicago a week ago.

But our flight was beautiful. We flew over the Grand Canyon, Lake Mead, the Rocky Mountains, all with grand views, ate steak again, drank wine and champagne. Jan's daughter, Jenny, was waiting for us when we landed in Milwaukee and helped us picked up the bags, except for my new backpack, the one with the film, autographed books and other good stuff. After reporting the missing bag, I doubted that I would ever get it back. It was too new and tempting. Fortunately, I didn't lose my travel journal packed in a suitcase. I'd never be able to remember all of our adventures on this trip.

Chapter 6

Jan on June 5, 1979

I don't get to skip a beat, though I did get to the office late because I slept longer in our own wonderful bed. It will take weeks to process all of our boxes when they're shipped to the store. Even to unpack and get things back to normal will take time.

My California trip was three vacations in one: the booksellers convention, a stimulating and exciting experience; the three-day cruise in a 31-foot ketch on the Pacific, relaxing, unique and heartwarming; and the rest of California's coastline.

Ironically Alex and Jenny were in San Francisco on the same Monday we were. When I found out that was to be, I asked Jenny to see Judy Chicago's masterpiece, but she missed this important art event and spent time with former neighbor and friend Marcia Kruse in Venice wind surfing in the Pacific while Alex was on business tasks. I must have driven close to Marcia's place several times and didn't even know she'd moved to California.

Carolyn gave me a hearty greeting like a puppy with its tail wagging, happy to see me back to take over my share of the work waiting for me. She's OK. Everything went well. Laura, Pam and Bob helped a lot when they could. But she said she was ready for a vacation now.

Not right away. We had to store our "Lakeshore Medical Center's signs at St. Agnes' Health Fair, seven 4 x 8 foam core posters and flyers stacked in our office, as well as Carolyn's seven beautiful banners that drew spectators to our tables and made our staff feel extra proud. All the preparations for taking over a large meeting room at St. Agnes' paid off while I was sailing on the Pacific from San Francisco to Catalina. Carolyn and our team plus Lakeshore Medical Center's skilled and caring staff volunteered their Sunday afternoon to educate the public about the seven Lakeshore Medical Center services offered only at our hospital.

Bea on June 7, 1979

Still no word of our lost backpack. Damn! They'd better find it 'cause I have precious film and autographed books in it. And the bag's brand new, too.

We heard from Jenny that Matt's selling encyclopedias to the people in stifling hot Dothan, Alabama, wasn't working out. I told him when he came into the store over spring break that those companies sign up college go-getters like him, fill them up with a lots of bull, and then abandon them to find their own way, even begging for places to sleep. I remember a couple years ago when I was the Director of Religious Education at church when several of them camped out at Emerson House. The boys were so desperate they came to church and asked Tony Logan for some for money and a place to sleep. Of course Tony helped them. And then they messed up my schedule and Emerson House..

When I told Matt not to get involved, I probably cinched the deal for him to do exactly the opposite. He was going to make lots of money from commissions. Ha. They send the best students to the hardest places to sell encyclopedias to people who need them but can't afford to buy them. Matt finally had called home and asked for help. He said he finally scrounged up enough cash so he could buy a used bicycle and then someone stole it. The police locked him up in jail for a night because he didn't have a peddler's license. Harry sent money to bail him out. How humbling.

Someone had better find my backpack or I'm going to humble someone at the airlines.

Jan on June 7, 1979

Dear Matt,

It's been quite a while since I've been able to write to you because I finally got an address to reach you. Of course, I've been thinking a lot about you and where you are. I'm sure Dothan, Alabama, and its people will give you a new understandings of another culture—from hard-working redneck farmers to the scary "Redneck types" like Bull Connor, the symbol of the fight against the Negroes when he ordered using fire hoses and police attack dogs against nonviolent protesters. Actually Bull Connor's bully tactics shown on TV helped bring about the Civil Rights Act of 1964 that he was trying to oppose.

You'll meet other good people, of course. Someone once told me that you, Matt, are the kind of person who never meets a stranger because you are so friendly. Still I am glad you're relatively close to the Florida state line so you can, if you like, make a break for more tourist-friendly country.

I remember driving though the Dothan area when we were on our way to Florida. You were two-and-a-half years old and Jenny, three months. It was my turn to take the wheel and while leaving Dothan to cross a tip of Georgia to get to Florida, the atmosphere of the newly darkening night became oppressive as I drove into a mossy tree-lined tunnel of a street. A roadblock appeared down the center of that street and I made a mistake and found myself in the wrong lane. I quickly recovered my cool and my direction and crossed back on the correct lane. Just then a state patrol car with two uniformed officers passed me on the left and they stared into our car, Grandpa's new Rambler, no less. Their rifle racks were visible and the look they gave me sent my imagination into seeing me spend the night in jail while my husband and two babies tried to bail me out in a backwoods southern town.

Of course I've known about the KKK and the freedom marches. I remember Selma. I woke this morning thinking of the three freedom marchers from the late 1960s that were murdered and buried at the end of a swamp road. I remember the Unitarian Universalist Rev. James Reeb being bludgeoned to death helping Blacks register to vote. Obviously, I am concerned about my liberal son in that environment and, obviously, I do have prejudices about atmosphere in that part of our country. But intellectually, I know that you are going to be all right and will make some friends or acquaintances and you will sell your books and reach your goals. But I will be happier when you come home.

We have many exciting new books in the store from our booksellers' convention trip, including sailing and boating books that we hope to sell to our marina weekenders and local boat enthusiasts. Our inventory is improving all the time, but we're still not making a profit. We're paying our bills through and have placed an order for the textbooks for Lakeshore Med School of Nursing students in August. The woman director of the school is trying to send us more business.

I've enclosed a Lakeshore Med brochure that has received some acclaim beyond Lakeshore Bay because it was noted in a national communications newsletter, *The Ragan Report*. Now each day I get a pile of letters at work asking for a copy.

Grandpa is looking younger every day after painting Lakeshore Bay's first long-distance walk/run event banners. It was a challenge that he conquered. Now people are calling in float paper orders. He's very happy having us in the building and Bea answers his phone when he's not there so he doesn't lose any orders.

I hope to hear from you soon and to find out how you're doing. I guess from what I hear, you have sold some books, but let me know how you are. I'll keep sending you some money through the summer months in case you need bail money. I know. That's not funny.
Love,

Mom
P.S. I'm very happy too.

Jan on June 12, 1979

Jenny graduated from Henry Thoreau High on June 6. Because of the small size of her alternative high school, the students and teachers know each other really well, and their families too—especially with Matt graduating from there two years before. The friendly graduation ceremony showed their closeness.

That's more than what's happening in Jenny's family.

I'd hoped by this time that Alex and I could have come to some resolution and perhaps even have gone to Jenny's graduation together. I mentioned this to her, but nothing came of it. Alex still carries a lot of bitterness as does Aunt Var and Sona. (Last Christmas with carols of peace and joy sounding jolly holiday music through a department store, Var embraced our friend Anna Spence and whispered to Fran, "I could just kill her!" In church after that, Anna described my former sister-in-law to me as "Hate Incarnate.") That hate etches hard lines in their faces—and hearts. It's too bad. To keep the peace for Jenny, Bea, my dad and I stayed on the opposite side of the gym and reception area.

The ceremony went well with a warm and happy message from her homeroom teacher and Rite of Passage adviser. She said Jenny was a warm and compassionate person and explained that during Rite of Passage meetings (where I was a proud participant), Jenny would always offer excuses for not giving a good report, and then she'd come through with great success. Then from a paper bag, Louise pulled out a stuffed duck, symbolic too because Jenny has a thing for ducks, and presented her with a "Not-So-Lame-Duck Award." After an initial blush, Jenny smiled broadly and showed her stuffed duck to the cheering audience.

Jenny managed her split families beautifully, bouncing back and forth visiting dad, aunt and cousin on one side of the room, my dad, Bea and me on another side—and many friends in between.

Last night Jenny and my dad came to his Father's Day and her graduation dinner. Of course, Chico was there too. He's so old. Dad showed us how Chico would teeter over when my dad moved him from his lap to stand on the floor. Sure enough, the dog keeled over. Chico didn't even snap at us like he used to do. I told Dad to stop with the tricks. I joshed him saying, "What would you feel like if we went to the nursing home when you are too old to stand up and did that on you?"

Independent Jenny started working at St. Agnes Food Service department when she turned sixteen and would get up at 4 a.m. to start the breakfast menu for the patients. Now she has two jobs: cooking at the hospital and making sandwiches at Hogan's deli.

She opened her graduation presents from us; important books, of course, and this is what I wrote on the front page in each of them.

> *The Women's Room* by Marilyn French
>> I wrote, "An angry book but educational," and quoted:
>> "Say 'Yes' to yourself, to your energy, your skills,
>> your thoughts as in individual, as a woman."
>> *****
>
> *Our Bodies/Ourselves* by the Boston Women's Collective
>> "You own your own body—"
>> *****
>
> Dream of a Common Language by Adrienne Rich
>> From "Transcendental Etude"
>> "…No one ever told us we had to study our lives,
>> make of our lives a study…
>> practicing till strength
>> and accuracy became one with the daring
>> to leap into transcendence…"
>> *****
>
> *Siddhartha* by Herman Hesse
>> "It seems to me," said Siddhartha, "that love is the
>> most important thing in this world. The world was

beautiful…The moon and the stars were beautiful, the
brook, the shore, the forest, the rock, the goat and the
golden beetle, the flower and the butterfly were
beautiful."

Jenny, may your life always be beautiful.

Bea on June 13, 1979

The airline called to tell me that my bag is officially lost and I should
turn in a value on it and its contents so they can send us a check to
cover the value of the lost items. We mourned the loss of the film
most. How can you put a price on all our pictures and the
autographed books that we had treasured? Damn! Damn! Damn!

Bea on June 27, 1979

Our artist of the month decided not to display so I'll do it. I bought
4 x 8 panels for three boat pictures painted on sails that I cut from
the panels, lashed them to rods to represent the mast and the boom,
and hung them in our gallery at the shop.

While Barney was busy on the phone with his little bit of 4th of
July business, Chico must have wanted a drink from his dish so
Barney took him off his lap and set him gently on the floor. I'd hired
in a plumber to check out the workings of our ancient toilet and basin
on the middle landing. Yesterday, a guy browsed around in our store
and asked me if he could use the bathroom. Though we hate to have
anyone go down to use those old fixtures, I gave in. Later I kept
hearing the toilet running and realized that this guy stole the ancient
copper float in the toilet tank!

Anyway, while the plumber was working on the middle
landing, he heard a quiet tumbling sound and watched the rusty-
brown fur ball of skin and bones roll down the nine or ten steps from
the open door of the first floor. Chico had fallen down the steps.

The stunned plumber finally gave out a yelp as Chico staggered across the landing heading for the worn wooden stairway of at least 24 steps ending on concrete at the lowest level of the building. It was too late. Chico was heading straight for that open space and stepped off and down again with me following him and Barney just behind.

For sure the dog was dead, but Barney talked to him as he picked him up into his arms and told Chico he would be all right. Barney took his Chico back up to the chair they share, wrapped him in his old towels to warm him, and the dog actually regained his breath. Thank God I didn't have to apply mouth-to-mouth resuscitation on that little old ferret of a dog. But I really felt sorry for him, and for Barney too.

The plumber was aghast! He told me it seemed as if the dog was trying to commit suicide, but Jan's dad brought "her brother" Chico back to live and love again—loving Barney, of course. Jan always says her dad takes better care of that damn dog than he ever took care of her, except for Chico's trip down the equivalent of three flights of stairs.

When I told her what had happened, she replied that she and her dad had a big talk recently and showed her where he stacked an aluminum box with a lid. "It's Chico's casket," he told Jan. "I want you to know about it in case I should go before Chico does. And when you come to the parade on the 4th, I'll show you the place in the yard where I've dug a square hole, but I've covered it up with soil and grass. But you can find it when you need to."

She assured him that he'd be around for a long time, but that she'd take care of the dog if something did happen to him. Ironically, they never discussed plans for her dad's funeral, except to find out that all his plans are on file at the Veterans Administration office.

Jan told me she guessed he didn't want her to be as informal with his burial as she was with her mother's remains. Jan buried Mildred's ashes herself. With her dad, Alex, Matt and Jenny as witness, she dug a hole next to her mother's beloved son Richard's headstone. Then Jan plopped the can of ashes in the space and planted a small bush over it. She would rest next to her Richard, the child of her first marriage. On June 1, 1931, she watched in horror when a car hit Richard and he was killed. Mildred had married Barney on January 1, 1930, and Jan was to be born on November, 14, 1931.

Jan on June 30, 1979

I have had an insightful moment looking into my future. I will be the one to die first and Bea will add her insight by writing a book about our lives.

Bea on July 6, 1979

Most of our family members met at Barney's front yard to watch the 4th of July parade on a beautiful day, and we stayed for a potluck lunch in Barney's backyard. The Manley's including Marge's mother, Nina, gave Jan's dad some extra company. Dear friends Marian and Sharon and Carolyn Schafer and her daughter Jane came too.

Lakeshore Bay always has a grand 4th of July parade, but it is not as grand as when the C. B. Anthony Sign Company made most of the parade floats. Was it just three years ago when Barney was honored as the Parade Marshall in the Bicentennial 1976 parade because of all the beautiful parade floats he managed to build since the late 1920s. We didn't have much to do with the parade since then, except for Barney who still sells float paper and advises amateurs on building their own floats. Good thing he didn't do more. Jan and the rest of us have enough other jobs to do. Barney looked tired after the parade, but this year it's not from working those long hours to build the floats. He was just tired. Sharon took his full-face photo while he sat quietly staring at her, seemingly oblivious that his photo was being taken. She had her own darkroom and yesterday she brought us an enlargement for us to have. Jan remarked when she looked into his eyes that she wondered what he was thinking.

Our lives have changed so much.

As is Jan's routine before the parade, she had me walk with her the half block north to the parade's line of march and beyond to watch others struggle with their last minute float problems as she had done for so many years.

Barney had helped Grace Krupp with float paper and creative ideas. She runs Orphan Critters where they never put animals to sleep. How can you not have a cute float when it's full of dogs?

But one black and white shaggy puppy didn't get to be on the float. Grace told us the pup couldn't make it in the parade for that long. Grace pointed out that the pup had vision only in one eye. The other eye looked at us from its fuzzy face with a floppy ear as if to say what orphans always wish: "Take me home with you."

After the picnic, we relaxed and sat in our very own yard next to our very own new but traditional wooden picnic table that we'd just built. We were quietly enjoying our drinks from our very own bar, but our minds were spinning.

Jan finally interrupted the stillness. "I'm sorry but I just can't stop thinking about that puppy."

"I can't either. I try but I can't get her out of my mind."

"Let's drive to Orphan Critters and see if we can get a better look at her."

"I'm starting to think of names already."

"Me too. Remember in England when almost everybody, even the trolley conductors, called everyone Luv? That's been going through my mind."

"Gosh. We haven't even considered getting a pet and you already have a name for one."

"Well, when we looked to buy this house, you asked if the tree in the back was in 'our' yard."

"What can it hurt if we just have a look at her?"

"Yah. You've heard that question in 1974. 'What can it hurt if we just let things happen,' and here we are in our own home together."

"Let's go. Just to look at her again." And we drove across town to press our noses against a dusty window and peek to catch a glimpse at this little black and white dog who was nowhere in sight.

I never imagined I'd be a seeing-eye person for a one-eyed dog, but that's what I am because I went back and signed the adoption papers for Luv the very next day. We took Luv's picture sitting on the new picnic table, and her chin is just a bit higher than the top of the coffee mug next to her.

Jan on July 6, 1979

I hope that all attending our Roosevelt High's 30th reunion had a fine time. I'm not going to back out of our class activities because I'm divorced from my high school boyfriend and am an out lesbian. I've been on every reunion committee. Alex quit coming, but I'm still their peer. I posted our wonderful and high-spirited Class of '49 memorabilia and entertained them with a slide show with snapshots from my old Brownie box camera and school pictures from the school newspaper and year book photo files that I gleaned from the publications rooms before school closed thirty years ago that summer. I combined them with other humorous photos and commentary of our classmates, threw in some feminist photos from my feminist clip art books: Arabian women in burkas, etc. At this luau informal summertime theme, my show had them screaming with laughter. But then again, they probably were plastered.

Jan on July 7, 1979

Matt came home from trying to sell encyclopedias in Alabama. What a relief. He came to see us at the store in the late afternoon and told us he never needed another character building experience. Too many doors had been slammed in his face and when people invited him in for a sales talk, he could tell they needed his books for their children, but they couldn't afford them. Another dent in his pride is that Bea's advice about not going in the first place came true.

It's good that Bea and I don't have to raise children together because we'd fight even more because of our different child-rearing styles. We even argue about raising the dog. I'm a crate person. Dogs should sleep in crates and not have the run of the house when we're away. Bea's not, so when we leave Luv in the basement, the dog whines and scratches the door until Bea lets her out.

Not only are our fights fueled by alcohol and stress and insecurities, families, puppy dogs and various stages of internalized and externalized homophobia, but each of us seldom fought with our husbands, especially in front of our kids. I usually gave in and Bea's husband usually did that. I promised myself I will not be a wimp nor be treated as a subordinate again. Nor will she.

Strange, but she is edgier and drinks more just before her menstrual period. I can tell because she marks her period on the calendar and I check out my notes about what happened before. She's often had to cope with various menstrual problems.

We both keep personal notes and calendars, but the reporting that I have to do at work drives me wild. I'm to keep track of everything we do and turn it into Randy, when the end results are quite obvious, or, better yet, Randy could just talk with me about what's going on. I don't even think he reads them because he seldom answers the questions I include in my reports. Maybe he keeps a separate file on me in his office, one that's different from my official file in the Personnel office. I'll bet he's collecting evidence on me just as I'm collecting my defense.

Chapter 7

Bea on July 8, 1979

Our life and love was calm and our schedule routine—like regular people until I was in our little bathroom off the family room, sitting on the toilet while Jan was taking a shower in our upstairs bathroom. I felt some water falling on me like rain and I realized it was coming from upstairs.

"Jan! Turn off the water. I'm getting all wet down here!"
"What?"
I pulled up my pants, ran upstairs and yanked the billowing shower curtains apart.
"Augh!" she screamed. "You make me feel like I'm in the Psycho movie!"
"Maybe you are¬—but I'm in Niagara Falls! Look at those tiles. Their weight is pulling the drywall away from the wall studs and the water's seeping downstairs and through that bathroom's ceiling. It was raining on me!"
After work hours, we tore out all the heavy ceramic tiles stuck to the crumbling wallboard that was leaning into the bathtub just waiting to crash onto the porcelain, and we carried out the debris to be stored in the shed until the rubbish men came. I went to the

lumber yard and bought materials, heavy rock lath 4 x 8 sheets. We hauled them home in Barney's Rambler station wagon and hauled them in! I also rebuilt the shower and tub wall as much as we could together, but Jan worked at the store on Saturday while I put in wall bond and a drop-ceiling over the tub. Jan taped and patched when she came home. Before all the new wallboard was installed, I cut a hole in the roof for a vent, teetered between the narrow roof and bathroom ceiling to connect all the vents and electrical wiring, installed glass shower doors in the new ceiling just in time to help Jan and Jenny decorate a car and a truck for the 4th of July parade. Barney, Jan and Jenny continue the three-generation family tradition—which now includes me.

Oh yes, while shopping for bathroom supplies, we also bought lumber for a picnic table and I put that together before the 4th.

This work was all done with no air conditioning in the old building and no air in the house either. The previous owners of our house had owned up to that broken, full-house air conditioning problem. Too bad they neglected to disclose the leaky bathroom that they patched back together, a job that required major work from us, especially when we couldn't afford to pay someone else to do it. What the Hell! After redoing the entire storefront, building bookcases and refinishing the floors, there's nothing I can't do if I put my mind to it.

Bea on July 29 1979

Even though Alex hates my walking on his Woodridge property in Door County, we invited Marian Dickert and Sharon Burman to join us last weekend. We warned them what was up and they were brave enough to come along with us anyway. I decided to take along my father's English Webley pistol, a huge, heavy old thing, and we could do some target shooting.

We let ourselves into the little trailer when we pulled in Friday night and we arranged for Marian and Sharon to sleep on the bed made from the table and upholstered cushions near the door. They slept in flannel pjs and were good sports about using the outhouse too. But what choice did they have.

It was fun. Different, at least. But Sharon, a nurse, once lived on a farm and Marian, an artist from Kansas, had lived in New York City before coming to Lakeshore Bay a couple years ago. We surprised them at daybreak when both of us in our regular sleeping attire—nothing—jumped out of our berth and out the door. We didn't want to run all the way to the outhouse so we just whizzed in the grass near the trailer. Our good friends were giggling when we leaped back into the trailer with morning dew on our skin and hoped back into our double sleeping bags for another hour of sleep.

During our weekend visit, we showed them all the artists' barns, shops and galleries, the lake and beaches, and treated them to a Door County fish boil. But we never knew what we'd find when we'd drive back on the land. Had Alex been there or was he sending someone to arrest Jan and me?

During the day with the clear horizon far ahead of us, we set up an old board we found in the woods against a rickety, well-weathered box. I loaded up the old Webley, paced myself about thirty feet back, and for the first time with this old gun, I set my feet firmly to my sides with both my hands holding the pistol. I cocked the gun and fired.

My three comrades kept far behind me with their fingers in their ears as we watched the stunned board shatter and collapse to the ground. Sharon took a turn too, but Marian and Jan hate guns and declined. "If Alex comes," Jan said, "all I want to do is get his attention—and if that doesn't work, maybe I'll have to shoot—but only at his toe. But he'd be scared enough just seeing me hold a gun, so I don't need to practice."

"Ha! You've misjudged him before, Jan—and lost."

"So it goes."

Chapter 8

Jan on July 30, 1979

July's schedule has been wild with Mr. Young's last official day tomorrow, with invitations, receptions, *synergy* stories, Nick's promotion to CEO—and it's going to get busier with special and on-going projects, continuing publications, even t-shirt design and ordering plus a new advertising campaign in the midst of a cost containment campaign. A free van service needs to be promoted because the new parking ramp is not finished and the new building used up the large parking lot to the south. Houses are being demolished for a new lot across the street. I'll have to plan for a ramp celebration and dedication as soon as that's finished.

My reports to Randy are a long list of A, B, and C priorities with check marks to show they're finished. Everybody's busy and most do not have time for my projects, except when I have to respond to the media or when top administrators tell me to get something finished. I try to keep a sense of humor, but I'm not above nagging when I'm desperate for information. That includes putting an "A" on Randy's weekly reports listing "Plan for salary negotiations: Please see me soon. 8/15 is Carolyn's date." But I'm aching for my well-deserved raise. Yet I never get an answer, except from memos for more detailed plans for the rest of the year.

One idea I had that I'm proud of is to create an illustrated Heimlich maneuver poster for restaurants to post with Lakeshore Med emergency number on their walls.

Another long-term project that I enjoyed was publishing the new expansion construction report in an easy-to read, inexpensive 8 x 11 format using Xeroxed photos and stories about the new building's construction progress. It was mailed to financial, political and community leaders. I had access to the entire project so I could take photos. I even had my own hard hat and made friends with the construction crews because they could read about how their work was appreciated. I recorded the building from the first ground breaking, tree topping and progress on each of the four floors, even the huge heating, cooling and generator systems.

After I received a certificate award from the national American Society of Hospital Public Relations for one of my projects, the award used the generic "he" for public relations director in it. (Most hospital workers are women; doctors and patients are not always male; and nurses are not always women.) I quickly wrote back and submitted my editorial from our state organization's newsletter on the importance of hospitals leading the change for using gender-free language. It was printed in the national newsletter and I was assured that future certificates of awards will use non-sexist language.

Of course, these accomplishments do not impress my newly promoted hospital administrators, Nick Dixon and Randy King.

Jan's *synergy* article in the 1979 Fall issue
"Nick Dixon accepts leadership challenge"

Since he came to Lakeshore Med in 1968, Nick Dixon's goals have been similar to his predecessor Clark Young: to champion a hospital organization sensitive to community needs, a place of feeling and caring and excellence, more than just a building that takes care of those who are sick.
And any changes involved in new management will not be major, he said. "More a matter of different personalities…"

"I don't want to be the authority symbol. I don't want to be where all the bad things happen."

(A personal note not included in the article, but while I was interviewing him for this article: I remembered how Nick hired me without letting the person doing the job know she was being replaced. She didn't find out until we met and I was the one who had to tell her that I had just been hired to replace her.)

Along with more responsibilities, he wants to give employees more credit and a greater awareness of the importance of each person's job...

"It's not just my job to see that the hospital is run efficiently, it's everybody's job...."

I am now working for my former Unitarian friend and neighbor and my one-time office mate and confidant, now his executive vice president, his henchman, Randy King. I remember when he was promoted out of our office to become the Director of Human Services, and I said, "Randy, you'll put the "Human" in "Human Services!"

Jan's editorial with Bea's "Fiddler on the Roof" in *synergy*
"Like a fiddler on the roof..."

The singular position of a hospital chief executive officer is similar to that of a football coach, a baseball manager, even—a fiddler on the roof.

Sound's crazy, no?
But in our little community like Lakeshore Bay (and other villages, towns and cities with hospitals like our own), you might say the hospital administrator is like a fiddler on the roof, trying to scratch out a pleasant, simple tune without breaking his or her neck.

It isn't easy, especially if you're trying to balance the expectations of physicians, your employees, your community, directors and trustees, consumer advocates, the government, health planners, rate setters, cost containers, etc.

And you're highly visible when you're up there all by yourself. If you're an innovator, you plan carefully but the risk you take might cause you to tumble: if you take no risks at all, you may keep your perch but become irrelevant.

You may ask, "Why do you stay up there if it's so dangerous?"

You stay because hospital administration is your career and it is a challenge to keep the balance and provide for people's health needs.

And they need, in a word, "tradition"—"the tradition" of community-oriented health care. The tradition of excellence, the tradition of local, voluntary, not-for-profit hospitals that have maintained quality care without controls from federal and state capitols.

Good luck to us all. Good health. Mazeltov!

Bea on August 1, 1979

Two weeks ago, we went to the Milwaukee Feminist Writers group and exchanged our some of our writing. I try to look as great as possible wearing black, looking slim and smart. Jan wears our Mother Courage t-shirt and hands out bookmarks to anyone who will take them. The main topic for this session was song writing led by Bev Glasner, and I sang two songs of mine. We'll keep in touch with these women for sure.

Mother Courage business is a little better now. The School of Nursing books arrived and students are coming in. Jan comes in after work and I go home to complete house projects like scraping, patching and waterproofing the basement walls with several coats and then while I'm still in the mood, I started sanding and painting the wooden siding on our house, one side at a time, and I finished it all in jig time. I took a break from painting for a change, doing the bathroom, odd jobs, making love a lot.

Luv's doing all right and fortunately Chico tolerates her. Barney loves her and occasionally the three of them go to lunch together. Maybe he'll even keep Luv when we are away from home for a while. I'm taking charge of the dog and bring her to the shop. but the neighboring business owners aren't happy when I walk the dog down block to the parking lot to find a piece of grass to relieve herself—and puppies need to do that a lot.

Jenny loves Luv too, but Jenny's dog Cooper, a rowdy black lab, is too rough to play with Luv. Jenny picked out Cooper because she was alone a lot in the big house when Alex went off on business trips. The dog was just a pup, but still he was large, gnawed on doors and practically ate the huge living room sofa when he was left alone while Jenny was at school and at work. He ran away a lot along the wild wooded area along Lake Michigan's bank across the street. Jenny has to bail Coop out of doggie jail when he gets caught running loose.

Jan on August 1, 1979

Last week on a full moon night, I drove us to a neighborhood park in Milwaukee's residential Shorewood suburb. After parking the car, we had to walk through a weird white painted and well-lit tunnel under an elevated railroad track. We emerged from what seemed to be an echoing womb except that we could hear our footsteps rather than our mother's heartbeats. When we emerged from the tunnel, we found ourselves entering a wide grassy and forested park, a bowl-like green sanctuary along the Milwaukee River. Women with candles were forming an inner circle and we were guided to form a line to the right, starting with the oldest women first.

Working our way to the head of the line, we were pleased not to be the oldest, but we were only fourth and fifth in line. Three Milwaukee women were ahead of us: Shirley, Mike (or Dorothy) and Regina. And after us there grew a long procession of women whispering together in anticipation of being in the presence of one of the founding women of the lesbian women's music movement who would lead us in a full moon celebration.

Kay Gardner, in a flowing ritual gown, stepped from the beamed-style clubhouse built on a knoll above us and walked down steps and across the grass into the inner circle of candles. She motioned the oldest of us to start walking so we could form a circle of over sixty women around the inner circle of candles illuminating her and her signer for the deaf. As Kay Gardner played her flute, we walked quietly to her extraordinarily pure tones. I could feel their vibrations in my soul and pulled tissues from my pocket to wipe away my tears.

Our circle formed while she played her music using rediscovered notes and scales from ancient times when women were valued as poets and musicians. "Moon Flow" and "Lunamuse" resonated through us, out onto the bushes and trees, up the hill and along the river, uniting Nature with Her flowing water, all of us together under the moon and the stars.

No urban sounds blocked this magic. Only the rippling river accompanied her voice as she sang and then spoke of our heritage and the values of our women's lives. We have evolved and are evolving, she said, and she asked us to speak out, in turn, the names of our maternal grandmother, our mother and our name. I often thought about the power that I inherited from the women in my life, but I have never had the opportunity to honor their spirit with others in a ritual. Now I can—and with others in this reverent circle. One woman said she didn't know who her mother was; some didn't know their grandmothers' names. A few cried. I shouted my mother's name, Mildred Anthony, to the heavens after speaking Emma Lueckfeld's name and then my own. I may have used the shouting to cover my vulnerable emotions about my mother's being schizophrenic.

This was our very first women's spirituality ritual, and we finished by holding hands and singing several choruses of "We all come from the Goddess, and to Her we will return, like a drop of rain flowing to the ocean."

Later we talked among those nearest us. Julie Kuiper, Mike's friend, told us that she had been Kay Gardner's host and that Kay sang and played on Julie's piano and her flute every day. Julie said that Kay Gardner is studying the effect of musical vibrations and its connection with color and nature and the healing of the body and mind. And Julie told us that this ritual with Kay Gardner was possible because she had just performed in concert last night at the First Unitarian Society of Milwaukee.

Kay is already a part of our woman's music herstory by playing flute and harmonica on the groundbreaking album, *Lavender Jane Loves Women*, created with Alix Dobkin and Patches Attom in 1974. They actually used the word "lesbian" in their songs on the album.

When I got back to our Mother Courage Bookstore, I played the record and read her album comments about her life that is similar to our lives except that she is a bit ahead of our transition—and becoming well known.

Kay wrote about reading *The Feminist Mystique* back in 1963 when she was married and a mother. Controversy about the book raged among her friends and she related that her "…ex-husband said I was unbearable to live with and I returned to my housework and my role of wife/mother." (My first feminist book that inspired me was Simone de Beauvoir's *The Second Sex*. Bea told me she's read so many, she can't single out one that influenced her the most.)

On the album, Kay referred to "…the late sixties when such articles as 'The Myth of Vaginal Orgasm' were distributed on crude newsprint. I read them with shock and fear. "Those tracts were written by a bunch of dykes," I said to a friend who later became my lover."

She wrote more on the album: "Sylvia Plath's poems were the next influence on me…Here was a woman I could identify with." (My poet was Adrienne Rich but both Bea and I read Plath and Anne Sexton.) "Soon I was reading every piece of feminist literature I could get my hands on. I was living in Virginia at the time, still married, very active playing…and teaching flute…"

And here she says on the album: "And then I fell in love with a woman. Head over heels! Where had I been all my life? This was the real me and I was beautiful! My eleven-year marriage ended, and I returned to college."

(Returning to college was what put Bea's marriage on the rocks. And I know what Kay Gardner felt about being head over heels in love with a woman.)

Her story continues: "Soon afterwards I met Alix Dobkin and between my work with her and my participation in an invigorating and radical consciousness-raising group, my mind was made up. I could contribute to the Women's Movement through my best talent, music. (Mine—ours, is our bookstore.) "So here I am, and here we are. Lavender Jane loves women!"

Signed: Kay Gardner

Chapter 9

Laura Williams on August 11, 1979

Well, Pat Holmen and I taught an assertiveness in-service for nurses last night. I don't know what administration and the physicians think about encouraging nurses to be assertive, but Pat and I got an OK from our Director of Nursing Donna Durand. We planned this evening carefully not to sound too revolutionary and we had a great turnout teaching Techniques on Assertiveness Training for Women in Health Professions. Tri-Technical College is setting up a Woman's Bureau that deals with women's issues so we had a good excuse to teach this revolutionary material.

Pat and I made them laugh at situations nurses fall into when doctors treat them as subordinates and how to respond or adjust so-called superiors' perceptions without sounding too abrasive. I hope administration doesn't think we're being too subversive, especially with nurses in a few other hospitals becoming unionized, but Pat remarked that it's time we change those ideas that nurses are "doctors' handmaidens" and "we have to work our wiles" to get the best treatment for the patient.

We invited Jan to set up a Mother Courage book table with all of their books on the subject, and she took orders for books she didn't have that we recommended for nurses. The three of us agreed that each order was to be picked up at the store. Some of the women didn't like that, but we asserted ourselves and insisted they go to Mother Courage so they could see all that was there for them to read and to learn.

Bea on August 12, 1979

I remember March of '75 when Jill and Joel announced that they wanted to live with Jake! They're leaving me! For him! "You're the strong one, Mom," Jill deduced, and Joel nodded. "Dad needs help more than you do."

Suppose your kids say, "Ho hum. We've decided to live with Dad," or "Guess what? We've joined the Army."

> My children. My precious children.
> The thing that made my life purposeful.
> My propagation, part of my immortality.
> My babies, my beings in whom I invested my
> complete self.
> What of them? Two are grown and gone; Uncle Sam's
> children now.
> And two said, "Hey Mom. Guess what? This'll kill
> you, kid.
> Guess what we decided to do. Just for fun we're going
> to live with Dad.
> Hell, we've lived here in this house all our lives and
> we need a change.
> Ho Hum. Mom. You won't care, will you? You ain't
> home much
> Anymore, anyway. You're so busy. This will give you
> your freedom."

What did I do? Jan was at Woodridge so I couldn't tell her of the radical surgery that came with my divorce. Wounded and bleeding, I went to Marge's and her friend Charlie was there. I was crying but now I'm angry and strong. We went to the Eagles Club to dance and later she decided to share, to send him with me to cheer me up, I suppose, so Charlie had me for the night—or I had him. Whatever.

Jan on August 15, 1979

Most divorced couples fight over custody issues with children; we battled over our forty-four acres of Door County land we call Woodridge, a tiny strip of stones and trees, an old immobile travel trailer, a barn that we built, and an outhouse. To me it is a priceless piece of Mother Earth, and She's not creating any more. This land was for my children's future and I intended to have them throw my ashes under what I called "Mother's Rock" in the middle of the land blessed by birch trees.

Even when I was there with our family or straight couples, my lover Bea at home was with me in spirit. My internal dialogue filled my inner self.

> I want to share a rainbow with you—
> a rainbow spanning across the moist, warm air
> from the turbulent spring wind-swept lake
> bordered by the fresh, new green grass,
> greener than Easter-basket-grass green,
> but alive—alive as I feel,
> full of newness, full of life, full of colors,
> broad and rich as the lush, double, perfect
> rainbow that I want to share with you.
>
> You have taught me what love is.
> You have unified my forces
> of emotional, intellectual and

sexual passion into a whole
—a feeling wholeness,
a knowing wholeness, a being wholeness.
You have taught me what love is.

I notified Alex that I was claiming visitation rights to Woodridge on the weekend of September 21 to 24. I answered the phone during supper on August 29 and Alex told me that he would not allow Bea Lindberg to go on the land.

"Who do you think I'm to go there with, my children holding me by the hand like it's a visit with my crazy mother in the insane asylum? Well, we'll see about that!"

I still had keys to the trailer and the barn.

"From the desk of Alex Carnigian" on August 30, 1979
Subject Door County-9/22

1) Bea Lindberg is specifically excluded from using or staying at Woodridge.
2) Please limit groups to 10 or less.
3) Please call for update on use of new facilities.

From Attorney Conrad Sanders on August 31, 1979
Dear Mr. Carnigian:

Jan Anthony has consulted us with reference to your response to her requesting the use of the Door County property for the weekend of September 21 to 24.

Our client cannot accept your condition that Bea Lindberg not accompany her. The stipulation and divorce judgment contained no such condition and in our opinion, it cannot be reasonably implied.

Similarly, your arbitrarily attempting to limit our client's guests to nine is not acceptable. Jan has informed us that the property's facilities have heretofore comfortably accommodated many more than that number.

Yours truly,
Conrad Sanders

Jan on September 12, 1979

Dear Matt,

Just a note to let you know that I'm thinking of you and am hoping that everything is well with you for this new term in Madison.

I'm planning on taking a weekend at Woodridge and have been looking forward to seeing the place again after more than two years. I want to go from September 21 to 24. Then I'm off to LaCrosse for a public relations meeting with Wisconsin hospital PR people.

Love,
Mom

From Attorney Conrad Sanders on September 14, 1979
Ms. Jan D. Anthony, etc.

Dear Jan:

Enclosed is a copy of the curt reply from Attorney Kerry to my letter of August 31 sent to your ex-husband.

In consequence, you may have these alternatives:

1) Make the commitments he wants.

2) Use the property with your friends, risking a confrontation if he arrives while you are there. You would have no use of the building, unless you can manage to get in.

3) Bring a legal action for an interpretation of the language used in the divorce stipulation and judgment. This would involve expense to you, and probably several months would elapse before an answer could be obtained.

Had I appreciated that Alex's warped, petty attitude would continue this long, I would have urged a more specific definition of your rights when the stipulation was being drafted. Have you disclosed this matter to the children? Perhaps they could help him see how immaturely he is acting.

Very truly yours,
Conrad Sanders

Kerry's letter to Sanders dated September 12, 1979

Dear Mr. Sanders:

As you know we represent Mr. Alex A. Carnigian. We would appreciate it if all correspondence involving Mr. Carnigian be sent directly to our office rather than to him.

It is my opinion that Mr. Carnigian has title to the Door County Real Estate and has the right to control the use of the property. It was the intention of the parties that Jan Anthony have the right to use the property and it was contemplated that she would use it with the children. The divorce judgment does not give her the right to have large groups on the premises and I am sure you can understand why Mr. Carnigian does not want Bea Lindberg on the premises. Since the divorce judgment does not grant any of these rights to your client, we must respectfully decline to acquiesce in her demands.

If you have any further questions in this matter, please advise.

Very truly yours,

Thomas C. Kerry

Jan's journal notes on September 14, 1979

Transition toward selfhood=frustration

Adrienne Rich's poem from *The Dream of a Common Language*

"Mother-Right"
  (for M.H.)
Woman and child   running
in a field   A man planted
on the horizon

Two hands   one long, slim   one
small, starlike   clasped
in the razor wind

Her hair cut short for faster travel
the child's curls grazing his shoulders
the hawk-winged cloud   over their heads

The man is walking boundaries
Measuring   He believes in what is his
the grass   the waters underneath   the air

the air   through which child and mother
are running   the boy singing
the woman   eyes sharpened in the light
heart stumbling   making for the open

I will retain my visitation rights to Woodridge without petty and arbitrary patronizing restrictions that attempt to demean my intelligence, my judgment and my fair and agreed upon use of Woodridge.

Now there's unhealthy hate and bitterness, a waste of effort and money for attorney fees and legal action, and continued hostility after two years of separation and divorce plus many years before of an eroding marriage and relationship—since 1968.

There's tunnel vision of laying the blame on a single person.

Our children see me now as a happy and productive person—and peaceful. How does this image compare to those whose bitterness still exists.

Time, time, time for anger and hate to die.

Jan on September 19, 1979

Dear Matt,

Your father is really giving me a hard time about my right to visit Woodridge. I'm afraid I will have to take legal action in order to use it and that will take months and money that is a waste for all. I gave up my financial claim to the land to preserve that space for you and Jenny for your future use. A settlement of the case for my half of the property would have perhaps forced the sale. I did not want to have this happen so I settled for simple visitation.

He continues to have tunnel-vision hate for blaming Bea as the cause of his divorce even though the cause of the divorce began many years before that with the eroding of our relationship.

This continued hostility after two years of separation is unhealthy. Hate and bitterness must stop after all this time. It's unnatural.

On Saturday, Bea's son Joel was married and I attended with Marge and other friends and was warmly accepted by her children. Her husband was even considerate and friendly.

Continued confrontations to the last ditch of vengeance on your father's part are harmful to everyone who still carries this in their lives. It creates unnecessary trauma every day and especially in your major life events: graduation, homecomings, marriages, childbearing and parenting.

I think I've had enough of others' hate and anger and uncompromising demands. I want to hurt no one, and I do not want to give up my rights to whatever I have left.

Remember when Jenny was burned after spilling hot grease on her chest when she pulled a huge turkey out of one of St. Agnes' food service ovens? I had to sneak over to the house because your father has forbidden me never to come there again. I called Jenny when your father was at work so that I could go there to see her and do whatever I could for her. How terrible for Jenny to be in pain and for me not to be able to care for her when I was able to help.

He continues being incredibly unreasonable and I know you do not want to cross him, but I would be so grateful if you could help me tell him that his restrictions on my use of the land are unfair and arbitrary and will lengthen the fights and frustrations and bitterness he has.

You and I share a lot when we can. I've been honest and open with you and you probably know me better than many sons know their mothers. If you can help me in any way to keep my rights to use the land, to visit with you and Jenny at home and at Woodridge, to visit with your future spouses and children when the time is right, to keep my space open for me when I need it, to continue to have in my will that my ashes be placed under a rock in the small woods in the center of Woodridge, I certainly can use your help.

Love,
Mom

Bea on September 25, 1979

We'd packed our tent and gear to head for Woodridge again. The tent came along in case the doors were barred, but we didn't need it. We opened the trailer and barn doors and Jan cut the grass while I unloaded the car and settled us in for our forbidden visit, staying in the cozy trailer rather than the barn.

Jan cried when we arrived at Woodridge. She really needed this visit to enjoy all the pleasures and beauty of Wisconsin's rock ridge of a peninsula. We drove to my old stomping grounds where my parents build a log cabin on the Green Bay side. On Lake Michigan's side, we shopped at Nelson's Hardware, a Bailey's Harbor landmark, to buy whatever you need—or don't need—and walked about my ex-husband's dad's old place, then through The Ridges wooded paths of wildflowers. It was warm enough to swim in Buckaroo Lake.

Enjoying Woodridge, we went into the woods to risk making love, to let down our guard from a hostile husband who may come storming on the land. Finally relaxed enough to slowly savor our bodies in Nature's fresh, open air, nakedly fragile, our hunger for this happiness strengthened and enveloped us in tenderness——first a simultaneous delight, then variations of childishly creative sensual playfulness in the shade. After resting as in meditation, we dressed to meet anyone, we sipped leisurely martinis in the sun and returned to civilization at dusk via Fish Creek's fish boil to eat the buttery and juicy meal with our fingers.

Our dog Luv loved all that too. She was so good and she loved the land as much as Jan's dog Pepper had in her many visits there before the divorce and then the dog's dying after that.

The fire ring and its sparks floating to ash before it reached the trees that encircled us brought back more memories, and the stars shined on us so brightly as we stepped from the woods to be under the clear night sky.

Jan on January 20, 1980

My dad called this morning to tell me that Chico, his tottering old Chihuahua, died while sleeping on towels held in his lap. Dad sat in his chair for hours for the dog to gasp its last breath. Gads! What am I supposed to do now? How sad. I can't imagine how my dad feels. But I hate that dog because he nipped at my kids, peed in my house, scratched his butt across my couch, and my father loved that ratty, popped-eyed dog so and took such good care of it—better than he took care of me. I heard stories that Dad would carry Chico with him into a bar for a drink and sit the dog on the stool next to him. Chico was the center of his life—even more than me. Bea said I should be grateful for that. It took me off the hook.

He needs help digging through a five-foot high snow mound stacked on top of the gravesite that Dad had dug and covered with wood and grass a couple years back for this eventuality. How do we get to it? I'll have to shovel it away, I guess. Dad brought home the aluminum casket he had someone make for Chico. He'd showed me where he kept it at the shop, but now I didn't have to find it and hand him this maudlin offering.

Ah, but a miracle happened just as we were standing outside surveying the snow pile. I had called Jenny earlier about Chico, but she didn't tell me that Matt was home from Madison—and my son drove into the backyard armed with a gas-powered ice-fishing auger. He climbed to the top of the pile and, following my dad's supervision, started drilling into the icy pile to find the burial spot.

It took a while and I excused myself to get back to a meeting at work that I was missing. I was freezing too, I said. Dad offered me a brandy, but I begged off and let Matt save me from witnessing the interment.

In the interim, my dad and his grandson discovered that Chico had stiffened up and now he wouldn't quite fit into the gaudy aluminum casket lined with tacky red plastic cushions my father had made from leftover materials at the shop. Matt told me that the two of them stood over the deceased dog that now couldn't fit into the casket as my father had envisioned. Matt waited at his grandfather's side and finally took the initiative to bend Chico's legs a bit off kilter and push the dog down snuggly against the soft foam to make him fit. (I hope this doesn't imprint an undertaker's career on Matt's mind.) Before closing the box with its silvery aluminum top, my dad took out his seldom-used disposable camera to take Chico's picture in his casket, his final resting place. He took several and finished off the roll of film.

Matt then climbed on what remained of the pile for the entombment, respectfully planted the coffin squarely into its place and piled chunks of dirt and snow back over it. Grandpa would smooth it all out and plant grass to cover the square in the summer, he said. They paused in reverence before they went into the house where my dad offered Matt to join him in a sacramental taste of brandy. Later at home, I had my martinis with Bea who chose a shot of tequila and a chaser of Mexican beer in Chico's honor.

When I called my poor father to see how he was doing, he seemed OK, but I'll bet the brandy stiffened him up too.

The Bay View Times on May 7, 1980
"Network' formed for working woman"

The Women's Network was founded in 1979 to bring career and professional women together from many areas of expertise and share experiences and exchange information.

In many professions, career women are isolated from their peers. Often, the professional woman is the only woman in her work group. These women are usually excluded from traditional "old boy" networks where men exchange information over lunch, coffee breaks and at meetings. The Women's Network provides a natural support group for women who might otherwise be alone in the work force.

Networking for women is more than a local phenomenon. Variations of the network have been established in every major city of the country. Women everywhere are finding the "network experience" to be the highlight of their workweek.

Now, in Lakeshore Bay, working women have the opportunity of expanding their network of contacts to get jobs, find a doctor or a lawyer, or simply to seek advice. To promote this self-awareness speakers are invited to almost every meeting.

Beth Johnson is the founder and president; Sue Sura, the Network's public relations director; and Robin Witte is chair of the Network's directory with over one hundred members. Her area of expertise may be utilized through the directory that each member receives. A newsletter provides members with news of upcoming events as well as individual accomplishments within the community or their firm.

If an individual were to compare this organization to a male counterpart, hopefully, it would match the Rotary, Elks or Kiwanis. What these organizations have in common is spirit, enthusiasm and a commitment to mutual non-competitive support.

Chapter 10

Jan on June 2, 1980

I ran out of my allergy pills and went to pick some up at the drugstore. While there I bought the paper because there seemed to be time to read the *Milwaukee Journal's* massive Sunday edition, and coincidentally, to check out job want-ads.

To my surprise, our friend Rachel Sandler's photo appeared in today's "Life/Style" section in a feature about women and guilt.

Rachel Sandler insists on our partnering with her to illustrate, publish and market her manuscript into a book for children who have been abused. Bea is stubbornly holding out on the project because of our stretched-to-the-limit finances.

And there Rachel was in a sideline box on page 6: "How to stop the guilties."

These strategies for dealing with guilt are suggested by Milwaukee Public School psychologist and Transactional Analysis specialist Rachel Sandler.

- Rectify what you can and let go of the rest.
- Accept and view the past as unchangeable.
- Discover what you're avoiding in the present.

• Accept yourself and your choices, whether others dislike them or not.

• Check your value system.

• Assess the real consequences of the actions that make you feel guilty.

• Check grandiosity—the idea that you are the center of the universe—and give up the myth.

• Choose a partner and tell the person what you're feeling guilty about. Have the partner repeat it to you and then react to it as though it were the other person's problem. (Invariable, says Sandler, you'll be more compassionate and forgiving when you hear the story coming from someone else.)

Ha. I definitely agree with all that, as I do with most of what Rachel has counseled and joshed with us since our first TA Intensive Workshop at our church's Emerson House in 1973.

I definitely do not believe in guilt. It's a useless emotion. I have made mistakes that I am sorry for and have sincerely apologized for most them. But I do not dwell on them forever. "Get over it," has helped me. "Get on with life," helps too, except for my career when I must continue to pursue excellence and fight for equality and get a paycheck.

In the main article, the reporter explains that in one of the first Woman-to-Woman conferences five years ago, "...an astounding overflow audience of some two hundred women" had Rachel repeating it every year, and every year it's filled to capacity.

"It's not that Sandler has anything against guilt itself. In fact, she believes it is essential to a civilized society. Without it, you have a bunch of incipient sociopaths."

I thought to myself, "It sounds like some guys I work for."

The paper's story continues as Rachel explained that in school she had dealt with children who seem to have no sense of guilt, no conscience. "One young man was asked how he would have felt if a blow he struck had permanently damaged another child's eye, he replied, 'I don't care. He shouldn't have messed with me.' Sandler finds that attitude chilling.

Sandler believes that many times guilt masks another feeling, one that is less acceptable for people to express—especially women. "It's OK for me to say I feel guilty because of all the demands made on me," Sandler said. "I can handle guilt for too long and then I get angry. I can attack or sink into depression."

Well, thanks again, Rachel. I'm not going to let depression get me because of my career. That terrible job review that Randy King wrote is still eroding my spirit. I'd better do something about it.

Jan on June 20, 1980

Dear Alex,

This is to notify you that I am claiming my summer week visitation rights to Woodridge starting on Friday evening, July 11 to Sunday, July 20.

Please have Jenny, or some other person if you like, get the barn, trailer and outhouse keys to me by Tuesday, July 8. I will be bringing guests with me from work or they will be joining me there. If you like, I will be happy to contribute my efforts to any extra maintenance tasks while I'm there, like painting, cutting the grass, etc.

If you have made plans to be at Woodridge during any part of that time, please let me know by Wednesday, July 2, so that we can reach an agreement on any scheduling problems.

Your cooperation in this matter will help to heal old wounds that have been hurting too long and for the wrong reason. It's time for a sensible, peaceful resolution,

Sincerely,

Etc.

cc: Jenny, Matt, Conrad Sanders

Jan on July 10, 1980

I discovered this note from Alex in my office door mail slot today, Thursday, at 11 a.m. It is noted 3:30 Tuesday. Obviously I don't check my mail slot often because the hospital courier hands me the mail several times a day. I'm happy I was out of the office because I'd have been stunned seeing him looking through the window at me.

Jan,

I tried to reach you Tuesday without success; we needed to have a talk. And I'm leaving for Detroit tonite. So—

I'm in the process of disposing of Woodridge. It's becoming a source of continuing irritation to me so I'm solving the problem for us both. I've discussed things with both Matt and Jenny.

I'd suggest you make other plans for this weekend and next week.

It would be helpful to me if we could discuss Jenny's schooling, Matt, etc. If you're interested, I'd like to tell you some things about my life, too.

I apologize again for not gathering your stuff. It's my top priority and should be done by month end. In view of my traveling every week, it has not been a top priority in my life.

Jan on July 17, 1980

Bea and I went to Woodridge anyway! When we stopped at the Reiker's farmhouse to get water, the newly widowed Frida Reiker, whose family sold us the property, wasn't there but her surprised daughter, Jane, welcomed us and we loaded up our water jugs from their milk house. Alex changed—or he hired someone to change all of Woodridge's padlocks. Undaunted, we copied the I.D. numbers on the bottom of each new padlock and searched through the lock sections of nearby hardware stores. We found and bought new locks sets with the same I.D. numbers and the keys to open those barriers that were to keep us from fulfilling my property rights.

Dear Jenny and Matt,

It's Friday at Woodridge and I'm spending my first full week here since 1977.

In spite of your father's threats to keep us away and of "disposing" of the place, I arrived to stake my claim and to become a part of this important land again. The air, the sky, the trees, the lake are all so dear and so vital to nourish my soul. I gave up my financial rights so that your father would not have to sell this place. I signed my name on a slip of paper called a "quit claim deed" during the last minutes of being in divorce court. I assumed your father would be fair and honest and reasonable about the trifling request that I visit this place for a few days each year.

In spite of this all, my week has been more than I could ask for. Through various means we gained access to every building—through locks and double locks, and we cleaned up the trash, fly bodies and mouse turds, took down the vandals' toilet paper streamers and "shit house" sign in the barn and made this place a gentle resting haven again.

Each day we did tasks to add to the pleasure of this environment. I wrested the grass back from the weeds and gave the area a trim look again. We collected wood for campfires. I cleaned out the outhouse. We took away trash. We fixed the lawn mower and added new propane gas to one of the tanks.

With three guests the first weekend, Carolyn Schafer, Jennifer Kindle and Sue Manning, we walked down the path to find stones and bones. We went to a late night jazz session in a barn near us. We ate fish boil and talked and laughed 'til after 2:30 a.m.

We're waiting for the next batch of friends, Betty Willing and Joanne Zekas to join us soon for this weekend. They'll walk into a homey and clean, friendly barn.

Yesterday Frieda Reiker surprised us with a visit. The place looked so great and we were so happy to talk with her as another strong woman. We had that in common as well as mutual respect for each other.

I told her I was happy that we still could be friends and we nodded affirmatively to each other. When I came here last fall, she was so surprised and happy to see me. She didn't know what had happened to me, she said. She asked Alex about me once. "Where is Jan?" she asked, and Alex said only, "Just like in a book, all chapters come to an end." She didn't know by that if I were alive or dead.

We talked a lot: about work, about Jane's deer hunting, about our having a pistol and a rifle here for protection, about being widowed, about being divorced, about our bookstore and how we want to help people find strength and answers to their concerns.

I asked her if Jane's husband still cuts the hay off the front land and she said no, that Clyde asked Alex two times for permission to do so and that Alex gave him no answer. This upset Clyde and maybe that's a reason why Clyde is so friendly to the two of us. Helpful too. I saw no reason why he can't use the land, especially when we get water and watchful protection from them.

Speaking of water, Buckaroo Lake is beautiful. We have a little two-person raft that we take out there with the dog and when Luv tires of swimming, we just lift her in it and she rides out with us. It's good to hold our swim suits while we take a quick skinny dip.

Last night the stars were exquisite. The smoke from the campfire rose straight up to the sky and we talked about primitive women making pots for their use: to carry oil, store seeds and food, to add to their civilization and create goodness out of the earth and fire; to preserve and even to hold the ashes of their lost loved ones.

This whole place gives me a connection to the earth, to the past, to the future. If it is taken away from us, I'll probably find another tiny piece of land somewhere, someday—though I don't know how I'll be able to afford it.

What about you and your space for the future?

And for what reason may we lose it? For spite and jealousy, ownership and show of power over others, which are the immediate reasons, plus the lack of nurturing self-worth that caused me to leave everything else behind me in the first place.

Alternatives can be considered. I'd love to come up here and share the chores. I have no hostile feelings, no anger, no hate. What I do feel is hurt, kicked-in-the-stomach hurt that I'm tired of feeling for so many years.

Your father writes that he wants to talk about your schooling and he'd like to tell me something about his life. I see very bleak chances of doing this if he disinherits you from your land and tries to thwart me from my sharing it.

But I am concerned about your schooling and your lives, and therefore I propose that the four of us have a meeting as soon as Matt gets back from California so that we can jointly discuss any issues, conflicts and resolutions about any of your problems and concerns.

And I feel that your father should seek some professional counseling about the continued cancerous hate and rage that he carries that may cause him to make irrational decisions that affect you both immediately and me in the long run.

Divorced couples do heal their wounds and join together with family and friends for the good of themselves and their children. The past can be buried so that the present can be perceived with clear and positive behavior. Life can be lived with understanding and hope and cooperation. No one needs to suffer any longer.

I'm reclaiming some simple Woodridge objects to take home, to make whole again or to use with joy: my old banjo, the kalimba thumb harp, my mother's typewriter and one favorite rock.

I'm sitting in the barn writing this as the clean wind washes past the sleeping dog next to me; it cools me and freshens my hands, arms and face. I see some of the trees that we had planted on a Mother's Day weekend are growing taller over the weeds. They survived better than machine planted ones. I clipped grass and weeds from around the trees close to the barn.

The leaves sing their songs with the birds and the bugs. The weeds and the wildflowers wave back at them. There's a rumble of thunder coming from where the clouds have turned to solid gray moisture. The thunder, the rain will sweep over us soon and the sun, white clouds and warmth will reach us again after that.

Jan on October 16, 1979

Identifying other lesbians is almost impossible. Estimates are that at least ten percent of the female population is lesbian. That's a lot of women. If only all of us were able to come out at the same time, and gay guys too, we would transform the world. We can only guess about our role models whose true selves are well-hidden, as Greta Garbo said, "I vont to be alone."

Well we don't want to be alone. At lunch in the cafeteria last week with new staff Sam and Liz, I discovered that they were actually gay and lesbian and "live together" in a little apartment in Lakeshore Bay to hide it. Sam's a jolly tall fellow and Liz has a lover in Milwaukee who's divorced with two kids. Liz's lover and her ex-take turns living in the same house so their kids don't have to be shifted back and forth. They swap the apartment when the other parent is "at home" with their children. So some couples, whatever their mates, do get along.

A few weeks ago, I invited Sam and Liz to our home for supper so we could share more of our lives without being overheard at work. It was then that Bea and I decided to form a lesbian support group that would meet at our house. Each of us would seek out those women we knew who could be trusted and could be comfortable together. We met last night for our first meeting. Sam couldn't come. Women only.

When Bea had a gut feeling that a woman or a couple of women customers were at least close to being lesbians, she'd carefully slip them a note saying that we're having a rap group for women identifying with women-only issues. Well, a dozen brave ones as singles and couples came to our home, and after that we decided that we would meet at various women's homes—like a secret society. We could bring others into the group in the future, but we would have to ask others in the gathering before if it's OK to invite new women.

It helps to identify with lesbian women as a group, that your primary emotional attachment is with women, to be around them in an open and honest way. Through the bookstore, we can help them find events and ways to attend the larger woman-identified culture. A woman may not be having genital contact with another woman and still consider herself to be a lesbian. One of our women is a nun in her mid-twenties.

We discussed what I was reading from *Lesbian Sex*, the book by JoAnn Loulan: "…that only you know how you feel. If you feel that you're a lesbian, then you are. No one else can make that decision for you. It's hard to be part of an oppressed group; being a lesbian automatically qualifies you as part of one. You receive no rewards from the dominant culture, no special discounts. Being a lesbian has to be its own reward, in and of itself."

And one of the rewards is finding our "sisters" and bringing them together.

Referring to "the larger woman-identified culture," Bea and I went to another annual Wisconsin Women in the Arts at the Madison Park Inn last weekend. We took advantage of home hospitality for a change and we were put up in the basement rec room. That gave us the privacy we wanted. After our customary cocktails in our private room and our international supper at a Madison cafe, we went to the conference hotel to hear the featured speaker Diane Gelon. She showed *The Dinner Party* slides and urged us to support the project with contributions. Of course, Chicago needs to find more places to exhibit the monumental piece; museums are turning her away. We talked with Diane for a few minutes about our spiritual feelings of seeing *The Dinner Party* in San Francisco and how we sell Chicago's books at our store.

The evening's entertainment included a performance with dancers wearing pastel shades of veils to dramatize nuances of the classical myth of abduction of the Goddess Demeter's daughter Persephone with leafy maidens, mothers and crones hovering all about the principle characters as seasons change while Demeter mourns the loss of her kidnapped daughter into the earth and celebrates Persephone's return to please Demeter who makes the earth again becomes fertile. A narrator would have helped the effect, and we got bored compared to previous years' presentations.

Our new Milwaukee friend and musician Bev Glasner played her autoharp and sang feminist songs as the best performer that night—one worth waiting for.

A hefty, bearded woman wearing old bib overalls asked Bea to dance with her. She's met us at the Feminist Writers' group and my lover teased me about being miffed at my not being asked to dance as we slipped out the ballroom doors. This conference was not as good as the others we had attended in the past. Perhaps they're running out of funding while we're also running low on money.

Jan on October 22, 1979

I finally endured our salary review that was due September 16. Randy keeps demanding that I get organized and then he doesn't meet his own responsibilities to us. I'm still on an "exempt" status with a 32-week schedule though he knows how hard and how many hours extra that I'm working for the hospital. I'm on an annual salary too, which means no overtime. From a study that I included six months ago in my state PR newsletters, PR salaries ranged from $13,800 to $28,500 with the median being $18,700 from available figures in 1977. I was earning $15,000 up to this day. Now my new raise takes my salary only up to $16,200 and I'm still on the low end of the salary spectrum, no matter how hard I work and how successful the results are.

I read somewhere that the Equal Pay Act of 1963 makes it illegal to pay a woman less than a man receives for the same work. Ha! Where do you find that and try to enforce it? And keep the job you have?

And where is that Lakeshore Med rule that says a supervisor and a subordinate cannot live together? That's the hoax Nick and

Randy devised to get rid of Bea as my assistant after we bought our house and moved in together. I don't speak about "assertiveness" when I'm the most compliant to the power over me. I have to be or I'll be fired too, right away. Gads! It's easy for these emotions to consume me.

I'm also writing Mother Courage's *Courier* newsletter and staffing book tables workshops around town on some evenings and weekends. It seems like every day when I get to the bookstore, I'm the one who empties the wastebaskets and sweeps the floor. I feel like the janitor partner when it comes to making decisions around here.

Quit whining, Jan.

Bea on October 23, 1979

Jan is so depressed about her raise. Hell. At least she doesn't have to wait all day for a customer to come into the store. At least she has a salary and benefits and can see people at work. Yesterday she surely spoiled my day off when she came home in a rage. After a few drinks and supper, we played pool and that helped her calm down for this evening.

She couldn't get back to sleep after she woke at 3:30 a.m., so we had ourselves an interlude. That helped me too.

Jan on October 29, 1979

Trick or Treat! Well, it turns out that the trick is on me—and our School of Radiology students who volunteered respond to the recent media coverage of Halloween candy tampering. More than one hundred families took us up on our offer Sunday to x-ray Trick or Treat bags to scan for inserted razors or needles because of the national scare that came from some out-of-state lunatic who was reported to have put razor blades into candy apples that the kids collected.

We were actually unprepared for the crowds and worked our buns off trying to keep the kinky lines of costumed youngsters and parents happy while they waited for us to spill out their bags and carefully return each bag to their correct person.

Randy, one of his current girlfriends and his new associate, Chuck McCarthy, stopped by to see how things were going and helped us out to speed up the line and get panicky people back to their peaceful homes. Of course we didn't find anything, but the scare that some copycat ogre would hurt our children on this once playful holiday added more to the fright than fake goblins and ghosts.

And in Maple Grove, they're still burning a fake witch over a huge bonfire with little kids running around the flames. I suppose having kids stand in line to get their candy scanned for sharp objects is better than resorting to celebrating symbols medieval femicide. My commentary in *The Bay View Times* last year on what this truly means in the history of women—and some liberal men who sacrificed as heretics, but also what impact that must make on today's children watching some human figure being burned in effigy. I try not to believe that the media is more interested in the morbid than in the merry news events. I didn't realize it, but our local newspaper was feeding the fear by taking pictures as people were lining up at Lakeshore Med and witch manikins were being burned in our Maple Grove suburb.

Jan on November 3, 1979

We had something to celebrate yesterday when we dedicated the new parking ramp with music from St. Mary's High School band, balloons, little souvenirs, apple cider and homing pigeons.

Employees, board members and trustees, administrators and guests walked with helium-filled balloons to the main ramp entrance with Clark Young, Trustee Gerald Walter and Nick Dixon leading the way. The neighboring high school band waited at the opposite entrance and I was poised with my contact person from the Homing Pigeon Club who had about twenty or more birds (not doves as in Disneyland) in cages hiding in the wings.

Of course, Nick Dixon told everyone how wonderful this ramp was for the whole community and when Mr. Young fired the starting gun, Mr. Walter cut the ribbon and the uniformed high school band started marching toward us with its "76 Trombones" blasting at us under the ramp ceiling as if we were all in an enormous, ceramic tile-lined bathroom. People let go of their blue and yellow balloons and the pigeon man opened the crate doors and let loose the birds who swooped into the sky following the balloons in the wind. Everyone's cheers added to the joyful noise.

One pigeon, perhaps in shock from Mr. Young's starting pistol shot, stayed in the cage, and the handler reached in to grab it and release it. In its dizzy state, it floundered on the ground, danced a couple hops and just happened to fly up Board member Peggy Miller's skirt. She let out a howl. The pigeon barely recovered from its detour and flapped away like a Dodo bird to try catching up with its feathered friends and the balloons heading east, brightening the gray clouds of a Lake Michigan November.

With all the noise, few heard Peggy's surprised yelp being goosed by a pigeon. When I apologized for the pigeon, she told me that she had wanted to wear slacks in the cold wind, but her husband suggested that it more appropriate for her to wear a skirt. Luckily my old friend kept her great sense of humor and Randy couldn't blame me for what happened.

Bea on November 20, 1979

The store activities quicken with holiday newsletters to promote Christmas sales. In preparation for the long hours we're going to have to spend at the store, Jan's helping her dad get rid of the "gold mining sluice" he rigged up to funnel the rain leaking from the roof along the chimney and through the ceiling into a hole next to a radiator pipe that led to the basin on the landing below. He didn't want to spend any money on his shop and home because he believed the State of Wisconsin or Lakeshore Bay County would end up owning it all because of the unpaid bills he'd acquired during the lost decades of Jan's mother's confinement in these public mental institutions.

Jan talked him into fixing the roof and then we tiled the ceiling in his office and workroom behind our book store. Her next plan is to paint the rooms while she's minding the store and waiting for some Christmas customers to come in during her evening shift. Together we paneled those walls that were too cracked to fix. He's so happy to sit in a clean and well-appointed office again.

Our lesbian rap group is becoming successful as we get to know each other. It's liberating just to be ourselves. All of the women are younger. They're concerned about coming out to their parents and we're concerned about how we come across to our children.

A couple nights ago we were invited to the Shannon's again for three saunas and two dips in Lake Michigan, and of course, Jan was at the old ping pong table zapping balls around with the guys. Months ago, I realized what a great exercise program that would be for us so we moved our living room furniture around so we could fit our ping pong top from our pool table in the center of the living room and play some games at home. That really went over with our rap group women, families and guests who now visit exclusively downstairs in our family room.

Bea on December 2, 1979

The bookstore business is picking up after a slow November. To help me get through the days, I've been having a drink or two. Times will get worse. We'll be opening the store 'til 8 p.m. starting December 4 through 3 p.m. on the Christmas Eve.

Just before Thanksgiving Day we invited Matt and Jenny for supper on one night and my kids over for another supper. That would free them all to be with their "regular" families on the holiday, and it gave us a beautiful Thanksgiving Day together, just the two of us where we cooked a turkey, watched the parade and movies on TV and made love.

But Jan had to go back to work on Friday, found Administration's five-page questionnaire to complete by December 15, and came home to have one of those "Friday night freak-outs." She drinks a couple martinis with me and I don't remember the one wrong word I may have said, but she started yelling—and I yelled back. Our home turns from an island of peace to a drunken battleground for equality. She says she will not submit to being subordinate as she did with her husband. She will not be put down again! She's never learned how to argue, she says. But she's learning.

I went out shopping alone over the weekend and bought a microwave today. That will be our Christmas present.

(The scenario goes like this.)

Unable to sleep, Jan sat up in bed with a newly rising orange moon lighting up the shadows between them. She looked at her own nakedness under the glow as a healing blessing. Bea, always restless, expecting some one, some thing, woke and looked to her partner. "What's the matter! Did you have a bad dream?"

"I just woke up. It must be the moon's usual power on me." And she threw the rest of her blankets, exposing her bare body to comfort Bea with love. That doesn't solve all the problems, but Jan is always ready if that's what Bea wants.

"I'll get us some wine," and Bea headed downstairs for the bar, not hearing Jan say quietly, "That doesn't solve problems either."

Returning to sit cross-legged on the bed, Bea handed Jan her glass and as usual, they toasted, "To us!" and swallowed a hefty gulp.

Facing each other with each knee touching her lover's with the wine and the moon warming them in their cool bedroom, Bea seemed ready to embrace when Jan asked her, "Why do we have to fight like we do?"

"You always seem to blow up, Jan, over something trivial."

"It may be trivial to you, but I don't want you to tell me what to do or to order me about. I get enough from that prick at work."

"You get mostly love and support from me and from others. Why do you have to act so edgy with me?"

"I'm afraid I'll lose my job and how are we going to support ourselves."

"Hell! The bookstore won't support us. I'm giving Jill cash to take over the store on Saturdays and it's more than I'm probably making myself." With false bravado, she finished her wine.

Jan inhaled, taking advantage of the moment, "And I'm afraid that I'm going to lose you again to alcohol. I do not want to be abandoned and left alone again to make everything all right with everyone and with my own grief."

"You're strong, Jan. And I'm OK. I know how to handle alcohol," as she lifted her glass to Jan and finished its contents. "You know what I really have trouble with? Being a lesbian. Oh, I laugh and make jokes at our rap group and I try to advise others about living as a lesbian, but I'm pretty shaky about it most of the time. You know the story. My brother committing suicide because he was gay. I'm almost glad my parents are dead so they can't disown me like they did him. And I don't really know if my kids hate me or not."

"If you love me, and I know you do, I guess you are a lesbian."

"Well, who says I can't change sometime, go back to the old days."

"I don't know. Maybe. You've tried hard enough for both of us to stay straight. You've always said you tried to send me back to my family—how many times. But I hope you won't change because I want to be with you for the rest of our lives. I am a lesbian, Bea, and even if you don't want to be, you are too. And I'm proud of you—except when you drink too much, like in Las Vegas."

"Shit. Don't ever mention that place again. In rehab, so-called experts drilled it into me that I have a disease—alcoholism, but I know I can handle it. I know I really messed up our hospital trip there, of all crazy times and places to get wasted." She straightened her spine. "Hey! Damn it! When will you get over that! Forget about it?"

Jan put down her glass and touched Bea's arm. "That self-destructive behavior scared me then and it always will. I've lived with these fears since my mother's crazy behaviors—my fear of her killing herself. It seems to haunt me always—even now when I still don't know what I'll find when I come home."

"Yes. But that's what I was doing then, drinking myself to death. That's how I made it through those days and weeks without you—when you were with Alex. I'd numb myself out so I didn't feel so empty. I was so lonely I wanted to die. But I don't feel that I will lose you now."

"Most people fear being abandoned and lonely and it becomes desperately lonely when someone you love prefers to drink and pass out in her chair than to be with you."

"But you have it too, Jan. Alcoholism. Don't kid yourself. You just hide it better."

"Maybe. But we've been reading about women's health issues just in the past several months and it makes me think you have PMS and an alcohol problem. You've always acted unpredictably just before your period started. No one even knew about PMS until recently when women started researching the condition. It all makes any depression much worse. Alcohol doubles its effect before your period and sometimes even after. It causes twice as much craziness. And that doesn't even factor in how you feel about your being a lesbian."

"Look who's talking about crazy? That's you too."

"Yes. Sometimes I can't stand the pressure and I lose control. But I love you and I will never give you up. I haven't before and I won't—ever. I promise. I will not lose you. We can make a life together. We will make it together."

"You make shit into sunshine at work, Jan."

"But Bea, I don't want to have to do that about my life, too."

Tired finally, they comforted each other and wiggled about with Bea spooning into Jan's body and Jan's arms embracing Bea. Together under the warm covers, they looked through the window toward the smiling moon, now white and higher in the clear winter sky.

Chapter 11

Jan on December 28, 1979

The three Christmas Eve services at our Unitarian Universalist church celebrate the Winter Solstice with "Let there be light" as our Rev. Tony Logan enters the darken church carrying a lighted torch. Soon the lighting of candelabrum illuminates the sanctuary. Hanukkah words in English and Hebrew are spoken over the lighting of the Menorah and candle-holding folk dancers circling the room. Betty Hanneman introduced the dance to the church and now our dear Anna Spence and one or more of her three beautiful daughters always lead it. As usual, Alex, Matt and Jenny sit on one side of the church and we sit on the other until we join with Jenny in the Candle Dance. That must infuriate Alex, but performing the Candle Dance is a tradition—and Jenny's too, but now she decides to stay with her father rather than dance with us in the line.

The first of the services is a children's manger pageant with the wolf making peace with the lamb, and the children are dressed as shepherds, lambs and the wolf, the Magi, angels with halos, and Mary, Joseph and the baby. It's a joy to watch each child grow from little lambs to the wolf who can learn to follow the script or be angels with speaking parts.

This year, the two adult-oriented services that come later in the evening have Tony Logan dressed as Mary telling her side of the Christmas story. He always dresses up as one of the Christmas story characters, including King Herod, but his Mary was one of his best performances. After singing traditional carols, a glowing rainbow, projected from the back of the sanctuary, curves its colors against the wall, organ pipes, wreaths, above the bower of Christmas trees and poinsettia on the altar. The rainbow in church takes my breath away in awe and I break out in tears hearing Jim Henson's and Kermit's "The Rainbow Connection" with Tony playing the banjo with the other musicians. I barely sing the song because of my joyful tears of affirmation at experiencing the rainbow light cast over all, giving an even deeper meaning to this holiday. "Lovers and dreamers and me…" I try to sing, thinking "and us together—all of us, no matter how or why."

Balls of mistletoe stream down a wire from the ceiling portal and the church goers embraced each other in the happiness of the sun coming back to make each day longer and sometimes even brighter, to celebrate religious freedom, and to sing "Silent Night" and "It Came Upon A Midnight Clear," written by a Unitarian minister, "…From angels bending near the earth to touch their harps of gold, 'Peace on the earth to all good will from heaven the news we bring.' The world in solemn stillness lay to hear the angels sing." Then in the last stanza, to sing "…when peace shall over all the earth, its ancient splendors fling, and the whole world give back the song which now the angels sing."

(The scenario goes like this.)
The Carnigian holiday was hollow compared to times past but they pretend it wasn't. Jan's absence seems less painful than last year, but Jan is still a phantom in the spacious house that's sometimes empty when Alex is on business and Jenny is with her adopted family at a downtown restaurant and tavern. Jan's even a shadow when the house is crowded with Alex's family and friends, including the Dixons, making wine and bagels and having homemade wine-tasting contests. They all cluster around Alex, affirm him, hug him now—and he lets them.

"But it's like living with a terminal disease," he told Marge recently. "And I've lived with it for six years now, even longer perhaps, before I knew what was going on. She betrayed me not only with another person, but she's put me and the kids in our own closet because we can't really talk about her or tell others that I lost my wife to another woman and that she became a lesbian so they can try to understand what happened—and that our divorce is not my fault."

"What's going on is quite obvious to a lot of people," said Marge. "It's not your responsibility to keep Jan's lifestyle a secret."

"But I don't know who the people are who know about it: my immediate family, Jan's dad, a few other friends like Diana Dixon. I started talking with Diana last summer after walking along the lake. She or I would be sitting alone on our porch."

Alex sighed, "I'd like to get this depressing burden off my back. It's Jan's perverted story to hide, not mine. Jesus! My wife and the mother of my children is a lesbian! And she is so damn obvious with her feminist commentaries in the paper and that fucking feminist bookstore!" He almost bit his lower lip with the anger in those "f" words. "I didn't do anything wrong. Nothing I tried would change her. I did my best, but I only seemed to make it worse."

"You're right about all of that. I tried to stop her from throwing away everything she had, but she didn't listen to me either. Listen! She didn't alter her way of life to hurt you. At least I don't think so. I know she didn't want to hurt Jenny and Matt, and I feel that she really didn't want to hurt you."

"The kids are coping with it all right, I guess. We don't talk about it and they don't seem to be losing any friends. Jenny gets moody, but what teenager doesn't. She's working out a deal where she's renting out one of our rooms to a girlfriend. That way she won't be alone when I'm off on business trips. At least she doesn't have to fight with her mother to break from that so-called 'mother-daughter bond.' Jan took care of that when she left us."

Marge presumed, "I suppose the negative effect on the kids of your divorce is less stressful than that their mother is a lesbian."

"I don't know and I can't analyze that. What's worse is that perhaps theirs and my entire belief system is shot. My dreams of marriage. Even my own self-confidence." He whispered, "Even my manliness is compromised. She's the only woman I've ever had. I don't know what to do. I'm embarrassed. How can I live with the fact that I've lost my wife to another woman?!"

"I'm a good listener—and your friend, Alex," Marge whispered back. "And I'm probably the one person who knows the most about everything. I'll be your safety valve. Hell, I'll be a key to help you unlock the door to your side of that closet."

Bea on December 31, 1979

I'm BBQing steak outside tonight and will finish off this year with champagne. We pop the cork out the family room window and Jan says it's a great surprise when she finds it during her springtime gardening. Celebrating this season started with a Winter Solstice party at Sue Samira's in Milwaukee.

We received three free frozen turkeys from a man who came into the store with extras for us to hand out because he had completed his route. We saved one for ourselves. Our poet and professor friend Carol Lee Savoli stopped at the store to give us a bottle of brandy. (Maybe someone gave it to her and she knew we'd appreciate it more than she. We'll take it! And she got a turkey. And thank you!)

We worked out several suppers here and there with our various families and friends, finally finishing our leftovers with a turkey divan brunch. We stopped by at Marge's to exchange our gifts and have a few drinks. It's hard to believe that she is the first in our group as a "gay divorcee" who seems to have never recovered from her ex-husband's rejection, even after all these years. She was my best friend as we went out searching for men to maintain our self-esteem, even when I was frantically in love with Jan. She was the first adult woman Jan had an emotional crush on before I returned to rejoin folk dancing and church and escape the madness surrounding my husband and family. After Jan told Marge that she loved her, Marge acknowledge that her love would always be a deep friendship, saying she couldn't respond to her in any other way, and she kept

Jan just close enough to use Jan's good will and deeds for her own comfort. Oh well. Jan's euphoric crush for her collapsed when she fell in love me, when our friendship evolved into erotic feelings and actions, a woman who loved her in return.

And all that bar-hopping Marge and I shared, some adventures with guys together made her my most intimate friend—but not a lover. Now all that's all over for me since Jan finally left Alex to be with me.

One night Jenny and Matt came over and had a good talk with Jan until 1 a.m. I went to bed early!

Carolyn and Jennifer Kindle came for a drink or two at our bar while each of them, together, held our Luv on their combined laps. As the conversation and consumption continued, Luv quietly slipped down between them to the floor. So far, Luv is the only one to fall from not one, but two patrons on our bar stools.

Jan told me she was pleased with the annual Lakeshore Med Christmas party, this year honoring the retired Clark Young. He went out of his way to find her posing employees and escorts' pictures while they are all dressed up for the party. He took her aside and gave her a book, *An Exaltation of Larks* by James Lipton, shook her hand and thanked her for all the good that she has accomplished for Lakeshore Med

We enjoyed a merry round of holiday visits with Betty Willing and her girls, Carolyn's, Marian and Sharon and our rap group where someone introduced a little holiday wine and our first pot smoking. That's what happens when you hang around with younger women.

Jan on July 31, 1980

Here comes another weekend at play with Marian, Sharon and our camper to experience the joy of canoeing on the Crystal River from Ding's Docks near Waupaca. Carolyn and her guy Roger canoed a month earlier and I decided it would be a great idea for us, too. Roger said it was a true test of relationships. If couples survive canoeing on the Crystal River, they will survive for life.

All went well at the old KOA campground on Friday night with a campfire and Saturday morning with warm temperatures and cloudy skies. Sounded great as we paid our fees and boarded a battered amphibious duck boat with dozens of others starting their Crystal River adventure at Ding's Docks. The Army duck towed a clothesline of canoes that made me think of a real mother duck with her offspring following after her in a row.

We wore swimming suits beneath our summer shirts and shorts, and we had our wallets wrapped inside plastic sandwich bags. Sharon put a half-used cigarette pack and matches in plastic and that went in her shirt pocket. As we anticipated our paddling down the Crystal River, we looked across the lake for another dock to land and reboard in our canoes, but all we could see were reeds and cattail clumps rising from muddy shallows along the small lake. On the duck ride, our instructor told us that the unique fiberglass canoes were designed especially for Dings Dock's clientele. They're lightweight and easy to maneuver for those not accustomed to the art of canoeing. We certainly qualified on that count. Only Bea had that experience in her teenage camping years. She and I had tubed, but three of us had never been in a canoe.

"Don't worry if you tip over," the guide advised, "except for the stretches of lake water that are marked as deep water. For the rest of the trip, you'll be able to stand up and get back in your canoe. It's not deep."

We looked at each other with firm resolve, our confidence returning as the duck ferried us toward the reed beds that appeared closer together on each side at the Crystal River's mouth.

"If you do tip over, you can jump right back in."

The skinny, sun-tanned guide added a warning, "When you do need to right your canoe to get in it again, it's nice and light after you dump out the water—and, be careful not to rub your legs against the outside of the canoe 'cause some glass fibers from our specially designed canoes can rub off and stick on you."

Marian whispered hoarsely in our direction, "I'll bet Chief Waupaca didn't have a fiberglass problem in the old days."

The sun began to break through the clouds just as the duck began to slow down. "There's where you'll be heading," the guide pointed, "and you can jump in the water now and pick out your canoe."

"Jump in the water? Where's a dock?"

"We'll get wet right away!"

"Oh well. Here goes."

And we jumped into the lake as another Ding's Docker guy in the water helped us haul our butts into a canoe and pass us our paddles as he pushed us away from the spring-fed lake toward the rippling foot-deep waters of the Crystal River.

"This water's warm compared to jumping off my boat into cold Lake Michigan," shouted Bea, my canoe captain who stayed at the stern so she could control the direction—and I should apply the power. Marian and Sharon didn't care which one was where.

Our two-boat flotilla followed the flow. Others passed us quickly to free their canoes from the jumble we all created at the start. I held my breath as we followed our friends over the deep lake that he warned us about and paddled smoothly so we wouldn't tip over here. Carolyn had warned me about her fears through this part, but she isn't a water person like Bea and I are. Still, I breathed more calmly when we reached the bubbling river waters. Sharon's breathing was almost to hyperventilation when she realized her cigarettes drowned when she jumped off the duck.

Within the three or four hours we paddled or dragged our canoes, we were often separated. Once we found them standing knee high in the water.

"What happened to your canoe?" we shouted.

"It's here," and they pointed straight down into the river. "We've been in the water more than in the canoe," Sharon added in an edgy, irritated tone.

Sometimes we'd have to get out to go under fallen tree branches or over boulders, but other than that, we never tipped once. I was cranky because I wanted to fall out and play in the water. Captain Bea insisted that I behave and not tip the canoe. "Hell, Bea. That ain't no fun!"

At times, the river leaves the wildness and actually flows along people's back yards and through a city park. At one stretch, our friends flipped into the water again and Sharon started scolding Marian who put on her blameless Harpo Marx blank look. Fortunately, one of the neighbors, being entertained by all of us while she sits in her lawn chair, called Sharon to come over and Sharon went. Surprise! The woman handed her a cigarette and gave her a light. "I know what you're going through," she said sympathetically. That Good Samaritan saved our entire adventure by giving Sharon a nicotine jolt to calm her nerves.

When the river widened into a city park, part of the river flowed as a little waterfall that we four sat behind in the little cave, sheltered from the power of the falls by the sidewalk above. I was delighted to see the world through the falling waters. Imagine how glorious it would be to go under a huge falls like those you hide behind when your chased by Indian warriors or the posse or when you touch the rainbows at Niagara Falls.

After that break, we went back into our canoes and sent ourselves shooting down a steep river channel with a sharp turn at the bottom. Then we were to climb out of the canoes and board the bus to go back to the parking lot. Of course we didn't go under, but our friends did, and the canoe behind them hit Sharon's leg. Poor Sharon. Poor Marian. Both of them also suffered from fiberglass prickles too. The "child" inside of me only suffered emotionally because my resolute Captain kept us upright throughout the entire trip—and was she proud of that.

Though we were exhausted at our camp, we found a swimming beach and played with our snorkels and masks while Sharon went fishing—and smoking. We slept soundly, two to each side of our little camper, but I wondered if their fiberglass five-o'clock-shadowy legs were cured after Bea and I applied healing ointment to each one during our campfire under the stars.

<<◇>>

After a leisurely breakfast, we packed up and headed for Oshkosh and the Experimental Air Show, parking among a mass of cars in farmers' acres away from the indoor and outdoor exhibits and landing strip areas. The event always brings hundreds of thousands to the show, and with perfect weather, we saw so many unique airplanes, flying machines and sky stunts. Bea took rolls of film, but not of the planes as much as of people with kids. She always has some project in mind and when I asked her, she shrugged me off as if not to jinx her creative luck.

By early evening, we were sunbaked and weary, especially when we had to search to find our car and trailer. Both Bea and I bought Amelia Earhart headgear with goggles and put them on while we sipped on a beer and edged our way through the rows of cars lined up to leave at the same time. The hot afternoon weather forced us to hang out the windows to breathe, but I looked cool at the wheel, like Amelia with my Earhart hat and goggles, my elbow resting on the window's edge as if in her cockpit, my hand resting casually on the steering wheel ready to maneuver into line, escape the gridlock and take off.

Three scruffy, sweaty fellows, arm in arm and walking in tandem while they kept each other from falling in a drunken heap, headed directly toward me. Nonchalant as an Amelia Earhart flying ace, I kept direct eye contact on them as they approached me with their cheesy beer breaths.

"Hello," I said in an appropriately high-class fashion. If I had worn a long, white, silk scarf, I would have tossed it back and over my shoulder.

"Hellooo," they responded, leaning toward me while bracing themselves against the car. "We like your hat!"

"Oh, yes. Thank you." Perhaps my politeness would turn them away.

And one bent forward to face me too closely. He smiled and grinned, "Hi Snoopy!"

That's all. That's me. Snoopy—and not Amelia. My lofty self-image deflated again. But this time it's all right. It's surprisingly funny. I accept being Snoopy—anytime.

Jan on September 2, 1980

Dear Rachel,

I'm stressed out about Bea's behavior for the last two months becoming similar to pre-Las Vegas trip that turned into a horrendous fiasco.

For about three times in the last two months she's used abusive language and behavior for minor reasons and then I blow up. When all passes, she never, no seldom refers to the previous events. Then there's a great surge of happy, calm and productive days.

I'm taking a course in assertiveness training with effectiveness training and conflict resolution. Maybe I can head off some hostility through that. But that doesn't do anything much for her except to perhaps give me some skills at defusing whatever it is that ticks this off.

Do you have any suggestions on a book on how to live with a manic-depressive alcoholic who's also going through menopause? If not, maybe I'll write one after this is all over. I'm exaggerating about the manic depressive stuff. Nothing's been diagnosed.

Work is grinding away too with incredible pressure and deadlines for a grand open house and dedication plans of the new building addition. I'm expecting thousands of people to visit the place in two weeks.

I ran across some pictures of you, us, our kids at Silver Lake light years ago. We haven't changed much on the outside.

Love.

Jan

Oh yes, if you want to comment on this, please mail it to me at work.

Rachel Sandler on September 4, 1980

Dear Jan,

I'm really sorry to hear that Bea may be going into a tailspin. I'm sure that you have tried almost anything I could suggest. There is a book by Albert Ellis entitled *How To Live with a Neurotic* or something very close to that. I think the key is probably in your "heading off" things and taking care of yourself. Bea has all kinds of options for help and she knows that.

I'd be happy to talk more with you if you wish. Call. We can meet for dinner or whatever. If you're coming in for the Woman-to-Woman conference, maybe we could spend some time together Saturday?

Much love,
Rachel

Jan on September 7, 1980

Dear Rachel,

Thank you so very much for your letter and invitation to see you at Milwaukee's Woman-to-Woman Conference. We've heard about it from our Lakeshore Bay Woman's Network. Bea and I are both coming and she's signed up to be in one of your sessions, which indicates the high side of her personality.

We reached a real low on the Friday, the fifth. Jill called me worrying about Bea because she closed and left the store in the afternoon. After talking with me, Jill brought herself and Bea's oldest son, Josh, to the house and they were able to solve to some key problems between them all.

Ninety percent of the time, life is significantly beautiful, fun, warm and creative—and worth it all. Then that premenstrual tension and other emotional, depressing factors take over more than alcohol, and life gets awful and I get the brunt of it.

After this last time, Bea said she would get some help. I don't know if she will, but this pledge was more sincere than in the past.

And I've been working too hard and too long for Lakeshore Med. After this Sunday's open house, I hope to do less—for my own sake. Oh yes. I've been job-hunting, but so far the interviews have been on my initiative. We'll be getting a salary review next week so we'll see. Working here is great, but Randy and a few other men get me down, and I am grossly underpaid.

When we do see you after Woman-to-Woman, we can talk over a drink or maybe have some supper.

Sincerely,

Jan

Bea on September 7, 1980

Sheesh! I really caught it on Friday when Josh and Jill walked in our house and found me after I became tired and fed-up and closed the store. Sure, I had a few drinks from my bottle under the counter. So what! Nothing new!

My two adult children sat across from me, observing me in my chair. I was alone against them. Why did I come home, anyway? I could have stopped and had a drink or two anyplace along the route. Jan's at work, as usual. She wouldn't know. I haven't been in a bar in years. Didn't even consider stopping for a drink. Too many old drunks in those places on a Friday afternoon. Anyway, we always have plenty to drink at home, and when I'm home, I don't have to drive any place.

After what seemed like a long time of their looking at me as if I were a bug on a pin in a Boy Scout's collection, Jill started out saying she was worried about me when she went to the shop and it was all locked up with the closed sign in the window. She phoned Jan, she said, and will call her again now that she knows I'm safe and at home.

"Just leave me alone. I'm tired—and bored. I don't have what it takes to be trapped in that store waiting for a customer, and when one does come in, I don't have the book in the store or it turns into a counseling session with me as the counselor."

"But what would you have if you didn't have your bookstore? What else would you want to do?" Josh asked.

I just stared at him. "Do you want a beer or anything?"

"We just want you to be happy."

"I am happy, most of the time. Hey! How did Jill find you? You're supposed to be at work?"

"That's not important. I took the afternoon off to fix some stuff in our apartment. But back to you. That's not happiness that we see. Josh was brave enough to say it. "We want you to be sober."

"Ah. That's what this is about. An intervention. Did Jan set you up to do this?"

"We are responding to what we see, and we worry about you."

"Why should you worry about me? I was the one who divorced your father and split up the family. Actually it was late 1974 when your father and I talked about divorce. And we had a truce for several months because we hardly slept together anymore. I thought I didn't care about him, but I did care because it was important to me. Sex had been part of our marriage, but it didn't happen; he was just not interested anymore. Then you and Jim joined in the Army and two days before the real divorce, you, Jill, convinced Joel and the two of you decided to leave me and live with your father."

"That's because he needed us more than you did, Mom. I've told you that many times. You were the stronger one and he needed us. He couldn't even pay his bills."

"I needed you too—and you wrote my piddly little alimony check each month for one whole year. I had to cash my alimony check with my daughter's signature on it. The only job I had was the part time one at church—and all of you left me with junk cars and teenage crap to clean out so I could sell our home and settle the divorce agreement with your father. Sell our home! And where was I to live after that?"

"Joel and I would have helped clean out the house if you'd asked us."

"Sure. Why should you help someone like me? I broke up the family and the home where all your friends could come to see you.

Now what do you say to them? That your mother is a lesbian. I don't want to be a lesbian. I hate it. I lived with Jake for twenty-one years. How can I be a lesbian? Just because I fell in love with Jan? Hell! I wish she were a man. Actually, it's good that my parents are dead. And Josh—You're going to get married in two weeks, and you have to drag along your lesbian mother and her girlfriend to the ceremonies and introduce them to all of your new in-laws."

"Oh Mom, we've known about all that for years—and so what! We don't worry about that. You and Jan just come to our wedding and have a good time."

"But what about all your friends?"

"They don't care either. They've known you since they were kids and they really like you better than any of the other moms. You're a lot more fun. You're like their family, their friend."

"Maybe I'll be better when the tension of your wedding is over. And I have to cope with Jake at the wedding and dinner while Jan makes herself blend into the background."

Jill spoke up, "I've added up all my new relatives that I have now and came to a grand total—and that includes Jan, of course."

"It's so strange," said Bea, "that Jan drinks too and nobody jumps on her. I'm the one who's labeled as an alcoholic. And all our rap group of ten younger lesbian women worry about telling their parents about their lifestyle and I worried about telling my kids and their friends."

"That part's OK, Mom!"

"And I promise to behave at your wedding, Josh," and the three of us talked until Jan came home. They baked a couple pizzas and had a casual conversation. When they left, I went to bed.

Bea on October 11, 1980

Jan's gone bananas on me. She hasn't acted so happy in months. Going to the Holly Near concert at Milwaukee's Mount Mary College put her over the top. Though she's almost forty-nine, Jan's joy had her skipping like a kid, arms swinging up the long sidewalk to the auditorium with Marian, Sharon and me walking behind to enter the theater and blend in with all these women, an astonishing crowd after the little back-of-the-store concert at Sistermoon Bookstore. The two of us had been to one of those little concerts a couple years back when pioneer lesbian entertainer Alix Dobkin performed to a stacked crowd of women so packed together at that bookstore that Jan and I had to prop our butts against the rim of the storefront pane's metallic frames. We practically froze our asses off from the icy condensation with all those hot breaths crystallizing on the winter-weary windows.

Last October we drove to the UW-Milwaukee Gay Pride Week's performance of Robin Tyler, the first lesbian stand-up comedian we've seen. The auditorium filled up with college kids and some of us adults. We didn't know many people there and felt comfortable in that gay-affirming atmosphere with jokes and repartee based on our lives. Among all of the "inside" comments about not being out, she remembered being closeted in an all-girl's school for a while, but temptations were strong to find mutual "sisters" among the students—and faculty. Tyler said she went on a school field trip for her acting class and was outed as a lesbian in front of her theatrically animated, somewhat hard of hearing drama teacher who responded in an affected accent, "Thespians! Thespians! Of course, dear. We're all Thespians!"

At this Holly Near concert, the almost eight-hundred women seemed to be mostly lesbians wearing jeans and plaid shirts or dressed to the nines, tuxedos and all. A few men kept quiet and tried to look unobtrusive; four were listed in the program because they helped with childcare. Where did they come from? Could they be gay? What a din of conversations, greetings, laughing, even noisy hugging that echoed from the entrance hall and bounced back from the stage.

"Holly Near with Adrienne Torf" included our new friend Bev Glasner as the opening artist! Our first women's music concert! Jan could barely stay in her skin. She hugged women she knew from Mother Courage, from our lesbian rap group, and new Milwaukee friends, She even hugged the ticket-taker and thanked the women she recognized of Hurricane Productions, Inc. for taking the financial risk of producing their first event.

We've played Holly's four records over and over at the store. And she's so cute and respectable looking. Did you know she was once a Partridge Family kid and did some movie and theater parts, including *Hair*? But she chose to be a political activist who went on tour with the FTA (Free the Army) Show with Jane Fonda and Donald Sutherland. We could read that all in the program (except for the Partridge Family stuff) that printed ads sponsored by women's businesses, health centers and attorneys, environmental action groups, politicians, unions and the NOW Chapter that meets at the Unitarian Church West on North Avenue. (Those Unitarians again!)

Like the feminist and lesbian energy fueled by women's bookstores and alternative publishers, the alternative music scene affirmed and gave voice to those who had come out of the closet or are just out for an evening of freedom. Excitement filled the hall with the historic Milwaukee concert and Bev Glasner was great in her warm-up for Holly and Adrienne.

Something else on stage was different. Miriam Ben-Shalom was interpreting the words for the entire concert in sign language for the hearing impaired. We heard that Miriam had been discharged from the Army Reserve because she is a lesbian, and an out, visible lesbian—and she's fighting the discharge in the courts. Jan said her own struggle seemed monumental, but at least she didn't have to take on the U.S. Army.

Ben-Shalom uses her whole body rhythmically as well as sending out the ideas and concepts of songs and impromptu stage banter with her face, hands and body language. At times, I would catch myself concentrating on the signer's moves rather than the performer.

Leave it to the lesbians to accommodate deaf persons at a music concert.

When Holly Near and Adrienne Torf came on stage, the crowd went bananas too. These women chose to come out as lesbian entertainers early in their careers and are courageous role models.

When Holly sang "Imagine My Surprise" about her loving another woman, guitarist Meg Christian, she justified the existence of women loving women in her audience with her honest affirmation of that love. WOW!

In "Imagine My Surprise" she sings of rugged women like pirates Anne Bonny and Mary Reed and "Lady poet" Emily Dickinson pouring passion through her pen. "I never knew your poems were meant for me…Imagine my surprise!"

Many of her songs called for social action to stop violence and injustice, but the audience response raised the roof when she sang "Something about the Women" and "The Woman in Your Life Is You."

We were too wired to go home, so one of our friends suggested we join them at the woman's bar called The Beer Garden. Jan followed the street coordinates and found the Germanic helmeted-looking building, phantom-like with boarded-up windows and a barely lit sign over the side door. But when we dared to enter, the saloon was bursting with lighted neon signs, cigarette and cigar smoke, and women laughing, drinking at the huge square bar in the center of the main room and dancing in smaller rooms to the side. That's where we found a table and went to the bar to get our drinks.

But Jan grabbed me by the arm and said we have to dance now to "Funky Town," the funky song that we danced to at our first lesbian bar and heard while snorkeling off Isla Mujares on our Cancun trip. One of the 44-RPM records that I like to play that I kept for myself after giving most of the others to my kids. Another was "Oga Chaka Oga/ I can't stop this feeling/Deep inside of me…" and "I Honestly Love You" with Olivia Newton-John. I'd play those over and over again.

OK! And we wedged our way to the dance floor.

> "Gotta make a move to a town that's right for me,
> Town to keep me movin'. Keep me groovin' with some
> energy."

And I gyrated my hips just like the old days. I can still hang in with the young ones. Jan loves it when I do that, and I'm so pleased when I surprised the others watching us.

> "Talk about it, talk about, talk about, talk about
> moving'.
> Won't you take me to Funkytown."

Well, those rhythms heightened my thirst even more, and we brought a pitcher of beer and glasses to our table. I should have bought two pitchers right away as more friends squeezed in to join us. For some unknown reason to me, Jan began challenging women to arm wrestle with her. Honestly. What does she have to resort to burn off her excess energy? Well, good sport Marian took on the dare as they squared off with women circling them. Marian's usually shy, but she wasn't tonight. Jan bared her old tennis arm; they put their elbows on a cardboard Blatz beer coaster and squared off. After customary grunts and groans to stifle laughter, Jan wrestled her opponent's hand to the table and asked for more. Marian said, "Two out of three" and was taken down again.

Jan relented after her second round of knuckle crunching when one of our younger friends stepped in to take on the champ, and she drank her beer as a tired but proud and happy loser—along with Marian. Let the younger ones carry on.

Jan on October 20, 1980

We headed for Milwaukee's Red Carpet Inn to see what Milwaukee's Woman-to-Woman Conference was all about. We had so many choices of what to attend and there were vendors with products to appeal to women and organizations to recruit us.

Bea went to Rachel Sandler's workshop and I went to a writers' workshop and was frustrated by the shallow topics the panel of authors wrote about, especially the fancy-hatted, bejeweled woman who wrote romance novels and is quite successful, I guess. After their talks, I asked the panelists if any of them made a living by their writing.

One of the organizers announced at lunch that because of the growing turnouts for Women-to-Women, next year's meeting will be held at the huge new MECCA downtown, so she urged everyone to get the word out to other women to volunteer as workshop leaders and give their time to volunteer with all the work.

Our Lakeshore Bay Network women planned to have a drink after at the cocktail lounge, but we were to meet Rachel Sandler who's known us since our church TA weekend sessions years ago and has counseled Alex and me in our conflicts over my love for Bea and my quest for equality. Rachel insisted on meeting us. While waiting for her, we had a drink with our local crowd of Network women, and we celebrated the strength of purpose that we shared from all of the electrifying woman energy surging through us for the entire Saturday.

I just wish we could generate more energy for Bea at Mother Courage.

Rachel found us and directed us to a quiet corner for our second round of drinks, as she described again her serious problem as a school psychologist, a problem that everyone in her field has, and requires our expertise. She wants a book for children to relate to so she can help them talk about being abused.

Abused children and adults do not talk about it. They keep it a secret as if it's their fault. Bea knows that. I know that. And Rachel thinks the three of us can publish a book to open up lines of communication and free the abused from the nightmares they keep inside. She'll write it; she almost has it finished.

"No. We can't do that. We don't have any money," was Bea's immediate response.

"We'll split the cost three ways."

"That's one way for you and two ways for us," Bea replied. "Mother Courage isn't making enough to barely support me let alone pay the cash I give to my daughter to sit at the store each Saturday. It's a good thing we don't have to pay rent."

"Wow!" I said with brilliant phrasing. "I work with a good printer for the hospital."

"That's what I mean," Rachel explained. "Bea can do great illustrations and you know all about PR. I have the credentials and know what to say in simple terms that a child would understand. What a team we could be!"

"Jan! We can't afford to do this and I can't do the illustrations. How does one illustrate child sexual abuse, for Christ sake?"

Knowing she wasn't going to get anywhere with today's meeting, Rachel asked us to mull it over. We shared a few stories and left for home. But I knew this wouldn't be the end of this. Rachel knows how to get her way.

Bea on November 5, 1980

I did not want to publish Rachel's *Something Happened to Me* manuscript. We're losing money in the bookstore and I don't want to spend any—but Jan wants to do it and Rachel insists that the two of us be her partners. Why us I don't know. She's created copy for a children's section and then guidelines for adults to use the book in therapy, for opening ways to communicate with a child. Jan will produce and promote it and those two demand that I illustrate it.

I didn't think I could do it properly. How do you illustrate child sexual abuse? I finally captured an idea that could work. It did work and they liked it. I had been saving picture ideas of sad-looking individual girls and boys and I sketched them, including a couple of my church school photos of my students when I was the church's Religious Education director. The pictures I had taken at the Oshkosh air show inspired me to draw happier girls and boys with an adult or adults so that the first lonely child saying, "Something happened to me" at the beginning of the book could see at the end, girls and boys with an adult or a family and know that each is not alone.

Jan developed a format with lots of white space to capture the isolation felt by children at the start of the book. The white space fills the emptiness with adult helpers and more words as the book advances, hopefully opening a path to trust and to talk to an adult who can help them.

Jan's format also conforms to what her favorite printer can do with the presses the company owns—and at a reasonable cost.

I have to admit that I am getting excited about it now.

Jan on December 1, 1980

To plant the idea of Mother Courage bookstore for their gift giving in the minds of about fifty of my Women's Network colleagues, I volunteered to take a turn speaking to them at Lakeshore Bay's Eagles Club. Of course I plugged our bookstore, subtly, I hope.

"Your Days Are Numbered" is the title, and I've written each item on individual note cards. I started out with forty cards but didn't need them all when other women stood and contributed their own cheeky testimonials to the merriment. I'd been writing down ideas for several months, and now I could use my notes for healing laughter and hoots and howls after most of each statement. My comic pacing was great at the start and grew almost to perfection. When I finished, I was flushed with pride and joy.

"Good afternoon women! You're not paranoid, but you know your days are numbered—

"When you've taken a two-week vacation to go to the Virgin Islands, and nobody at work knows you've been away.

"When you haven't seen your dear old friend and co-worker for several days and then she tells you—five minutes before she leaves on her vacation—that she's going off to Greece with your ex-husband.

"When your college intern, who considers you as her mentor, changes her career goals after witnessing what you have to do to make a living.

"When your grand open house celebration of a new building includes releasing helium-filled balloons and a flock of flying homing pigeons—and a disoriented dove dives under the skirt of a woman board member. (Flap arms. Make a Wahoo sound imitating woman board member when she fumbles around with the bird under her skirt.)

"When the handsome male employee pictured prominently on your company's annual photo calendar gets arrested for selling cocaine.

The first woman added, "When the young file clerk wears her three-piece dress-for-success suit every day with a see-through blouse—and becomes your supervisor after six months at her job."

Another joined in. "When you find out you're training a volunteer to do your job."

"Great! Keep it up!" I said and turned over another card. "When you get angry on payday!"

"When your boss finally asks to see you—only to tell you to order an engraved plaque—and you're supposed to be in charge of corporate communications."

Another volunteered, "When he fires a subordinate who is having an affair with his father because working with her would make him uncomfortable."

After the amazement of the women, I regained the momentum. "When your boss mandates that you make arrangements to meet with him once a week and he never returns your calls or memos to confirm a time and date.

"When your boss reports to his professional review peer that you're making $3,000 more than you are really making.

(In a reflective and puzzled mood.) "When the handsome young student who used to share your office and tell you the most intimate details of his life—becomes your boss."

Someone added this old joke, but it too made them laugh. "When you've just been artificially inseminated and you see a clone of the Hunchback of Notre Dame slip out the fertility clinic's back door."

Good thing we were in a private room for this meeting. Even the waitresses were laughing.

"You're not paranoid, but you know your days are numbered—

"When your first (Hold up index finger.) written job evaluation in ten years (Hold up ten fingers.) is a three-page, (Hold up three fingers.) typed and single-spaced document, that ends with the sentence, (Put up both hands with fingers making quote signs.) 'The only reason you're getting a raise is because there's hope for improvement.'

"When you wake up in your apartment on the morning after the party you've hosted and remembered that your boss was the last guest to leave." (Roll eyeballs. Look befuddled until I pretend to get the idea by raising my index finger.) "—And then you remember why.

"When your boss sexually abuses your best friend and you know about it.

"When your boss sexually abuses your best friend—and others—and you know it and he knows you know and you better not let anyone else know and you better not talk to his boss, or even be seen alone with his boss —to tell him your concerns. (Take a deep breath.)

"And when you finally tell his boss, hoping to stop this harassment, you lose all chances for a promotion because he labels you as a troublemaker.

"When you're searching for your best friend. You're afraid that she's drowned herself in the lake and you see your boss sitting alone in his black Lincoln Continental in the beach parking lot." That spooked the audience.

(Shift position, slower pace.) "When you ask the employment manager to help you hire more help, and you ask the compensation manager to help you get your raise, and they tell your boss that you have a bad attitude because you're telling people that you're over-worked and underpaid.

"When your boss tells you 'just because you feel cheated and underpaid is no excuse for a bad attitude.'

"When your boss tells you that the only way to get a salary increase is to find another job. Then you panic at finding a pink slip in your pay envelope—" (Pull a pay envelope out of pocket and draw out a pink slip of paper.) "—And discover the slip of paper promotes Mickey Mouse's Magic Kingdom Club." (Crush the pink slip and throw it away.)

"When your boss starts playing 'Oh Come All Ye Faithful' at the managers' Christmas party, and everyone circles around him at the piano across the room while you're the only one still at the bar.

"You know your days are numbered—

"When you shout out in your dream while you push your sleeping husband out of bed saying, 'Wake up! My husband's coming home! Can you find your way out the back door?'"

And another women hollered out, "—And your husband gets up, dresses and goes."

And another added, "When you find your husband's insurance policy and see that he's changed the beneficiary—naming your best friend."

Bea added her bitter quote, "When you'll be forty tomorrow and your husband always said that when that day comes, he'd trade you in for two twenties." She paused to wait for the groans to die down, "And later when your teenage daughter writes, signs and mails you your alimony check."

Another stood and tossed out this one, "When your husband finds your well-worn and underlined book titled *Creative Divorce* that you've hidden among your lingerie."

Then a Women's Bureau instructor added, "When you've been asked to teach a course on parenting and you're fighting to keep custody of your kids."

And another could have made this up—but who knows? "When you find a pair of women's underpants in the glove compartment of the car and your husband claims it's his." And then she added,

"When your husband asks you for a divorce—at your daughter's wedding."

A young woman confided, "When you're planning to meet with your lawyer about a divorce—and your pregnancy test comes back positive."

Another inspired woman added, "When the bill comes for your husband's vasectomy while you're paying the last installment on having your tubes tied."

(I didn't say this out loud; I slipped Bea this paragraph on one of the cards while the hubbub continued throughout the room.) "When you finally have found one person who nurtures and supports you, who's fun to be with and a friend, who enhances your self-esteem and your sense of personal worth, and who returns your love in the same way as an equal—but who happens to be of your same gender."

And after much more laughter and a few tears, I concluded with a grand gesture, "Remember! Your days are numbered—so let's celebrate and make every day count. Happy Holidays, everyone!"

Bea on December 31, 1980

We entertained family and friends with food and drink at our own Mermaid Inn family room bar throughout the holidays.

Jan's dad hasn't been feeling too well but certainly enjoyed our supper with Jenny and Matt. One day when I was out of the shop, Jan had a long talk with him, and Barney confided in her that his body needed touching. He felt depleted. Empty. I don't think he expected her to do anything about that but just listen. She didn't know what to say, either. He used to go to a chiropractor regularly for hands-on treatments until that guy died, and then he tried a new chiropractor who put him on a revolving and rotating table and let that manipulate his body. Finally Barney had to see regular doctors who hand out pills or admit you to the hospital where you may get a back rub from a nurse if you're lucky.

It's too intimidating now to find a professional masseuse

because of the controversy in Lakeshore Bay of having too many "massage parlors" whose unlicensed women encourage their male clients to "finish the job" by paying more for a final masturbating massage. The paper is full of news about the city setting new standards and trying to stomp out these "services." It must be embarrassing to be seen going into one of the many new "health spas" around town, and Jan didn't recommend that to her father.

Barney misses his dog Chico, too. Jan told me she should have shown more sympathy for her dad when that dog died, that she should be more understanding about him and his struggles. He certainly has taught her many lessons about accepting people—and loving and respecting us. I know my own dad would have disowned me as he did my brother. But Barney loves what we've done, especially with his shop. I think our being here every day gives him greater happiness than he has had for a long while. I suppose our feminist politics remind him of Jan's mother taking hold of whatever she decided she could do—and did it—until she fell mentally ill for most of their married lives. Barney does have a neighbor lady friend, however, who goes out with him. They visit and watch out for each other. I think that's about all they do though. Who knows? He never says anything about her to Jan nor to me.

Jan's still seething with anger with her bosses at work and is responding to leads for a new position and sending out job query letters with résumés to those she knows in industry and non-profits, colleges and universities. She loves her hospital job and the people she works with, but they too are becoming frustrated and angry because those who are creatively managers and/or are sympathetic to Jan seem to be on the receiving end of unfounded injustice and intimidation.

Now that the Christmas season is over, our sales are really slow, and the weather is freezing and dark, snowy and blustery. I've been through a lot of negative stuff about the store this year. I feel trapped. It's as if I were in a river, drowning in my own boredom and my disappointed expectations. The store is not a financial success and

I'm terribly disappointed. But it is still in business. If Barney charged us rent, we'd be out of business for sure.

We've planned a vacation. We're going to Cancun. Ole´! We're closing the shop and heading for warmth and sunshine and new adventures. Like the Judy Garland song, "Forget your troubles, c'mon get happy. You better chase all your cares away..."

Chapter 12

Bea's Mexican journal starting January 19, 1981

Jan and I left O'Hare airport on Sunday at 10:10 a.m. for a Sunflight tour to Cancun in clear but cold weather. We almost froze standing on an outdoor stair ramp in our warm sunny-weather clothing waiting for the plane's door to open as jealous January winds whipped through our tourists' bones aching to leave the penetrating cold for warm Gulf breezes. The crew finally let us onto the plane to fly up and over the biting wind and billowy clouds. The sky opened in time for us to see the mouth of the Mississippi River below and study the stretched-out flume of the brown Delta meld with the blue-green waters of the Gulf.

When we got close to the Yucatan, we could see a barren coast until we flew directly over Cancun with its new hotels and sandy beaches. It was hot when we got off the plane—and sunny! Our Hotel Carousel bus waited to take us to our vacation home! Our room is on the first floor with a view across the beach to the ocean. We can walk out through the glass doors onto our own patio, and the white sand beaches are only a few steps away. We checked out the swimming pool, the beaches and boats, and at 5 p.m. we had our group orientation in the dining room where they told us about all the day tours we could sign up for—but not for us.

We headed out on our own, hopped a local bus into town where the stores were open, and we could shop. We found a little restaurant that Carolyn and Roger recommended from their recent trip. After enjoying a couple margaritas, I devoured red snapper in garlic and Jan, a shrimp dinner. When we returned to our room, we enjoyed the fresh air of our patio, the view and our drinks, without ice cubes— as we were alert to avoid Montezuma's Revenge.

Monday: Our great Mayan breakfast, a local version of ham and eggs, was served in our hotel dining room in a separate thatched-roof building. We grabbed our cameras and gear, hopped a bus and went to Cancun's outdoor market with vendors waiting under corrugated-roof stalls waving flies away from their offerings of red meat and chicken hanging from hooks or ready to be cut up on the vendors' warped wooden counters. We studied the various forms of chili peppers and decided to buy limes to go with our drinks.

We entered a car rental office exactly in time to catch two guys pulling up with a Volkswagen Safari—The Thing! "That's what we want!" we shouted at the clerk—a white Thing with the top down. It was the only one they had. The guys tumbled out laughing and handed us the keys. They had just driven back from Belize.

What fun it was for us to drive and be free of tour busses and transportation constraints. After we bought groceries and more supplies, we loaded our Thing and drove out to the end of the developing tourist area on Isla Cancun to check out the lovely deep and wide sandy beach at the fancy and expensive Inca-pyramid-designed Sheraton. We scanned the posted restaurant and bar menus and prices and decided to drive back for a swim in our hotel pool with its swim-up bar. Then we enjoyed little siesta.

We weren't the only ones having a siesta. It seems that our rooms are the exact opposite of the next-door neighbors. Our headboard and frame seemed to be attached to the headboard in the next room. The thin plaster wall between us ricocheted sound indicating that they were honeymooners. Jan said she'd need to take a Dramamine to prevent seasickness from our rocking and rolling with the couple and their screaming orgasms on the other side of our queen-sized bed wall. We're not complaining because we rocked and rolled and made playful sounds too, many times before this, but now, perhaps, not as often, as long or as loud.

Tuesday: The alarm went off at 6:30 a.m. for a steak and eggs ranchero breakfast, and we spun the Thing out of the drive at 8:30 for a long drive to Chichen Itza. Jan drove for a half hour or so and I took over. We planned to stop at Valladolid for groceries and other essentials but Jan had an emergency! I stopped in the two-lane concrete road with no shoulder to put the Thing in a safer spot. Before I could really stop, Jan had grabbed some tissues, jumped from the car and ran across the dry and prickly brush to try to find a secluded place to drop her pants and relieve herself. She should have dropped her pants right on the side of the road rather than try to be modest because there was no bushy shelter when the urge forced her to crap on the crest of a little hill, making her more visible than ever. And was she stressed—especially when she fell and bruised her wrist and thumb plus her rear end and hip. Poor thing. Even though I was worried about getting the car smashed from behind should another car come along, I went up to her to help. I guess most natives are used to people stopping on the road. Good thing a tourist bus didn't drive by when Jan was so compromised, but she wondered what she would have done if we had been stuck on one of those tour busses.

Fortunately, we improvised, washing her backside with beer and pulling out the extra pair of shorts we brought in case it got too hot for jeans. We managed to get it all together again and drove on to Valladolid for gas. The little station had no facility for her to clean up. It took another hour with Jan in a state of shock and pain and embarrassment before we got to Chichen Itza. We parked, paid our admission and sought out the primitive public restrooms. Jan paid for toilet paper, received a square or two and then asked for more. (This was the first of our Mexican "facilities," and compared to the others, it was one of the best.) At least she could wash up with water.

Though shaken from her experiences dashing over and falling on sage brush and rocks under the hot sun, Jan wasn't going to let anything stop her. Of course she knew there would be no convenient ladies room at the top of what dominated the sky, yet we started climbing up the El Castillo Pyramid!

Wow. The tallest temple to the God Kukulkan with ninety-one steps on all four sides to the top, and it seemed almost straight up. The only assist is a chain along the middle of one side. And each step is high! You raise your knees almost twice as high as you would on a normal stair. The view was spectacular! We walked around the top platform—such vistas! Then we realized going down would be harder than up, but we made it, sometimes slithering down in our bottoms while holding the chain.

We turned the corner to see El Castillo's inner pyramid serpent stairs. If we had come at an equinox, the sun's light and shadows on the staircase makes the stone serpents seem to crawl up the pyramid. At its base was a doorway and more stairs inside, up to another and older pyramid top with steep sidewalls to hold on to but not as many stairs to climb to reach an inner chamber where a chacmool, a carved reclining Mayan male, held a stone dish on his stomach. With him sat a jaguar statue with jade eyes. It was so close and hot we could have fainted in there, especially when we climbed with your nose almost to the butt of the person in front who is also bent under the ceiling so low that you almost bumped your knee on your chin. If one of us did faint, there'd be no place to fall down because the line of tourists would hold us upright.

Down and outside again to take in a deep hot breath, we headed to the Sacred Cenote, a huge natural well said to be a site where human sacrifices were drowned.

I am always cynical about all this "human sacrifice" stuff. So many other reasons could explain what explorers found at these sites.

We rested and ate the light lunch and drank our beer that we had brought with us in Jan's backpack. Then we toured the ball court where teams of Mayan athletes struggled to send heavy rubber balls through stone-carved rings on each side of the arena. From our point of view, it seemed impossible to hit that ball through that little hole. And the losers were sacrificed after the game—supposedly an honorable way to die.

When we climbed the Temple of the Warriors with another impressive chacmool, we decided to repeat our silent vows that we made to each other at King Arthur's altar at Tintagel in England on our three-week European trip in our summer of 1976.

With a little more resting in the shade, we then we crossed the ancient path to the older ruins and the El Caracul, an astronomical observatory with slits in the walls to reveal the positions of stars on key dates in the Mexican calendar. This older section had other pyramids. The climbs here were much easier and we were happy we had done the hardest one first. Jan found a woman's purse on the Caracul and then found the owner around the bend. Both of them were so happy and went bananas together over her good deed.

I took tons of pictures and finally, having seen enough, we got in our Thing and started home to Cancun.

After Jan drove almost an hour, she said she was freezing in her shorts and had to change into whatever she could find in the back that was warmer and dryer, so we stopped in a rush and I took over the driving. Darkness set in for about the last one-and-a-half hours and the driving, though straight and flat, was scary because we'd swiftly come upon giant speed bumps that propelled us into the air past unlit villages and people, dogs and pigs in the road, plus drivers coming the other way who refused to dim their lights as if we were playing "Mexican Chicken."

We're both freezing now and the damp jungle fogged our windshield so we couldn't see the side of the road. Jan stuck her head out of the windowless door to tell me if I was headed straight or veering off the concrete. If I went too slowly, I feared we'd be hit from behind and if I went to fast, I was worried about the hazards at the front end.

We didn't install the Thing's windows. We didn't even know where they were. And we couldn't stop because of our situation, especially when I needed Jan to be my side vision out the door. How could it become so cold when it was so hot just hours before?

"Ole´! I have the answer!" Jan shouted as she reached into her backpack and found our half bottle of tequila. She pulled out the cork and offered me a swig from the bottle and then she took hers. Its fuel continued to warm us from the inside out as we forged into the blackness ahead like bodacious banditos dragging off our tequila and waving our bottle out the window, hollering and daring fate to run us off the trail.

We were happy at last to find Cancun and our hotel. A blessed wall of warmth hit us when we reached the shore roads. We devoured a fantastic meal when we reached our hotel. Jan had lobster bisque and I had squid and I was plastered from relief after all the tension at the wheel. One more problem stayed with us, however. We could barely walk up or down steps or curbings. It even hurt to sit down on a chair or the toilet because our leg muscles were so strained by climbing up and down the Mayan pyramids. But that gave us an excuse to walk together arm in arm in public as we limped up and down the uneven pavement.

Wednesday: Xel-Ha's nature preserve is where my new diving buddy Jan experienced her first mask and snorkel swim of her life with such exciting new creatures and coral gardens seeing so many colorful tropical fish and urchins I can't name right off—all in this sheltered lagoon. She was a good pupil. We had checked our clothes and camera, and rented our snorkeling gear. She trusted me when she took my hand, stepped into the clean and gentle body-temperature water and floated face down without hesitation into the clear, pure water. In a true bonding ritual, we swam along together holding hands while breathing through our snorkels. Through our masks we observed Mother Nature's beauty of the sea with rays of sunshine rippling through the watery vistas. We were almost alone together in the sheltered lagoon. After an hour we emerged like Goddesses of the Sea, renewed our energy with lunch and beer while resting in the tropical shade, and then we immersed our blessed bodies into the awesome water again. This time we headed to the other side where we saw masses of multi-colored parrotfish, jacks and a small barracuda.

We heard a voice calling out over the water and lifted our heads. "Look out! There's a barracuda down there!" shouted a man who leaped out of the lagoon onto a rock.

"Don't worry," I reassured Jan. "It's only a little one and it won't hurt you unless you attack it." She trusted my knowledge and we continued on, pointing to the beauties below that rested on the pure white sand.

Jan raved about the experience; she was glowing with happiness. I was proud to teach her how to enjoy what I have been able to do in my other life with my kids. I thought she'd soon be ready to learn to scuba dive. We reclaimed our clothes and drank fresh coconut milk through a straw in its shell. Jan was delighted to have sighted a toucan and an owl on our drive back after visiting the seaside ruins of ancient Tulum.

We replenished our bar supplies, (Jan has a thing against hotel room mini-bars.) and mixed our cocktails until we realized that putting our lime wedges, peel and all, in our drinks was the cause of our frequent trips to the john. How dumb can you be! When we felt refreshed, we went into town to eat crunchy Mexican chicken and pork enchiladas in a small outdoor restaurant and we listened to the Mariachi music spilling from various bars around us. There aren't any bugs here now. Amazing! They must all be buzzing around the open food market.

We drove the car around the small main street in the evening and later we watched crabs and turtles along the beach.

Thursday: We hustled in the a.m. because we had to catch the 8:30 ferry for Isla Mujeres, the Island of Women, from the village of Put Sam. We made it in plenty of time, but we had to back the Thing onto the boat. Jan backed the car in line while I bought the bulletos (tickets) for the forty-minute ferry ride. We chatted with a bird-watching couple from Rochester, New York, who travel around the world searching for birds. They drove a camper and were touring all over Mexico.

We drove the car off the ferry and through the little island town, found a dive shop, rented some well-used snorkeling gear, headed right to Graphon Bay, and helped each other change into our suits beside the car. We'd had enough of Mexican changing and public bathroom facilities—besides both seemed to be non-existent.

We stepped down a rough stone path to the sea, settled our stuff under a palm, sat on more rocks to don our fins and backed into the sheltered sea with small, white-capped waves against the shore. Wow! With some currents, it was quite different from yesterday's lagoon. A reef, mostly limestone, runs parallel to the shore. The water along the reef is perhaps eight to twelve feet deep with fish, fish—clouds of parrotfish, yellow tails, some that flock together—in schools, of course. Jan did fine until she became a little nervous when she choked on salt water from her mask that made it down her throat. We rested and when she said it bothered her, I told her to pretend it was a Margarita. She did and it worked. That's all she needed, she said. The salt didn't bother her anymore. She told me later, "I can tell you used to be a teacher of children with learning disabilities, 'cause your techniques surely work on me."

The second time out the shallow channel between the reefs, we just floated, kicking our fins slowly for a long distance. Jan and I held hands and she let me do the swimming for a second day in a row. I had a leaky mask, but I managed. Jan's at least was nice and tight.

We saw beautiful fish all along the reef—too numerous to mention. We'd keep pointing out the good ones during our gentle swim beyond the pier until more wave action rocked us around a bit. I spotted a coral encrusted Cerveza beer bottle and dove down to grab it to add another treasure for my diver's collection. We swam onto the beach, took off our fins, walked and waded back to our personal gear so we didn't fight the waves and current.

Going out again, our swimming area began to be crowded. Floating along with our masks, ears and faces under water, we were shocked to hear and almost feel the loud beats of "Funkytown." Jan almost choked again, reminding her of our first visit to Milwaukee's Sugar Shack, a lesbian bar. Then we felt another type of motion as people began dropping in the water near us. We stopped and surfaced to discover a Cancun tour boat was playing the tune with their swimmers, oblivious of our presence, jumping off the boat rails like depth bombs off a destroyer. Soon it seemed there were almost more people than fish.

We swam to another pier and called it a day for our snorkeling adventures. We made it up to the Thing and put our clothes on over our suits, which were almost dry in the afternoon heat.

We decided to make a pilgrimage to the ruins at the bottom end of the island—a temple to Ix-hel, a Moon Goddess.

We could see it far off the road and rather than walk, Jan drove the Thing straight up and over a rocky no-road. The Thing was made for that after all, she insisted, and we drove out as close as we could to the ruins to celebrate the women's images in a small temple that is falling gradually into the sea.

Our timing made us head back to town and be the first in line for the return ferry. We didn't want to be left behind on the island so we parked our Thing and bought a late lunch across the road. We were starved. I had a delicious caracole (sea snail) salad mixed with chilies. Jan ordered a shrimp dish that seemed to contain an entire minced garlic bulb. She loved it, and the dark Leon Negra cerveza tasted really good under our straw-covered shade at the outdoor café.

We walked along the beach while waiting for the ferry and found a conch bone yard—piles and piles of conch shells. We stopped in a few shops and then it was time to board the ferry. We were the first car aboard and parked on the main open deck. We climbed to the next deck and were no more than settled when it began to rain—and the Thing had her top down. Mother Nature poured torrential rains upon us! We were under an awning but the needle-like raindrops still sprayed us. It really didn't matter 'cause it cleared up fast, and we passed the time with some kids from Nebraska and Iowa who talked to us for quite a while. When we opened the door to our Thing, the water that didn't drain through the holes in the floor, flowed out before we drove off the ferry. We didn't mind being wet again.

After buying more supplies in town before returning to our hotel, we rested at our hotel, showered off the salt water, freshened up and returned to town to check the car back to the rental agency. Afterwards we found a nice restaurant, Viva Zapata-Viva Juarez, and ate fine Mexican food while being surrounded by banditos and banners of sinister revolutionaries staring at us with rifles drawn. Jan ordered "Diablo" and raved about its flavors while the trumpets of the Mariachi band blasted away.

Now dependent on local transportation, we boarded a crowded local bus and sat in the rear, bounding off the cracked plastic seats when it rode over something while the floorboards let billows of exhaust permeate the air and our ever so swimmingly clean lungs and bodies.

Friday: More time in the sun after waking early enough to write my notes before eating steak and eggs at the hotel breakfast area. The sun was bright and terrific on the beach as we just loafed for a change. Jan made us a little lunch and we had a most relaxing swim in the hotel pool and drank margaritas sitting on underwater barstools at its swim-up bar. We came in to our room to enjoy a loving interlude and a siesta with the honeymooners thumping about next door. Both pairs of us stepped out onto our patio at the same time and the newlyweds gave us such a strange look as if to realize that the noise on the other side of their wall was thumping by two women.

After we dressed, we hopped the bus to the Cancun Convention Center and toured the museum. I was the guide and interpreted most of all the labels at each display—even though I don't understand Spanish. Jan's jaw dropped as she tried to read the display cards while I translate their meaning in "pigeon-Mexican." I'd had three years of Latin in high school and we both thought I did an excellent job of providing insight into the history of the Mayan culture for my lover who was in joyful awe of my remarkable interpretation. We stopped at a pizza place (Can you imagine?) for a beer and music and watched and listened to the Convention Center's Mexican band

and dancers. At a little restaurant, Jan ate soft tacos with grilled cheese and guacamole filling and I had some with beef filling to finish up our restful day.

Saturday: It's a little cloudy and cool this leisurely a.m., and we didn't go to breakfast until 10. We chatted with a nice couple from Indiana. When we returned to our room, we plugged in our Magic Wand vibrator to use for the first time and all the electricity in our building went off. It went out just before we were ready. So—we pulled out the plug, rechecked to make sure our door was locked, and we did what comes naturally! Ho! After a little siesta, we slowly consumed a late lunch and tried to rest on the windblown beach with cloudy skies. On this, our last day, we finally took time to enjoy our beach and it wasn't comfortable, but I came in and wrote more in this journal while Jan read and slept. My hand is tired from writing!

We're ready to fly home and return again to travel along together on the unmapped, zigzagging, unpredictable journey we share.

Chapter 13

Bea on March 8, 1981

Our lesbian gang met at our house last night to see if we could salvage the group. We're ready to dissolve but we agreed to meet once more. I guess we have to part our ways, but they'll still come to the bookstore and there'll be parties with some of these women, at least at our house, I'm sure.

There are no sales at the bookstore but there's plenty of snow and freezing weather. Fortunately, our little Toro snow blower is lightweight because I have to pick up and set the damn thing on top of the snow and let it blow its way down to the sidewalks and driveway. And we have to do it at home and at the shop where the west winds blow so hard that it whips snow, whistling and swirling, through the corner show window's metal molding, ruining our Valentine's Day, Susan B. Anthony's birthday and other displays.

I stretched three canvasses and starting painting for hours to pass the time. We play canasta in the evenings and I win. I also bought a guitar at Goodwill and am refinishing and refining it. I also made Jan a stool in the shape of a box for her garden tools for a Valentine present. I cut a heart-shaped handle for the seat. I enjoyed making it from scraps in the wood box near my workbench. When she tried it out after I gave it to her, she said she'd have a heart imprinted on her butt all through the gardening season.

We started an indoor garden with some unidentified seeds that were given to us by a young friend who stopped by to visit and sat chopping seeds from dry green leaves that she saved in a pouch. The pots are in the sunny window in our house.

I've been under the weather. My throat bothered me for weeks. I went to see the local ear, nose and throat specialist who prescribed antibiotics. Then he sent me for a xerography that indicated that nothing was wrong. He made me feel as if I was imagining this and said he would have to refer me for psychotherapy. To hell with that crap. I even went to Dr. Burch for further check-ups on the throat business, but he said I'm in fine shape otherwise.

Ha! I'm not crazy. I actually passed a salivary stone this morning from a duct under my tongue while I was washing up and getting ready to go to the store. That's what was hurting me all this time. I stopped by to show it to my doc to have official proof that all my complaining had a cause. Now, except for my arthritis, everything is OK!

Bea on April 11, 1981

To cheer Jan up a bit from her stress at work, I proposed having a dinner party for those women who have been divorced recently, are soon to be divorced or have been for many years.

Our strong and determined Debbie, one of our friends from our lesbian group who became a Unitarian, was settling for shared custody of her two children and would also be responsible for paying child support. She didn't want to fight her case in court. She has neither lover nor partner. She has to be free of her husband.

Andrea is an old friend of Jan's, and their children grew up together in their southside neighborhood. In fact their two daughters were born at Lakeshore Med at the same time and were in the nursery together. Andrea and Jan helped to create the Montessori school and four of their children attended. Jan was somewhat surprised to learn about this divorce because she and her husband were highly respected citizens with four children, but then Jan remembered she never heard her friend laugh except for the times she came into Mother Courage with her woman friend. "If she is divorcing to be a lesbian," Jan commented to me one day, "then I can't be so bad."

Of course, we included our wonderful Carolyn who, years before, left the divorce court and went straight to the welfare office to apply for benefits for her harassed self and her six children. While waiting for the social worker to interview her, Carolyn picked up a battered old *Better Homes and Gardens* Christmas edition, opened it, remembered the better home and income she left behind, and then she allowed herself to break down and cry. She had stopped being a Catholic convert and got a job making dental apparatus at a local firm that hired artistic types to do this work. Some of those people happened to be Unitarians, and Carolyn signed up for Bea and Marge's adult UU Religious Education workshop on "Employing Your Total Self." She then completed her college education before taking my place at Lakeshore Med and coming to work with Jan.

Another was artistic and sensitive Rita, a straight UU friend with three children whose husband was older, demanding and controlling. She couldn't stand living with him any longer, and somehow, despite being another Unitarian, Marge hired her as a Lakeshore Med dietitian's aide. And Jan hired her as an artist to help with the Lakeshore Med displays.

We enjoyed exchanging our stories, laughing and crying together—and celebrating our courage.

Bea on May 25, 1981

Gads! It's my birthday again. I don't feel old, except for arthritis in my knee and back. And I guess I'm not that old, considering the alternatives.

I returned to business and the store on Tuesday to give Betty

Willing employee training, but it seems as if her primary goal as an employee is to go out somewhere to have lunch. She was shocked that I never eat lunch at all.

We also worked on digging in the earth, building boxes for Jan's intensive gardening plan, installing a patio block walk and planting seeds according to Jan's *Organic Gardening* magazine.

A couple days ago, Jill called me and asked if I could come to her. She has a virus or some kind of infection, she said. Her boyfriend couldn't be with her 'cause he went fishing and left her all alone. So I dropped everything and spent several hours with her and we had a long talk about important issues for women—for mothers and daughters. Jenny was here when I got home and we shared more conversation over supper. Wow! What a Daughter Day.

I felt the surge of poetry again.

> Women are reborn many times in life—
> Reborn in puberty when their own blood promises
> life—
> Reborn with each child borne—
> Reborn in love quickened in passion—
> Reborn when intellect flashes insight.
> I was born again on each of my birthdays—
> Overwhelmed with the greatest gift of all—Life.

Jan on June 2, 1981

About a week ago, Rachel came to work with us on her manuscript. All our ideas felt flat and Rachel left for home while we headed out to Shannons', where they are building an addition to their house that encloses their hot tub with huge, translucent roof and sides to cover their new swimming pool and yet be clear to see the stars, the moon, the beach and the Lake year 'round.

To get around the party area we had to walk like acrobats or pirates on the wooden planks at sea that Shannon and his carpenter friends built around the pool and hot tub spa. Many of our UU friends joined in the water fun, including Bob Sawyer and his handsome new partner Louie. Of course, we stayed with the hard-core skinny-dippers and wine drinkers until about 3 a.m.

To walk through the house to get into our clothes and before we were to find our car in the country darkness, we helped each other stagger along the narrow wooden scaffolding near the pool. Both of us clutched our hosts' huge white towels to cover ourselves when we aren't in the water. Quite tipsy, slightly intoxicated, partially inebriated, I lost my balance and tumbled sideways off the unsteady planks. Fortunately I landed against the pool's new teak edge with my full weight on my upper right arm and shoulder. I didn't break any bones, but I barely missed falling against my neck or perhaps even my temple, which could have finished me off—right next to their new pool.

Bea leveraged me back on the scaffold and covered me again as we stumbled together to change in their dressing rooms. She found our car and folded me into the passenger seat to drive us home without being arrested or hitting something or someone. My arm sported an indigo brown bruise for weeks—and my pride hurt too. I was thankful, however, that I survived and no one else was truly injured. As is our custom, we woke in the morning and make the best of it all by jokingly creating a headline or two: "Nude UU divorcee breaks neck falling from plank" or "Lesbian saves nude partner from drunken death."

The next day, Bob and Louie had their own reunion gathering before they returned to San Francisco. The picnic was at a gay teacher's house a few blocks down the street from our house behind a stockade fence along the sidewalk and around the back yard. Who would know? There goes the neighborhood! Lots of our UU friends, young and old, joined the crowd, included Anna Spence and her beautiful daughters who were always part of our Mother and Daughter Door County weekends before I surrendered that land in my divorce settlement. We laughed together with Bob, his new friends and old. We sang songs and told wonderful stories that sealed our circle as another loving family, even if our own six children are elsewhere.

Talk about elsewhere, last night we were invited to a "punk party" house-warming made up mostly of gay guys—including our hosts' friends from Chicago and around the state. Dick and Pat are church friends who live downtown on the second story apartment above their flower shop. Bea and I dressed in costume, according to our invitation. "Punk" seems to have a number of meanings and gave us liberty to wear almost anything. Sorry to say, we had to park about a block from the Main Street apartment and walk through Downtown Lakeshore Bay dressed like escapees from *The Rocky Horror Picture Show*. Slightly embarrassed in our costumes, especially with all the storefront lights lit, we finally entered into the skinny entrance door squeezed in between the stores and climbed the long flight of steps to reach the high-ceilinged, narrow apartment they had restored by blasting all the paint and plaster off the walls and ceiling to expose the original wooden beams and reddish, turn-of-the-century bricks. The walls and movable room dividers are covered with our younger host's dramatic abstract paintings. The couple redecorated by collecting furniture of the near past except for their giant Lincoln-era bed with its dark, imposing headboard seeming to support the wall. Their open-grid kitchen shelves are filled with Depression glass and colorful Fiestaware—dishes I remembered seeing at my Aunt Ora's house when I was a kid. And of course, our florist hosts decked their halls with boughs of tasteful, glorious arrangements of foliage and flowers.

As usual, I chose to dress comfortably as a Haight Asbury hippy panhandler in a torn, tie-died t-shirt with a peace sign sewn cross my chest, a rainbow bandana around my head, baggy jeans and holes-in-the-toes tennis shoes painted with peace slogans. Bea became the hit of the evening with lengthy, beaded and bangled necklaces tied below her cleavage to cascade down the front of her flowing black blouse over her black slacks. Of course, my lover adorned herself with artistic make-up appropriate for a high-class dame from the Age of Aquarius. Her sparkly silver shoes, like the rest of her costume that came from the resale shop, made a hit too, especially with one fellow who followed her around wanting to buy those shoes right off her feet. He kept bugging her until she hid them under the sofa and changed into the comfortable shoes she had carried in a bag with the host gift we brought.

Other guests came as "punks" or artistic Bohemian non-conformist, yet some did not "dress up," as the invitation suggested. Many of the out-of-town friends looked like Olympic athletes—young and bronzed and muscular in summer shirts and shorts. We'd never been to such a crowded gathering of handsome gay guys and a few women like us, plus our hosts' party-going mothers and straight friends too. Nor has Lakeshore Bay held a party like it before—as far as we know.

An "Anita sees the light" headline caught my eye, a newspaper clipping by Sydney J. Harris pinned on their neat kitchen bulletin board, and I asked to borrow it to make a copy for myself.

Harris writes, "I never wrote a line about Anita Bryant when she was peddling orange juice and petitioning against homosexual rights because when such people are in the public eye, they consider every knock a boost. Now that her world has come unstuck, and she is beginning to reglue it, I feel free to point out that she is a better person than when she was so busy being a 'good person.'

"In a recent interview with a women's magazine, she admitted that she had acquired the Valium habit, had become dependent on sleeping pills combined with wine, and had even contemplated suicide as her marriage was breaking up. Responding to her husband's charges of unfaithfulness, she confessed, 'I can't say that I'm totally innocent.'

"Instead of the smug, self-righteous crusader for the home and family, she can now say, 'Having experienced a form of male chauvinism among Christians that was devastating, I can now see how women are controlled in a unChristlike way…the problem is that most men are insensitive to women's needs.'

"As for gays, she now feels that 'The church needs to be more loving, unconditionally, and willing to see these people as human beings.' Her eyes have also been opened to 'valid reasons' for militant feminism.

"Finally she sounds like a person who has lived and loved and suffered, not a radiantly smiling face on a candy-box encased in velvet and wreathed with roses and totally insulated from the realities of life.

"A bad marriage (It was never much good to begin with.) almost wrecked her—but it also saved her because she grew rather than shrunk, expanded her range of sympathies rather than shriveling into self-pity.

"The Lord, we are told, works in mysterious ways, and I believe it. Sometimes being dragged to the depths is the only way we glimpse a vision of the heights; being desperate and disconsolate and defeated is the only way we redeem ourselves from pride and self-satisfaction.

"In pain, Miss Bryant is starting to be a Christian now, which she only thought she was before. 'Live and let live' has become her creed, which is approaching St. Augustine's 'Love, and do what you will.' She is no longer passing judgment on who is 'moral' and who is not.

"The visible church may have lost a militant member, but the invisible church has gained a soul. The Moral Majority may be frowning, but the Eternal Majority must be rejoicing that she has put down the frosty glass of orange juice and picked up the warm chalice of charity. As Santayana once wisely said, 'It is easier to make a saint out of a sinner than out of a prig.'"

At 5 o'clock this afternoon, Bea hosted a baby shower for Jim's wife with all Bea's nieces, her daughter, daughters-in-law, even her ex-husband's wife, her old friend Angie. Between the two of us, we are a great team and entertain without having to tell each other what's to be done. We served corn and spare ribs minus cutesy baby-shower games. No games! But this was like a job with all the other activities going on in our lives. Oh well. First-born babies don't wait to arrive on their mother-in-law's schedule. Bea's soon to be a grandmother. My woman will be a grandmother!

Chapter 14

Bea's article in *Feminist Collections: Women's Studies Library Resources in Wisconsin,* Vol. 2, No. 4, Summer, 1981

(This is the second in a series on feminist bookstores in Wisconsin. The first featured Madison's Room of One's Own that opened in 1975 and the third will be Milwaukee's Sistermoon, the fourth, Oshkosh's Kaleidoscope. With over seventy feminist bookstores in the country, these four are in Wisconsin, two are in Chicago, one in Minneapolis, Minn., and one in Iowa City, Iowa.)

"Mother Courage Bookstore and Art Gallery Is a Personal Statement"

As the "personal is the political," we, Jan Anthony and Bea Lindberg, are Mother Courage Bookstore and Art Gallery. Our personal histories made us feminist who saw the need to open this bookstore.

Our business is formed as a partnership. Jan works full time as the director of communications at a local hospital and I manage the bookstore.

People ask us why we named our store "Mother Courage" and we always say, "Well, there's the anti-war play by Bertolt Brecht; there used to be a feminist restaurant in New York City by that name featured in Rita Mae Brown's *In Her Day*; and we're both mothers with courage. Besides, it's a catchy name."

Both Jan and I came to feminism by long and circuitous routes. We met nearly twenty years ago when we were Sunday school teachers at the Unitarian Church in Lakeshore Bay. Jan has two children and I have four. Jan worked many years before her children were born, and off and on during her twenty-five year marriage. I got pregnant during the first year of my twenty-one year marriage, and except for a year or so of substitute teaching, I only had a part-time job during the last year I was married. After my divorce, I was that person known as "the displaced homemaker." Jan and I reestablished our friendship and discovered we had "Come a long way, Baby."

In our consciousness-raising experiences we shared a couple of TA marathon workshops, a women's rap group, several Wisconsin Women in the Arts conferences and lots of books and magazines that are the bibles of the women's movement. We had become committed feminists.

Before Jan's divorce settlement, we conceived Mother Courage. As a member of Wisconsin Women in the Arts, I was invited to show my nude paintings at Madison's Room of One's Own Bookstore. We spent some time there with the exhibit and over dinner at Lysistrata we struck a spark about opening our own feminist bookstore in Lakeshore Bay. Jan and I decided to put our divorce money where our mouths were as far as the feminist movement was concerned.

Mother Courage opened in October of 1978 after months of sheer hard labor. We located in a storefront in Jan's father's building that hadn't seen a clean-up since 1950 or so. The roof leaked badly. There were only two or three old lights. The floor was black with grime. The place was piled high with old stock, boxes and debris. We cleaned, painted, sanded and lit it up. I built the bookshelves and the counters. (We covered the counter tops with laminated Lake Michigan nautical charts and I attached a real ship's wheel to the ten-foot long cabinet and display table that ran down the center of the second room. Kids could stand at this big operating wheel and pretend they were steering a ship. I liked to pretend to do that myself when no one else was around.)

I began organizing the business: ordering the inventory, setting up accounting procedures, doing all the tons of things that go into opening a business. I also went to the American Booksellers Association beginner bookseller school for a weekend of intensive training in Colorado. Neither Jan not I had been in business before; we had never done anything in a bookstore, and, except for some sales clerk experience in our high school (Coincidentally, when we were teenagers, each of us sold 78 rpms records at music stores, Jan in Lakeshore Bay and I in Chicago.) and college days, didn't know a damn thing about the retail book business.

Well, we're still here. We have survived fairly well, except for a lot more gray hair and a bad case of anxiety neurosis. Our situation differs greatly from A Room of One's Own and Sistermoon. Both Madison and Milwaukee have strong feminist communities. Not so Lakeshore Bay. The feminist community here is in its early growth stage.

When we first opened, we were concerned about calling ourselves "feminist"—although we obviously are. Our rational was that we did not wish to turn anyone away. If we could reach any woman anywhere who was beginning to be positive about the feminist movement but was afraid to call herself a feminist, we wanted to reach that woman. We call ourselves a "full service general bookstore specializing in books for women," and we feature the largest collection of sailing books in the area. We do so for two reasons: first, because I am a sailor; and second, because our location is close to four recreational marinas. The other day a young man came in to the store to look at our sailing books. While he and I talked class sail boats, his female companion browsed around and finally bought *It's Your Body: A Woman's Guide to Gynecology*. I wondered afterwards whether she would have come in the store by herself to buy that book.

We do business with students, teachers and professors who ran a series of workshops on sexism and gender identity in the schools where we staffed an on-site book table. We also handle textbooks for Lakeshore Medical Center's School of Nursing. We have sponsored poetry readings, book talks, autograph parties, tarot card reading lessons, book fairs and have mailed several newsletters. We provide space in our tiny, elevated art gallery for women artists. We have had opening parties, special events and wine and cheese hospitality afternoons. We hold an annual Susan B. Anthony birthday party. We carry posters, records of women's music, buttons and bumper stickers, note cards and so on, but on a much more limited basis than the other feminist bookstores due to limitations of space and capital.

Financially we operate on an extremely tight cash flow budget. We are not in hock; we are abreast of all our bills, but we cannot increase our inventory at the rate we would like—nor pay me a living wage. We have reached a point in our business where we want to grow to better serve the women in our community and are looking for creative ways to do it. One of our goals is to bring some volunteers into the store to help. Up until now we have done it alone because we didn't want to exploit women if we were going to be making money ourselves.

Now that we know the realities of operating a business, seeking volunteers no longer seems exploitive. Last year I was only able to draw $1,753 from the business and that included $708 in paid health insurance. If Jan's father charged us rent, and if she and I were not living together, it would be impossible to continue running the store.

We hope that our local women's community will rally around us if we are able, with volunteer help, to keep the store open evenings and Sundays (and also to give me some freedom during the day). We can then plan more outreach programs, more in-store programs and more interaction with women more committed to feminism.

When I was a kid, I once entertained some silly ideas of being a missionary. Well, the thought crossed my mind that here in Lakeshore Bay, Jan and I are feminist missionaries. I hope that to survive and to grow we don't have to do as comedian Robin Tyler suggests on her record *Always a Bridegroom—Never a Bride*. I quote her, "P.S. Move to a big city."

Chapter 15

Bea on November 1, 1981

The photos I shot at the airshow inspired me to illustrate *Something Happened to Me* and we sent it to the printer last week, ordering 1,000 copies and publishing it under the name Mother Courage Press. It should be ready in two weeks. Jan's planned a promotional campaign by researching social service agencies and relevant journals and magazines to compile a mailing list with a media release and a copy of the book. Of course, that will cost us more in mailing, but it's cheaper than trying to advertise the book. Fortunately, she can cut and paste and Xerox copies for individual mailings or we'd be at the typewriters forever. Jan adapted this version for Lakeshore Bay and big city newspapers.

"Sexual abuse book helps victims communicate"

"Something happened to me," says the look in the eyes of the young girl from the cover of a new book for children, the initial publishing effort of Mother Courage Press.

The child's look shows that it was not the pleasant experience children are happy to share. "I feel different. I'm afraid to talk about it," she says in the opening pages.

Milwaukee school psychologists Rachel Sandler, M.S., wrote *Something Happened to Me* for therapists to help children talk about their experiences as victims of sexual abuse. But the book has a wider scope. Without being sexually explicit, the book may be for any child who feels unfairly treated or hurt. It affirms that in asking for adult help, children need not be alone. In spite of what others may do to them, these children are special and good persons.

As the simple, childlike statements unfold, the reader and/or the adult reading to the child uncover the feelings of child victims of sexual abuse. The feelings of fear and shame that may scar the child for life change as the book progresses, as the child finds adult help and comfort, as communications grow to reinforce the child's feelings of dignity and self-worth.

It will be of interest not only to therapists and others who work with children and families where sexual abuse has occurred, but to parents who wish to open a dialogue with their children about the subject.

Bea Lindberg's drawings cover the range of young children's faces, feelings and body language. The book's design by Jan Anthony isolates the child in the beginning, but as resolution and help evolves, communication grows and the children's pictures with adults helpers force the lonely, empty spaces to disappear, filled with positive holding and helping adult reinforcement.

Lindberg has taught elementary grades and learning disability classes at The Learning Center in Lakeshore Bay. A former director of religious education at Lakeshore Bay's Margaret Fuller Unitarian Church, she has worked in public relations doing writing, illustrating and photography. She currently manages Mother Courage Bookstore. Mother Courage Press is a new subsidiary of Mother Courage Enterprises owned by Lindberg and Anthony, the director of communications at Lakeshore Medical Center in Lakeshore Bay.

The large format paperback book retails for $4 and is currently available at Mother Courage Bookstore, 214 2nd Street in Lakeshore Bay, WI 42424

Bea on January 12, 1982

Jan's promotional mailings on *Something Happened to Me* are bringing in orders and we've been reviewed in several important publications.

The first biggie was *SIECUS Report from The Sex Information and Education Council of the U.S. Inc. of New York City*. The review wrote that *Something* sensitively explores the feelings of child victims of sexual abuse. Although the book was written for therapists as an aid in helping children talk about their sexual abuse experiences, it can also be used for any child who feels unfairly treated or hurt since it affirms that in asking for adult help, children need not be alone. Parents may wish to use it in order to open a dialogue in their family concerning sexual abuse."

In *Young Children*, the Official Journal of the National Association for the Education of Young Children in Washington, D.C., a reviewer wrote, "...The marvelous introduction and epilogue are written for adults and reveal the extraordinary care that the author, a school psychologist, has taken to assure the dignity and self-worth of children from troubled families."

My favorite review quote comes from a children's advocate Thomas Hysom in the *Sojourner Truth House Newsletter* in Milwaukee. He writes "...a sensitive, straightforward book designed to help children victimized by incest or other sexual abuse....They are helped to come to grips with unpleasant experiences beyond their control. Compassionate, competently rendered line drawings add immeasurably to the book, which is well designed to be easily understood and visually appealing. There is also room on each page for a child to draw pictures or write notes about personal experiences."

All right!

Jan on January 15, 1982

Matt is home! He survived the scheduled college trip and an extra six weeks to stay alone with an Indonesian family and study their farming methods—"slash and burn agriculture," he calls it—and research towards his Master's degree. I hear bits and pieces of his trip as he comes and goes, bearing batik fabrics for gifts and Polaroid photos of him sitting on the bell-shaped dome of the huge Buddhist Borobudur Temple built in the 9th century in Central Java.

His travels took him to the site of the original Krakatoa that blew itself to pieces and estimated to have been 13,000 times the force of an atomic bomb. Its remnants were underwater but Anak Krakatoa erupted when their group was there, sending out underwater lava flows that became an exposed island when the lava hardened. It became bigger and bigger and it exploded.

Once they were on a local bus full of frantic passengers with lava flowing near them. Matt speaks fluent Indonesian and asked the driver what he was going to do about it. The bus driver basically said, "Nothing. I have to do my job." And they continued hauling down a busy road, the driver forging on to his destination.

"It is humbling to be surrounded by smoke, wind, rain and ash. It made me aware of the force of the original Krakatoa. In some ways you want to get closer out of curiosity, but in other ways you're full of fear and want to escape."

He told about being on a boat going from Eastern Sumatra to western Java, and the volcano blew again but like on the bus, the boat was going to Java no matter what. "The passage wasn't turbulent but the air around us was."

We'll get together soon for a longer talk and some home-cooked food. He looks so handsome—and mature. Living in Third World conditions will surely give him a greater appreciation for what we have at home. But then again, he's always been grateful for whatever he's gained, even when he's had to work hard.

He's signed up to learn computer programming and he's going

to try to find himself a job while he's here living at home with his dad and Jenny.

I am blessed to have such a son—and a daughter, too.

Bea on January 15, 1982

I sent out my resumé and two job applications today. I can't take this boredom and working alone anymore. If job offers come along, I need to respond to them and keep my options open. I've been fine-tuning my resumé and I think I've submitted excellent cover letters, one to the Girl Scouts of Lakeshore Bay County who have a part-time opening for a PR director and the second to manage the UW-Oshkosh bookstore.

To the Girl Scouts I wrote, "I am currently the manager and a partner in Mother Courage Bookstore and Art Gallery and we are engaged in making new decisions about the business. Due to economic conditions and increased competition from new bookstores in the area, particularly at the new mall, our business has seen a $6,000 drop in gross receipts this year. Although we still managed to show a small profit, it is hardly enough to survive on. I feel it is time for me personally to put my talents, experience and abilities to use elsewhere. We may keep the bookstore open but cut down the hours. We specialize in women's books and have many loyal supporters in the women's community who would not like to see us close. Therefore a part time position would be ideal for me and I would look forward to devoting my energies and talents to the Girl Scouts."

I used similar information to Oshkosh's application, but I stressed that Mother Courage is a full service general bookstore specializing in books for women and we have the largest collection of sailing books in the area. We have exclusive contracts to provide the textbook needs for Lakeshore Medical Center School of Nursing. I wrote, "I feel that I would be the ideal candidate for this position, not only because I am confident that you will find my qualifications excellent, but because I know Oshkosh. I am an alumnus and have known and worked with so many of the professors and staff in the past."

My résumé is quite impressive with my latest qualifications "...in retail sales, publishing and free-lance art work. I set up the bookstore from scratch and have handled every aspect of it from bookkeeping, payroll, tax preparation, ordering, billing, inventory control, training and supervising employees. Mother Courage Press published a book last December which I illustrated and is selling by mail order around the United States, Canada, England and elsewhere."

I listed all the jobs I did as Jan's assistant director of communications: director of religious education, workshop leader, recruiting and training a church school staff of thirty-five adult teachers; community education programs producer with documentary sound film and slide shows and more.

Jan knows what I am doing, but she protects herself against facing the reality of changing the bookstore hours—or closing it— by not worrying about the situation until it becomes a reality. She knows how important it is to keep your options open, yet she keeps telling me to create options within myself through art and writing and music while keeping the bookstore alive. She doesn't say so, but I know she feels that it will be difficult for me to work for anyone, but that's because we had our interpersonal problems when I worked for her. That's not what I'm about. I can work with and for other people. I can lead, too. I've more than proven that in the past.

Jan on February 3, 1982

Our first "For Your Health" TV program was aired last night and I imagine only those who were involved watched "Taking Medications." It will be aired again on Thursday. We didn't get feedback from anyone. Pat Holmen was poised to answer questions phoned in after the program, but no one called.

We certainly did enough promotion. Our program sponsor, Emily Mills, and our program host, Laura Williams, had an excellent check-holding photo and story in our local weekly paper. Both women were smiling broadly. My article was printed word-for-word, as usual, and I quoted Laura saying—or I put words in her mouth, "Beyond providing quality patient care," said Williams, "Lakeshore Medical Center's next priority is helping to educate people to lead healthier lives. We encourage the public to join us in this new dimension in Lakeshore Med's educational programming."

Our friends at *The Bay View Times* won't print check-passing photos but they will take our money for advertising the program.

Now for thirteen weeks, we'll promote each show with flyers on patient trays and with stand-up cards on each cafeteria table. It looks like we're offering a wine list on those table cards. We distributed posters and flyers in physician and dentists' offices, beauty parlors and barbershops and mailed post card flyers to our PR mailing list.

We had to pull teeth from the cable company to guarantee thirty- second promos, and then they reneged on their promise. They did begin to highlight our program on their lighted bulletin board in front of their building. Big Deal!

Who knows if all this work is worth it? I'm tired, I guess, but working all these challenging angles is stimulating and Laura, Pam, and our cameraman Mark are fun to work with.

Administration wants us to cut back costs by ten percent so I spent time planning and typing three pages of options, including:

"A) Consider alternatives for more effective use of communications publications: eliminate *synergy* magazine for a one-or two-page spread in *The Bay View Times*. We'd reach a wider, broad-based audience of 45,000 readers rather than our 5,000 *synergy* readers.

Hospitals can't afford to send out our expensive and time-consuming, self-promoting magazines with all this cost-cutting scare going on. Of course, canceling *synergy* after eleven quarterly issues in three years also eliminates the publication that Bea and I started when we worked together as Lakeshore Med's PR team. I have emotional ties to that, but it's now become a drain not only on writing, designing and photographing it, but also maintaining the mailing list and getting it through the mail room. I'd go in there and see those *synergy* boxes sitting sometimes for weeks before the magazine would go to the Post Office.

And it's sent out to those people who already support Lakeshore Med. I brainstormed and storyboarded a unique alternative for several months and I submitted my plan as one of my entries to help cut cost yet continue to provide information that promotes the hospital to more people. Rather than continue publishing *synergy*, I proposed a one- or two-page newspaper "advertising" campaign called *Goodlife* with hospital news and features that provide "controlled" information to a wider audience rather than responding to "uncontrolled" media questions and stories that have become somewhat hostile in recent months.

It will also save printing and mailing costs to reach a community audience and potential hospital clients.

My proposal continued, "More than our TV programs, this campaign will reach and inform not only the community about health care information, Lakeshore Medical Center services, its quality staff and their accomplishments, it would also enhance employee morale and sense of responsibility. Lakeshore Medical Center would be in a proactive position rather than react to controversial issues like hospital costs and rate increases. Through this aggressive communications we will gain market share through community awareness of the value of this hospital.

"I know of no other hospital in our area, even in Wisconsin, that communicates features and news as full-page advertising on a regular, periodic basis."

My response was, "Thank you for your cooperation. Randy King will be contacting you within the next few weeks to discuss this."

And I received a poorly designed, boxed kitchen cutlery set for my efforts; the knife hurts your hand even if you only use it to carve meatloaf.

It's always a surprise to see Matt pushing an interoffice mail cart around Lakeshore Med at the beginning of the second shift. Marge must have broken the unwritten hiring rules like nepotism, hiring UUs, and supervisors and subordinates living in the same house, etc., by giving Matt a job while he's home and going to computer classes here. Of course, she's also hired her niece and other friends, but this is the first time since hiring our friend Rita Kline that Marge's hired another Unitarian—but Matt, who doesn't know about these so-called rules, is not living in the same house with Marge, or vice versa—at least, not yet. I don't see him much now anyway. But it's great to bump into him when I'm dashing around a corner at work helping produce our TV shows, or even better, to have him come into our office delivering our mail.

Speaking of a shaky economy, I heard that Alex's getting ready to leave his job because the company is downsizing and he's tired of traveling. I'm sure he'll negotiate a comfortable settlement after all those stressful long hours starting up their computer system and years of creating successful computer programs for the company and its departments, warehouses and subsidiaries around the country. I heard that he and Marge traveled to Australia and New Zealand to interview for a job. Is that far enough to get away from me?

Frank Tower in *Bay View Times* on April 18, 1982

"Making health entertaining"

There probably is no truth to the rumor that Lakeshore Medical

Center plans to get out of the hospital business and go into full-time movie making.

But even though it may not win any awards as best television documentary series of the year, Lakeshore Medical Center home-style "Health Risks" production provides a splendid example of closed circuit ingenuity.

Using a borrowed (from the library) camera and approximately one- hundred-fifty amateur actors, Lakeshore Medical Center turned out thirteen health programs for cable television. These segments will serve several purposes. For example, Lakeshore Medical Center patients can view them on closed circuit TV and the hospital also can use them for in-service training. Henry Thoreau High School has already requested to borrow the tapes for classroom use.

"A champagne public relations project on a beer budget," Lakeshore Medical Center Community Relations Director Jan Anthony called it. Better yet, the rates won't go up again because the entire series didn't cost the hospital a penny. Only two other hospitals in the country have attempted anything of the sort.

Patient Education Coordinator Pat Holmen set the tone for the educational films when she observed, "If you don't entertain, you won't educate." Anthony added, "Entertainment doesn't necessarily mean laughing, although in some instances, we did get people to laugh, even about health. We aren't trying to preach. We only want people to take better care of themselves."

In one sequence local antique car buff Larry Skogen is pictured driving down the street in a mint condition 1941 Buick, followed by a shot of an overweight, out of shape man also born in 1941. A point is made. Then, there's a shot of auto mechanics toiling at Frank Gentile's dealership and a timely reference to the fact that doctors essentially are body mechanics too.

Doctors love the series and there has been no difficulty talking them into being camera subjects. "Lakeshore Medical Center may tackle a similar series next year. If nothing else, it is enriching its own closed circuit television.

Anthony mentioned there were letdowns as well as challenges in the endeavor. "Like what?" inquired the columnist. "Well."

replied Anthony, "seeing yourself on television can be sort of a letdown."

Jan on April 29, 1982

In my weekly Randy King report, I listed our progress, including:

The TV series is finished with a party, thank yous, awards presentation and continue program promotion.

Lakeshore Medical Center new Blue & Gold plans: printing, advertising, t-shirt design, budgeting, entry & waiver forms, mailings, trophies, media releases, Auxiliary and employee involvement and training, route planning, maps, first aid, signage and decorations, run times and final reporting, route determined, police and street closings, praying for good weather, etc.

St. Agnes' Health Fair: Brainstorming to get fair ideas, exhibit development, St. Agnes' contacts, planning and implementation.

HPRW conference: preparing and presenting TV project to members and continue working on accreditation of Fellowship program.

At 3 p.m. on April 23, we had a cast party in the cafeteria, invited all who participated in the series in any way. Edited tapes showed out-takes of ridiculous, stupid-looking and tongue-tied program miscues. As emcee, I played my role as the promotions and PR person and all-around cheerleader by offering an award to each committee member.

I said, "From the beginning of this thirty-minute, thirteen-week program series, our committee worked to maintain Lakeshore Medical Center high standards of excellence on *For Your Health*. But in light of the realities of being TV production novices and being naive enough in such a short span of time to pull it off, I would urge them, quietly but realistically, that we could make some compromises with their highest expectations.

"I remember reminding them often, 'Keep this in mind. You

don't have to produce an Emmy winner for each program.'

"Well, we're finished now and we've done a good job. We've learned a lot about TV production and produced an excellent series. We've learned more about group dynamics too, in our committee made up of all Indians without a chief. We were all facilitators helping each other.

"But we haven't submitted any of our programs to the Emmy Awards committee—yet. So I've taken the opportunity to create a new award especially for our TV committee members.

"What award would be appropriate for this group of individuals? They were confident that they could meet this challenge, educated enough to have the savvy for the task, creative enough to come up with a different format and mood for each assignment, fun to work with and crazy enough to pull it all off with good spirits—a jaunty bit of swagger and some arrogance—perhaps to hide our concerns.

"Creative. Crazy. Confident. That's why I've named our award to each committee member the—Cocky Award!"

(My Bea had jig-sawed our logo roosters seven inches high, devised a block of wood for each to stand on and painted them golden to compete, on our scale, with Oscars, Emmys, Tonys, whatever.)

The audience cheered as each committee member received her or his award and then we all applauded back at the audience made up of our cast and helpers. Then we hit the refreshment table.

The entire project cost the hospital $286.90 plus staff time and videotapes.

The hospital decided to approve getting its own $10,000 TV camera and supportive equipment so we could do more programs for next year. But the real reason was to please physicians who wanted to document procedures and surgeries.

TeleCable TV said we provided them with the best local feature programming they've had. (Of course, we have to consider that they don't have much in the way of local programming except for sports.) They not only promised to repeat our programs throughout the year, but they will produce 60-second spots to use on sports programs and special events to fulfill their public service requirements.

Participating in this newer medium of expression energized our employees. They appreciated being singled out for their work and for their departments' value to the hospital and to the community.

Our participating physicians heard positive comments from their patients who viewed programs. An extra bonus was working with Laura and Pat and these physicians, giving them the opportunity to promote their expertise in an era that still frowns on doctors' advertising. It was fun getting to know them as people with a sense of humor and appreciation.

Chapter 16

Jan on July 22, 1982

Bea and I asked for trouble when we organized a weekend escapade with Betty Willing and husband Hank, Em Kuiper and Herman Schneider at Spring Valley Trails, Spring Green. We had camped there in 1975 with my Jenny and Marge's sons Tom, David and his girlfriend. We had such a wonderful time that we talked Betty and her gang into joining us, especially when an outdoor fiddling contest was to be nearby and we all would enjoy it, especially Betty.

Bea and I headed out early on Friday, stopping at several music and antique shops along the way. We set up camp after 3 p.m., and the rest arrived after 7. Hank was pulling a huge camping trailer rig he borrowed for the weekend. It was as big in scale as he is, and I swear he must weigh over 300 pounds. I don't know how Betty can survive having sex with him.

In contrast to Hank, out popped our dear little person Em, Betty's close friend and our church organist; Herman Schneider, a German artist who teaches sculpting and isn't much taller than Em; and of course our Betty who registered under her pseudonym, Harriet Peterson. We didn't know she had a pseudonym but we weren't surprised. She probably would have used that name in

Chicago when we were Three Sailors on the Town in the fall of 1974. Again we would understand why she uses it instead of her real name—in case she gets arrested.

We settled in at the far edge of the campground outside the ring of other trailers and campers, and our campfire's sparks joined the sparkling stars as we told stories, drank, laughed and sang. I brought out my harmonica and began playing when Em told us he had never played a mouth organ. I loaned mine to him and of course he caught on right away and played more songs. Herman's stories of being a boy in Germany and trying to escape from being sent to the front during the end of WWII would have been terrifying if he hadn't been so animated, standing and speaking with his accent slurring as the drinks flowed and his shadow danced menacingly against the leafy trees above him. It was as if he were part of "The Night on Bald Mountain" in Disney's *Fantasia*.

Hank told a few rude jokes before he scratched himself and went into the trailer to go to sleep.

I took a flashlight to walk away from under the tree line to find a quiet place to rest, and I meandered into an awesome sight of clear, bright stars in the night sky above the horizon and masses of glowing fireflies hovering over the fields, filling the dark land like the phosphorescence glow that flows on ocean waves. After I caught my breath at the sight, I made my way back to the campfire and tapped Bea on the shoulder. Without a word spoken, she followed me until we stood together whispering about the beauty of sharing this radiant bowl of sparkling lights against the darkness.

We remembered our lunch at the Blue Bayou Restaurant in Disneyland in 1979 where fireflies and bird songs filled the atmosphere that surrounded us before we were catapulted off on "The Pirates of the Caribbean" ride.

After a few minutes of quiet closeness, we turned to rejoin our rascally campers around the fire. But they had disappeared and the flames cast their light on an empty circle.

We heard muffled noise from behind us, but we couldn't see anything with our flashlight as we approached the sounds and voices all jumbled together.

"Betty! Betty! Are you all right?"

"Em! You fell on me!"

"No. I jumped to rescue you."

"Then I chumped too to rescue bot of you," said Herman standing in the rippling stream of water at the bottom of an eight-foot ravine.

"Well, you landed right on me, Em!"

"Oh, I'm so sorry, Betty. So sorry. Did I hurt you?"

"Nah. But I'm all wet now. And how are we going to get out of this ditch?"

Bea shined our flashlight down on three rumpled-looking, wet comedians looking back at us, shocked but seemingly uninjured. It must have been the alcohol that saved their relaxed bodies in the fall.

Both of us stretched out on our stomachs with our arms reaching over the edge to grab slippery hands and pull them out of their grassy gorge. I was surprised to find my harmonica in my hand instead of Em's grip.

"Take this first. I don't want anything to happen to your harmonica," Em said sincerely.

"Oh for Heaven's sake, Em. Let's get you out of there."

And with all our might and Em's determination to walk his sturdy frame up the side with help from those two down below, we got him out first.

"Keep Herman's accent, as in'Next ve take Betty,'" said noble Herman, who was poised and ready to give Betty a boost from behind—her behind. Up she came with a mighty screech, her hair disheveled and her clothes dripping wet.

We pulled up the brawny but wiry German munchkin with strong arms from years of sculpting massive clay statues.

Our giddy laughter grew louder as we brushed off the mud and tried to wring out our friends' clothing as they warmed themselves around the fire, drinking and toasting to their good fortune of being alive and unhurt. Of course, we disrupted the entire sleepy campground—except for Hank. We soon saw a large-scale flashlight making its way from the camp office to become the lady-in-charge who roundly scolded us for our noisy behavior, threatening to call the sheriff if we didn't stop it.

She wanted identification and that's when Betty's Harriet Peterson came in handy—for her. The rest of us could end up going home with a criminal record. Betty also turned the angry women's attack back on her. (I wish I had that skill. I could use it many times.) Betty sounded perfectly sober when she demanded to know why there wasn't a fence along that ravine. "Three of us fell in it and we could have killed ourselves or broken our bones. And," pointing to Bea and me, "these two would have grounds to sue you for negligence if we had died! We've got grounds to sue you!"

She backed down then and we promised we'd be quiet and go to bed. It must have been at least 2 a.m. and each of us went to our camper or trailer. But on the way, I discovered Em trying to sleep in the back seat of Hank's car and we convinced him to get into our extra bed for a good rest and try to heal up from his fall.

Our three ravine tumblers woke up in relatively surprising condition and we regaled Hank with their exploits. Bea took pictures to prove how deep the ravine was along with others in our various woodsy costumes as I started cracking eggs and frying bacon for their hardy breakfast.

Herman was walking around and mumbling, "My chews. My chews. I can't find my chews."

"What are you looking for?"

"My chews," he said pointing to his bare feet.

"Oh, shoes. Aren't those your shoes next to that tree?"

"No. My chews are gray and those are brown."

"Well, that's because they got wet last night while you were stomping around trying to save Betty—and Em."

The day was as warm and beautiful as the night was awesome. And I felt so much joy being in this beautiful Spring Green countryside with the beauty of a little Switzerland. I couldn't help it. I started, "The hills are alive with the sound of music..." and "How do you solve a problem like Maria..." Somehow I remembered every word and sang every note. And I kept singing the songs from the record that I had played over and over when my kids were toddlers.

After breakfast, we were to drive in one car to the Cave of the Mounds and to the open air Fiddle Fest concert. Betty said she wasn't feeling well so the three guys catered to her and they sat in an air-conditioned restaurant while the two of us enjoyed the Fiddle Fest immensely.

We met up to head back so we could grill steaks after cocktail time. I made a salad and again broke out singing and dancing "The hills are alive, etc." until Bea hollered, "Shut your von Trapp, Maria."

Martinis and steak always make me sleepy and we all were quieter around the campfire, and it was an early night to go to bed.

We loaded up and bid farewell to Spring Valley Trail campground—and we hadn't been arrested. We set off for the fantastic House on the Rock that had tripled in size since our last visit and included a gigantic indoor merry-go-round and multitudes of masterfully displayed collections: automatic musical instruments playing in concert when you dropped in coins; streets with storefront windows displaying a town's complete services and stores; a 200-foot sea creature among seafaring objects; themed buildings displaying autos and airplanes from several decades. It could drive you crazy and Em said, "Too much." We found him sleeping in Hank's car. Again, Bea and I were most enthusiastic about the remarkable music rooms, dollhouses and sea-faring scenes with the gigantic whale.

We parted for home in our own ways. That left us time for Bea to return to the shop we visited before to buy an antique autoharp and a piece of butternut wood for her to carve.

When I got home from work today, Bea sang me a folksong accompanied by the fully repaired antique autoharp.

Bea on August 9, 1982

Jan's promotional mailings on *Something* are paying off and *The Bay View Times* printed one of my illustrations on the top of

Sunday's front page with a lead, "Helping hand: A Lakeshore Bay bookstore extends a hand to young girls who are sexually abused."

The full page in Sunday's feature section started with a bold headline, "Something Happened To Me," written by reporter Mary Watkins. Two of Bea's poignant illustrations, one of a blond, white girl from the book's cover, the other of a Black girl with a cut line from the book saying, "I feel awful. It could happen again. Should I tell someone?" Her drawings fill several columns on the page.

Watkins writes, "In her book published last November, Milwaukee psychologist Rachel E. Sandler hopes to encourage more children and even adults to quit blaming themselves for having incestuous relationships with close family members.

"Oftentimes clothed in secrecy from childhood to old age, the scars of incest are protected only by a fragile scab, said Sandler, the author of *Something Happened to Me*. 'The wounds never heal.'

"The book is an attempt to '...educate parents on how to educate kids that they have a right to control their bodies,' according to Sandler. For that reason, the primer is being promoted by the bookstore as the first book with illustrations of children that deals with the touchy subject of abuse.

"Originally designed for professionals who counsel sexually abused youths, Sandler said her paperback has instead become a godsend, a silent confidant for abused children.

"'It's meant to be a comfort,' said Sandler, who has a private practice in Milwaukee and works as a psychologist in the city's public school system.

"'Kids try to tell other kids about what happened, but their friends absorb societal values too. They say: Yuck. Don't tell me about it.' Sandler said.

"'The book is meant to open conversation for a lot that's been unsaid, said Bea Lindberg, co-owner of Mother Courage Press and the book's illustrator.

"Adds Sandler, 'I think the most amazing thing about my book is that it was originally written for kids between three and 12, but now I realize I underestimated the age limit. It's for everyone.

Frustration with the severity of this problems combined with the lack of material available for use with children are the reasons this book was written.' Sandler wrote in the introduction to her book. 'Clearly the incest taboo is not operating to prevent it—what is operating is the fear to discuss it.'

"Sandler said her decision to write the book was based on her '...seeing a lot of abused kids and a lot of former victims.'

"The book was written after Sandler said she discovered there was a skimpy assortment of books available for sexually abused people. 'There are a few books for adults but not for children,' she said, and when she did find something, it usually was loaded with technical terms.

"'My experience with pre-adolescents is that they get embarrassed when asked to read something about incest. They get so caught up in the content they lose the lesson.' So, her black-and-white magazine-style book deliberately contains no sexually explicit terms, there's no mention of incest, no use of anatomical words and no real reference to sexual abuse. Its purpose is to absolve a sexually abused child from feeling any guilt,' Sandler said.

"For that, the $4 book is kept simple. It starts out: 'Something happened to me. I feel different. I'm afraid to talk about it.'

"Said Sandler, 'Children are real imaginative. They don't have to be hit over the head with a lot of terminology. When I hear (sexually abused) kids talking about it, they rarely make it sexually explicit. For example, when children are raped, they say they were "punched out,' Sandler said.

"Lindberg's illustrations are of forlorn-looking boys and girls. Some wear glasses. Some are dressed in rumpled play clothes, others in prim dresses. They have black and white skin.

"A girl starts out alone questioning the dilemma.

"'If I tell what will happen?' asks one girl. 'Will they think I did something wrong? Maybe people will be angry at me.'

"Then caring adults start appearing with the children in the book.

"'We talked about touching that feels good, like hugging and rocking and cuddling,' said one boy. 'We talked about touching that you don't like—like hitting, or touching in places that make you feel strange, touching when you're half asleep and pretending not to know about touching that someone tells you not to talk about.'

"The illustrations are gentle and cold at the same time.

"'Color was deliberately kept out of the book,' Lindberg said. 'I kept my sketches black and gray because black and gray was exactly the kind of emotion we wanted to express.'

Jan Anthony, the other owner of Mother Courage Press, said 1,000 copies were produced in its first printing. Most of the book's sales have been to social service agencies, Anthony said. But the behavioral science unit of the FBI and the government of Guam also have ordered copies, she said.

"Sandler said conservative estimates say one out of every four girls experienced some type of inappropriate sexual advance before the age of eighteen. That doesn't necessarily mean incest or rape, Sandler said, but also includes grabbing, obscene phone calls, fondling and indecent exposure.

"'Incest is often a closely guarded secret kept within the confines of a family,' Sandler said. 'We're trying to bring it out in the open.'"

"When it's time to tattle on daddy"

An additional story by Watkins filled several columns and half of the lower page and it described the detective work of Frank Scott, a Lakeshore Bay County assistant district attorney. Graphic details of actual victims made me cringe.

Watkins quoted Scott saying that incest is not rampant here but it "...happens with some frequency. I guess I feel sad. I know it will be a major problem for this little girl for the next thirty years and only the lucky few will resolve it in thirty years.

He's taken ten incest cases to trial in three years but another thirty or more were dismissed because the accused pleaded guilty. And he said he's hitting only the tip of the iceberg.

"The guilty person is the man who is initiating the assault. But when it comes to light it puts real pressure on the girl."

With psychological and physical details, the reporter describes his many cases and his frustration with the courts and his concerns over further traumatizing the victim in telling the truth to the court.

The scary thing is that many juries are prone to buy some version that the defense uses: that the mother was inadequate, the child was uncontrollable or the child was trying to get even for being disciplined.

"The defense is to cry rape," he said, "and juries are shockingly susceptible to that."

After this local newspaper exposure, several adult women came into the store to buy the book for themselves, including the wife of one of Jan's former employers. She told me something she has never told anyone. She'd never spoken about her being sexually abused as a child, and now I'm the one she confides in. I don't know how to deal with this—except to be a sympathetic listener as we talked together for a long time.

I found out that our little book appeals to more than social workers counseling abused children. I now have adult women come into the store and after looking at the book, they come up to me to tell me stories of their abuse—saying it out loud for the first time! I hope I'm responding to them appropriately and am a good listener for them.

It's hard to believe, yet it's true; women are keeping their abuse as secrets for all of their lives. I can only imagine how this may have affected their relationships with their husbands and lovers—with anyone in their lives.

Chapter 17

Bea on February 8, 1982

The pull of the moon lured me into inviting friends to our Mermaid Inn so Betty Willing, Joanne Zekas and Jan could join me to laugh at life's absurdities: jobs or no jobs, college classes and bookstores, discrimination, husbands, ex- husbands, bodily functions, survival.

Our family room vibrated with feminists' laughter ringing free, unfettered and ferocious.

Another friend, Betty Hannaman, returned from attending a week-long Jean Houston conference and Betty asked Jan and me to attend weekly Sunday session to explore what she had learned and to build upon Houston's intellect.

"Intellique," Jan showed off by raising her finger and saying words that Houston uses. Jan listens to Houston's tapes while she drives to work and quoted her saying "The universal energy that unites those who are open to this higher level of intelligence, creativity and spirituality."

"Yes, but Hannaman's group includes husbands and other males, and we know how they take over. I don't want to hear male voices tell me anything," our Betty insisted. "And I don't want any guru of any gender to lead me on any path. I think for myself."

"As do we all, my dear. As do we all," Joanne affirmed as she started getting ready to head for her husband and home.

"When shall we four meet again? In thunder, lightning, or in rain?" Betty cackled, and we joined in again over fresh glasses of wine, recalling the story of my cauldron of pumpkin soup scaring our lesbian sisters' circle last Halloween when they thought it had spiders and other creepy crawlers in it.

"What fun that was," Betty exhaled in the midst of her spiraling tendrils of cigarette smoke, "Why do we have to wait until Halloween to do it again?"

"You are always so impatient."

"Well! Why not!"

"We could meet here." I volunteered. "Unlike you two, we have no husbands nor children to cast a suspicious eye on our machinations."

"We've got the where. Now! When?"

"Oh! Look!" and Jan howled her customary full moon howl. "The full moon's lights are shining through our window."

They could see its aura of light around Jan, standing with the palms of her hands open and her arms out, in reverence of the moon.

"We could follow our body menstrual cycles and meet every twenty-eight days."

"And we could call ourselves Menses."

"It's obvious. We are supposed to meet every full moon. That's our sign. It comes every twenty-eight days as does a woman's menstruation, and it comes thirteen times a year, which is wonderfully witchy."

"That's why Julius Caesar, Emperor Augustus and the male priests recreated the calendar that we have now. They stole women's natural calendar. Nature's calendar had to be altered to take away women's power."

"And the male church took our sacred bodily functions. The priests put on long dresses and turned our birthing, breast feeding, menstruation and all and recreated them into the Holy Sacraments."

"Those men screw up everything," said our Betty.

"They screwed up our language and, of course, our religions.

All these masculine pronouns," said Jan she jumped on her favorite revolutionary bandwagon. "We'll never gain equality until we are part of the spiritual life of every culture. And we can't do that when all the god images are male."

"Remember how we penciled in gender free pronouns in our church hymnals?"

"But our denomination is changing all that and we're having new wording in our new hymnal."

"It's about time!" Bea thumped her glass on the bar. "And our group will be women only!"

"All Right!"

Jan left the bar to walk across the room to look at the moon again and explained that there is no "Man in the Moon" but an image of a woman on her one knee gently lifting her child in the air as in a celebration. I explained that Jan learned that from Libby Carson's mother who had been a missionary somewhere in Africa in her younger days. The Carsons lived downstairs of Jan's lower flat in the early 1960s and were UU friends who taught in our church school before I came along. Jan was sitting outside one summer's night after supper while toddlers Matt and Jenny and Libby's teenage daughter, Pam, played around them. The moonlight illuminated their multi-generational gathering with the children playing until the grandmother, the wise woman, attracted everyone's attention.

"Yes," Jan interrupted. "She stood before us pointing to the moon as if it were drawn on a chalkboard, and she said that the African women had changed her Man-on-the-Moon image to their interpretation of a mother and her child on the moon—plus other cultural differences that seemed so much more natural than that of the white Christian missionaries."

Betty and Joanne took their wine glasses and went to the window to stare out at the moon. The conversation quieted down, and those two were even quieter. We knew Betty didn't want to go home to her husband and she and Joanne could talk all night if they had the chance. Jan was exhausted and nodded to me. The two of us slipped upstairs to bed. The two of them could go to their homes whenever they desired.

Jan on March 22, 1982

As agreed, the four of us met on the March full moon to discuss who to invite into our group and what we would do. Bea dared to define us a coven. Her scholarship in reading many books told her that was what we are. She's absorbed Z Budapest's ritual books based on her Hungarian mother's teaching, on being the founder of her Susan B. Anthony Coven #1, and leading the first Dianic Yule ritual in Los Angeles in December 1971. Bea also used the work of one of Budapest's allies, Starhawk, and her invaluable and inspiring book, *The Spiral Dance: A Rebirth of the Ancient Religion of the Great Goddess.* Starhawk is one of my favorites too and she's becoming quite famous on her own as a priestess and teacher of the "Old Religion" in the San Francisco area. Another favorite new book of mine is Charlene Spretnak's *The Politics of Women's Spirituality.* We heard Spretnak speak at The Women's Building in L.A. when we were there in 1979 for the American Booksellers Convention. Our UU Beacon Press recently published Margo Adler's ground-breaking study of Neo-paganism and witchcraft across the country in *Drawing Down the Moon.*

Our dog, Luv, liked Z Budapest's *The Holy Book of Women's Mysteries* so much that she chewed off a third of the cover.

"Awareness of the Goddess movement is real and it's growing," declared Bea.

"We too will be a Dianic coven and invite other women, friends and acquaintances who are curious about the Goddess, women's spirituality, earth ceremonies and female energy in the universe," our Betty declared.

We assumed that each woman would be a feminist. In her book, Z includes spells and candles and magic, but we want to explore the magic that happens in the "sparking" (one of Mary Daly's words) that we make rather than restrict ourselves to anyone's magic candles, scents and formulas, especially being "skyclad" and kissing each other in significant places.

Elfin Betty really got into all this and asked if she or someone wants to try magic— "it would be for fun, of course. And what about calling us "witches" and using the word "witchcraft?"

We decided to downplay that aspect until it evolves within the group. We'll move in stages, valuing feminist spirituality first and then see in what directions we'll grow. Of course, any kind of women's circle is suspect to accusations of witchcraft. Right now we have enough to deal with, with being lesbians.

We decided to meet each full moon. That way our women could always refer to the calendar and know that our coven would gather at our house and we wouldn't have to phone or send out reminders. Every full moon at Jan and Bea's; whatever day of the week it landed on, that will be it.

We will all read and study, and we'd take turns leading the ritual, but we chose Bea to be the major ritual leader. Then the four of us agreed on the friends we'd invite into our coven that would meet at the next full moon. Because we'll meet at our home, we'll be a closed group of liberally religious feminists that we know could be trusted and would be comfortable with this experiment. We agreed to invite Carolyn from Lakeshore Medical Center, Marian and Sharon, Fran and Martha and Debbie as Mother Courage friends; Beth and Robin from the Women's Network; and Nora, our psychologist UU friend who is especially close to Betty; plus Joanne and Bea and me. Among the thirteen of us, six were UUs, ten are or had been married and twenty-seven children were birthed from our wombs, seven are lesbians—so far—and one is bi. In the future, we would like to keep at least thirteen women in the group, but we'll add others later, perhaps including daughters.

We heard that The Circle pagans from Mt. Horeb, led by Selena Fox and her husband, were coming to the new Brookfield UU church for a Spring Equinox celebration, so yesterday the four of us joined in the day-long event. I wondered if the prosperous Milwaukee suburban neighbors realized that pagans of all ages wearing floral headdresses and folk, Celtic and witchy outfits were dancing in the UU church and observing the ancient rites of spring.

Each of us attended different workshops to learn more of Wiccan and folk customs. I chose the session on the magic and medicine of plants, which included intriguing herbs, exotics and plain weeds, their legends and powers. Handouts were shared, but I could only remember that comfrey was our herbalist's favorite—Mother Nature's healing gift, she called it. "Eat it in the spring, cooked like spinach. Friendly bumble bees love its blossoms so there's lots of pollination going on—and it is great for your compost pile." She warned that it could be invasive, like most of the plants she described, so grow it in a contained area. I immediately had a vision of where to put comfrey in our yard—and how my compost could benefit from its rich witchness.

While my witchy sisters shopped for pagan articles and browsed among the books, I ventured in the church kitchen and discovered a huge bowl filled almost to overflowing with deeply dyed henna-red hard-boiled eggs; the surprise took my breath away. The group had saved yellow and red onionskins to create this natural blood-bold color—one color for all of these eggs. The bowl became the centerpiece of the food-ladened buffet table and though we were not a part of their group, they invited us to partake of their spring feast.

(For years, I focused on the egg as my symbol of worship. That is, if I needed a symbol. And here were dozens of my chosen symbol in an ocher-red earthy pigment as the centerpiece upon this sacred place of honor and delight.)

Of course, those of us in modern clothes stood out from the folk, but that didn't stop the circle from including us in their spiral and circle dances. We'd been folk dancers in the past and joined in the heady dancing to ancient pagan rhythms from the hand-crafted, hand-held drums, guitars, with various reed and stringed instruments making sounds and images from a hidden culture that is alive again from our ancestors and traditions that honor the earth.

We four, electrically charged, could barely wait to begin our own women's circle.

Bea to Jan on our April 1, 1982 anniversary

> You are the only Temple in which I worship.
> I am making icons to you.
> But in making icons to you, Earth Mother,
> I am making icons to all women.
> Everywhere in that Elysian plain,
> like the birds and insects,
> voices of women singing through silent hearts,
> and yearning with writing tools and paper,
> and drifting on the wind,
> chords and pipes and voices in the woods.
> The voice of women singing
> so right and natural—
> singing untroubled or simply ignoring
> for the moment the barking dogs,
> the sounds of technology
> just over the hill.

Jan on April 1, 1982

Dearest Bea,

> I still write poems to you every day in my heart
> when I think of our love and our life together.
> I am so proud to be your person
> and you to be mine. I love you—
> more and more each day, week and year.
> I'm yours,
> Jan

Bea on April 9, 1982

We held our first full moon circle last night. Everyone seemed comfortable because they trusted us, but I sensed some apprehension at what was going to begin on this night at 7 p.m. They each brought a small snack to share and a beverage to drink after the ritual. They placed them on the family room table and when everyone was here, we explained a few guidelines.

We want each woman to have space and time to share so we will pass a talking stick around the circle and she who is speaking should not be interrupted. (This didn't work out perfectly because someone would always ask a question or add respectful advice.)

We'll try meditations and be silent during them.

We could do a variety of rituals and we invite everyone to take a turn at being the leader and planning a ritual.

We must honor each other and not violate the other's confidence that is brought to the circle.

We must stay in the circle until it is closed, except for an emergency. No one will answer a phone while in the circle.

We can be free, free to cry and free to laugh. We can play. We do not have to behave as if we were in a church. We can imagine, make believe, create a power that will energize us.

And after each circle, we can talk about any changes or new guidelines that our group wants to try. Please do not bring new women into the group without discussing it with us all; they may not understand our secret meetings.

We lined up according to the oldest woman to enter the sacred circle in our darkened living room with the draperies closed over the large picture window. We were hidden from the outside world. At first Carolyn, who is in the midst of a hot love affair, was flustered to be considered the eldest, but when we convinced her it was an honor, she knew she had to lead the way. She chuckled in her bubbling, good-humored manner and led the women around the altar I had prepared.

We were creating our sacred space. A green cloth for springtime made a circle that covered a scrap of plywood set on our white shag living room rug that's comfortable for sitting if anyone wants to do that. I placed three tall white candles in my mother's candleholders in the center representing the Earth, the Sky and the Spirit Within and four different colored heavy round candles on saucers representing the four directions, one placed in each direction. I had placed my camping knife in the circle and after the ritual, a couple women kidded me; they had wondered what I was going to do with the knife. They knew that we'd ban any bloody sacrifices on our white rug.

Each woman placed some object on the altar that was symbolic or important to her. Jan had added her earth-red Goddess of Willendorf that Marian had molded out of Sculpy for her birthday gift, the Goddess she carried in her pocket every day. We encouraged the women to put down jewelry, a personal writing, books, photographs from their wallets, feathers, something borrowed from our shelves or flowers.

We provided a reading for women to respond to the directions I called out as I raised my unsheathed camping knife now sanctified as my "athame" to cast the circle. I raised the tool and called out each direction, guiding the women to face each direction as we call its name, holding arms up and outward.

I called, "To the East," and one reader spoke simplified words from Starhawk's book, "Hail, Guardians of the Watchtowers of the East, Powers of Air! We invoke you and call upon you. Come! By the air that is Her breath. Be here now!" The East candle is lit.

"To the South," and we turned as the next reader read, "Hail, Guardians of the Watchtowers of the South, Powers of Fire! By the fire that is Her spirit, send forth your flame. Be here now!" The South candle is lit.

"To the West," and the third reader said, "Hail, Guardians of the Watchtowers of the West, Powers of Water! By the waters of

Her living womb, send forth your flow. Be here now! The West candle is lit.

"To the North," and another read, "Hail, Guardians of the Watchtowers of the North, Powers of Earth. By the earth that is her body, send forth your strength, be with us now." The North candle is lit

We faced each other in the circle and by the candle flames illumination glowing on our faces, I spoke, "And to the Earth which is our foundation."

"To the Sky and the Atmosphere above."

"And to the Spirit within," as each candle is lit and the room is illuminated.

"Blessed Be! The Circle is cast!"

I taught them this simple chant and we held hands and sang three times, "We all come from the Goddess and to Her we shall return like a drop of rain flowing to the ocean."

We passed the talking stick and each woman could explain the meaning of her symbol in the circle and/or briefly highlight significant feelings that she wanted to share.

Jan had asked me to read Diane Mariechild's "Wise Woman" meditation because of the impact it had the first time she read a guided medication that asked a Wise Woman for guidance.

Someone may have fallen asleep during that, but I paced myself so it didn't go on too long. Then I had to play my guitar and sing my "Mother Earth" anthem as they joined in. There would be many songs and chants to learn and carry in our hearts.

I closed by reading from Starhawk's Chapter One, "Witchcraft as a Goddess Religion.

"Mother Goddess is reawakening, and we can begin to recover our primal birthright, the sheer, intoxicating joy of being alive. We can open new eyes and see that there is nothing to be saved from, no struggle of life against the universe, no God outside the world to be feared and obeyed; only the Goddess, the Mother, the turning spiral that whirls us in and out of existence, whose winking eye is the pulse of being—birth, death, rebirth—whose laughter bubbles and courses through all things and who is found only through love: love of trees, of stones, of sky and clouds, of scented blossoms and thundering waves; of all that runs and flies and swims and crawls on her face; through love of ourselves, life- dissolving world-creating orgasmic love of each other; each of us unique and natural as a snowflake, each of us our own star, her Child, her lover, her beloved, her Self."

We held hands and Jan said, "The circle is closed but not broken. Merry meet and merry part and merry meet again. Blessed Be!" And without having any "expert" telling me what to do, I took the initiative, encircled our ring of power by having us all bend at the waist, holding hands and raising them in unison shouting, "ALLL RRRRIGHT!!!"

After hugging and laughing, we rushed to find the food and drink, feeling exhilarated not only because our women's spirituality had been affirmed but also because we witches, straight and lesbian, had all come out of the broom closet together. We all agreed to meet again each full moon and to keep it our secret for now.

(Rachel Sandler gave Jan a copy of *Moon, Moon* by Ann Kent Rush after we had our first Transactional Analysis Intensive Weekend at church in November 1973. It was our first introduction of feminist spirituality. In it Rush explains the natural rhythms of the moon and its connection to the religion of the people then, forced to become a secret cult, but now women's groups are bringing full-moon light again to the earth and becoming "birth centers for social change.")

Jan on August 4, 1982

Full moon group ritual was my responsibility last night and I've been preparing and planning for it since early spring when I started composting. I subscribe to *Organic Gardening* magazine and became a dedicated compost person. I had dual goals in my composting: to replenish the earth in a natural way and to prepare for last night's ceremony. I had made two chicken wire bins four feet high by two feet wide, already holding some of my compost.

I put them far enough apart for each woman to walk between and through the secured the bins under the boughs of our small evergreen forest of four maturing trees in the back of the yard. Then I planted and groomed a vine that would join the two compost containers. I visualized the containers as Mother Earth's ovaries and the vine symbolizing her fallopian tubes.

A wild grapevine covered the chain-link fence between our yard and our neighbor's garage, creating a sheltered, shady green space with the ground being a cushiony carpet from years of accumulated pine needles. Sunlight would beam its way through boughs competing for open space to grow, but I pruned the dead lower branches so I could walk about and meditate in my secret sanctuary.

The growing branches with soft needles reached to the west, away from my compost "ovaries" and toward the setting sun. The vine flourished in the shade and the nourishing composted richness in each of the two "ovaries" with last year's winter leaves, this season's grass clippings mixed with garden and kitchen veggie waste that would eventually turn into rich, black earthy gold.

I created an altar in the center of our living room and we completed our opening rituals: honoring the four directions, lighting the candles, passing the talking stick for each woman's turn to talk about the theme of rebirth, the times of change, of new beginnings. Oh yes, each could preface that with sharing of some joy or concern, asking for guidance and energy, bad and/or good news.

We sang one of our favorite Goddess chants and a round, "The Earth, the Air, the Fire, the Water/Return, return, return, return./Eya, Eya, Eya, Eya, Oya, Oya, Oya, Oya./Eya, Eya, Eya, Eya, Oya, Oya, Oya, Oya. Then I introduced a combination of two songs: the Negro spiritual, "Sometimes I Feel like a Motherless Child' and George and Ira Gershwin's "Summertime" from *Porgy and Bess*.

Together we sang "Sometimes I feel like a motherless child, a long way from home" and then I combined it with "Summertime and the livin' is easy...with mammy and pappy standing by." I first heard that combination of songs sung by Mahalia Jackson when Studs Terkel interviewed her on his daily radio show. It's always meant so much to me.

I followed that up by having them blow out all but one candle that I used to lead them out the kitchen door, down the driveway along our lush and billowy garden. Then I whispered, "Hold hands in a line and follow me," as we slipped next the old shed and entered my sanctuary to make a circle of women around the compost rings and their center vines. I'd lit citronella candle pots to illuminate the area and the sun began to set in the west. We held hands in the circle and sang Bea's anthem, "Mother Earth."

"It is summertime," I said, "and the living may or may not be easy, and some of us may not have mothers and fathers standing by—or siblings either. Sometimes we feel as lonely as though we are motherless children. It makes me think of another song my mother and I would sing when I was a child and we were washing dishes together."

The candle light flickered and shined under my chin as I softly sang in a little girl's voice.

> "When I was born, my ma and pa,
> They looked at me and said "Aw shaw."
> My uncle called me "a little fritz"
> And I've been a step child ever since.
> They always, always pick on me.
> They never, never let me be.
> I've been so lonely, so awfully sad.
> It's been a long time since I've been glad.
> But I know what I'll do, by and by.
> I'll eat some worms and then I'll die.
> And then you wait, you just wait and see.
> They will all be sorry that they picked on me.

"Fortunately, when we're feeling bad and sad, we may look to each other and inside our strong selves to find the resources we need for new beginnings." I explained what I had done to create my compost womb and laughed quietly because we didn't want to be heard by the neighbors.

"I am going start you on your way through the birth canal of this womb so you are rebirthed by Mother Earth. Bea will be the midwife on the other side to catch you."

And as planned, I smudged Bea with sage, and she stepped over the fallopian tube vine between the ovarian compost rings. She put her arms forward to lead her head and body through the lush evergreens.

Then I smudged the next oldest and started her on her path to be greeted by Bea on the other side who whispered in each woman's ear, "You are reborn in the name of the Goddess."

Though one or two seemed a bit nervous about blindly stepping through to the growing darkness of the branches, as each one followed through the boughs, she discovered the reborn women to welcome her and honor her rebirth.

When I came through as the last to be reborn, we returned to the feast inside with the centerpiece being a Dirt Cake made of gummy worms, crushed Oreo cookies, chocolate pudding and served with a little red shovel from a brightly-colored new sandbox pail. We lit more candles and sang "Happy Birthday to us all."

This morning I smiled at Carolyn across our desks as we exchanged our good feelings gained from last night's full moon rebirthing ceremony.

Bea on February 16, 1983

Susan B. Anthony's birthday sale yesterday brought in $110 much needed dollars I need to do some creative bill paying and keep the store going for another month. Otherwise, business is terrible. Some weeks have two or three days of zero sales. I refused to get too depressed over this same old story, but waiting for a customer to come in is wearing on me. And the snow is terrible with over eight inches piling up day after day, plus all that Toro snow blowing I do at home and at the front and back sidewalks at the shop.

I'm considering all my career alternatives and took Barbara Sher's *Wishcraft* book off the shelf and started studying it. We heard her speak at our first American Booksellers convention in Los Angeles in 1979 and we've promoted the book's creative concepts ever since. It's "how to get what you really want and how to find hidden strengths, set goals and a timetable for achieving it." It starts with understanding the real me and helps me brainstorm my problems into action. I've underlined many important passages, but most importantly, I set up affirmations for my life while I'm sitting in the bookstore waiting and waiting for business.

My affirmations are
   • I am a very intelligent and creative person.
   • I can do anything—and do it well. As Jan often tells me,
I am a Renaissance woman.
   • I am a beautiful woman. Jan tells me that too but I scoff it off.
   • I deserve to be happy. I deserve the total happiness
I have with Jan.
   • I am rich beyond measure.
   • I have it all and then some—and I deserve it.
   • I deserve to be paid for my Goddess-given gifts and talents.
She continues to reward me in full measure f
or the incredible talent She has given me.
   • I radiate health and energy.
   • My gifts, my contributions brighten the world.
   • I have warm, loving relationships with my friends.
   • I am the creator of my life.
   • I am now creating my life exactly as I want it.
   • The light within me is creating miracles in my body,
mind and affairs, here and now.

My goals are
   • Work/Career: I want a satisfying, responsible day job. Meanwhile I'll close Mother Courage, sell the stock and fixtures, rent or sell the building and recoup some of our

investments. I could do retail, real estate, banking, substitute teaching or be a teacher's aide.

• Money: A job that pays $8,000 minimum with medical insurance, paid Social Security, real returns on our Mother Courage Press books, a balanced budget with tax shelters covering our properties. Our combined income should be near $40,000, but it will be lots more!

• Lifestyle/Possessions: Scuba gear, a videotape recorder, a camera and an underwater camera, a microphone and amplifier, the little VIC word processor, a spa and sunroom, and a new car for Jan.

• Relationships: A new job and new friends.

• Creative self-expression: Painting for art shows, repair my harp, make a new song tape, work on my musical, novels and my memoirs.

•Leisure/Travel: Florida, Egypt, British Isles, Caribbean sailboat cruise and scuba diving in Hawaii and Tahiti, swimming, boating, tennis, golf.

• Personal growth/Education: Become proficient in computers, earn a Masters, Ph.D., art courses, be healthy, trim, in control.

My success list includes so much.

• Art and Crafts: building my seven boats, musical instruments, woodworking, repairing and remodeling.

• Music and Drama: writing two novels, PR articles, poems.

• Career: my teaching; a business manager, bookseller and publisher; UU religious education director; Lakeshore Med public relations with Jan (before I was dismissed because of an unknown rule that a "supervisor" i.e. Jan "and a "subordinate" i.e., me "cannot live together"—after we bought our home in 1978).

• Photography: producing movie, slide shows and darkroom processing.

• Sports: boating, sailing, scuba and swimming adventures.

That long list shows me what I really want: To work for someone else. I do not like the solitary responsibility of being in business without benefits.

> • In my dream areas of work, I want challenges using my creative brain, to be innovative and busy working with my colleagues, to have responsibilities and to delegate work.
> • I don't want to work evenings and weekends or work with merchandise that takes special ordering or have tedious, empty hours alone.
> • A far-out idea would be to run a dive shop, sell and rent sporting goods and mopeds.

Chapter 18

Bea on October 15, 1987

Our sending *Something Happened to Me* out with the media releases to professional journals, appropriate newspapers and magazines made the three of us celebrate this successful project that helped so many, including us as Mother Courage Press. Jan's marketing sense made Shakti Gawain's affirmation our reality. Jan says it every day, "This or something better is now manifesting for me in totally harmonious and satisfying ways for the highest good of all concerned."

Then other authors writing about sexual abuse started submitting manuscripts but Jan grew weary of editing sexual abuse manuscripts in her precious free time.

Mother Courage Press expanded, took on other topics, and our book list grew. We began displaying those books for several years in a booth at the American Booksellers Trade show (ABA) in whatever city they met. Our clever little booth drew so much attention that other small presses asked to be placed next to our high-priority end of the aisle booth. Every year, Down There Press won the prized place and staffed its booth with playful people selling illustrated adult books and interesting toys.

Those exciting ABA weekends brought tons of action, many contacts and a few orders. Jan and I took turns staffing our booth or scooping up free books from other exhibitors: trinkets and treats—sometimes even a glass of wine.

To attract people to the small press area, the ABA arranged to have the book autographing area near our displays. A few of our Mother Courage authors who came to the ABA autographed their books even though we were small publishers.

To get our share of autographed books to bring home, we stood in line and chatted briefly with Shirley MacLaine, Jane Russell, Jesse Jackson and others.

When Muhammad Ali walked slowly down our aisle, everyone stopped talking and stood toward him to honor him. Though he staggered some from early stages of Parkinson's disease, he walked straight and strong.

Ralph Nader stopped and asked about our books—and about us. He signed one of his books and gave it to our author who wrote *Fear or Freedom, a woman's options in social survival & physical defense*, and she signed hers and gave to him.

A sax player across from us noodled music throughout the day, and when England's Prime Minister Margaret Thatcher marched passed us to autograph her book, our guy played a jazz version of "Hail Britannia." Surrounded by her bodyguards and without a nod, she forged on straight ahead.

One time Jan stayed at our booth and was concerned because I was missing for a long time. But I was having so much fun joking with Loni Anderson, Burt Reynold's beautiful buxom wife. She was staffing her booth while "Burt was scouting the crowds," she said. Loni wanted to produce a line of artistically appealing calendars of semi-nude women. She enjoyed my talent making risqué slightly double entendre remarks so much that she gave me a hug—and What a Hug that Was!

<<<>>>

The word went out at the Washington, D.C.'s ABA that our feminist small press publishers were organizing. We met in Nancy Bereano's hotel room. She's Firebrand Press. I think I have all the names: Barbara Grier and Donna McBride of Naiad, and women from Calyx, Cleis, Kitchen Table Women of Color and Seal presses plus Onlywoman Press from London. We became a loosely organized bunch for more clout by joining together to help each other. Our informal name was Book Babes. And Mother Courage was there at its beginning.

We talked about the imposing, huge black banner with large white letters attracting people to the new Amazon, an on-line bookstore that's challenging the big chains. What would on-line sales do to our small presses, independent booksellers, especially our women's bookstore network?

We decided to meet every year at the ABA and next year it's in another fantasy land, Anaheim, CA.

Jan on July 21, 1990

Bea's pioneered in an exciting and completely new trend, desktop publishing using her Apple Mac skills and determination. Sometimes Bea would work ten to twelve hours a day and when she'd doze off in her chair after our cocktails and supper, I see her fingers moving as if she were on the computer keyboard.

One sunny room in our house is packed with reference books, file cabinets, a drafting table, laser writer printer and three Mac computers. Together we apply our professional editing and promotion abilities while I continued my hospital career. However, Bea is the CEO, our editor-in-chief, finance expert, managing editor, distributor and shipper filling all the orders and more.

"Jan! Today I sent 48 *Somethings* to Australia and whole box to the State of Hawaii and I gave permission to publish *Something* in Israel in Hebrew and they'll reverse it from back to front."

She'd tote heavy boxes, calmed author egos, paid royalties, etc.

Though desktop production had been shunned as inferior by many press colleagues compared to costly typesetting and page make-up, Bea changed minds by leading workshops at women in publishing conferences and she was invited to do the same, with all her expenses paid, to present a workshop at the International Women's Booksellers Conference in Barcelona, Spain. The Macs were in Spanish but she knew them so well that she dismissed the guys, set up the electronics and proceeded in English. The potential computer users learning from Bea accepted desktop publishing's value to advance women's issues through their books and publications.

This technology brought creative power into our lives—and freedom too, to expand our business and our goals. To have this instrument in our hands is awesome.

Bea and Mother Courage are a respected entity among women of the international feminist small press movement and women's booksellers network.

Dear Mother Courage Bookstore, You've touched many lives and they're not going to forget you. You're not dead. You're just not living at in your store anymore. We'll resurrect you! You'll be living in our home. There's an office there with two Macs waiting for you and your stories. You're going to be stronger.

Mother Courage did survive, publishing 25 titles including Unitarian Universalist friend and author Charlotte Cote's biography of Olympia Brown, 13 novels and sailing adventures written by straight and lesbian authors, including those written by Bea and me. Mother Courage books sold across the USA, Canada, Europe, South Africa and New Zealand. Even the island country of the Seychelles off the coast of India bought *Something*. Foreign rights sales for *Something* were made to publishers in Germany, Mexico, Australia, The Netherlands and Israel where they printed the book in Yiddish from back to front, as is the custom.

Now we didn't need to depend only on local customers. We went farther with Mother Courage. We simply relocated our dream—and Bea—from the confines of the bookstore on 214 2nd Street in Lakeshore Bay.

Afterward

Bea on September 25, 1998

"Mother Courage Press Herstory"

Bea Lindberg and Jan Anthony are Mother Courage Press, a feminist/humanist publishing company that now has 25 titles in print.

Bea and Jan expect to continue publishing books by women and expanding their helping/healing books, women of courage biographies, women's spirituality guides and lesbian lines. Their motto, *women preserving life,* and their continuing goal of publishing bibliotherapeutic books and books that preserve and enhance the quality of life from a feminist perspective is reflected in their logo which shows a life-preserver ring blended into a woman's symbol.

They began with their first book in 1981, *Something Happened to Me* by Phyllis Sweet, while they were still in the feminist bookstore business as Mother Courage Bookstore and Art Gallery. The bookstore lasted for five years until two chain bookstores opened in a new mall, and the very month that *MS.* magazine listed Mother Courage among the other feminist bookstores in the US. *MS* has since listed them again among the nation's feminist publishers in an article by Andrea Clardy.

Bea as CEO publisher, editor and computer expert is responsible for the "day-to-day" operation of the publishing house: art direction, production, distribution, public relations and finance. Jan is a co-partner, editor, proofreader, design and marketing person.

Twelve years in publishing have given them a unique perspective on the book business when coupled with the five years as booksellers. They both have added experience in teaching, journalism, photography, graphics and freelance writing.

Bea writes under the name of B. L. Holmes (*Rowdy and Laughing, Mega and Senior Citizen*) and was the illustrator of the book *Something Happened to Me* and Jan's book, *Amy Asks a Question, Grandma, What's a Lesbian*. Bea also did the cover painting for *Banshee's Women*.

Bea and Jan gauge the herstory and the direction of the press by the titles they have published. Beginning with two books on child sexual abuse, Mother Courage Press now boasts seven books for survivors of sexual abuse and two books for the prevention of abuse: *Why Me? Help for victims of child sexual abuse (even if they are adults now)* by Lynn B. Daugherty; *Something Happened to Me* by Phyllis Sweet; *Rebirth of Power, Overcoming the Effects of Sexual Abuse through the Experiences of Others* edited by Pamela Portwood, Michele Gorcey and Peggy Sanders; *The Woman Inside, from incest victim to survivor* by Patty Derosier Barnes; *Helping the Adult Survivor of Child Sexual Abuse, For Friends, Family and Lovers* by Kathe Stark, *Fear or Freedom, a woman's options in social survival and physical-defense* by Susan E. Smith and *Warning! Dating may be hazardous to your health!* by Claudette McShane.

Why Me won the Editors' Choice award for young adults books in the *Journal of the American Library Association*.

Mother Courage published its first lesbian novel in May 1987, *NEWS* by Heather Conrad, and its second novel, a lesbian romance for the middle-aged crowd, *Night Lights* by Bonnie Shrewsbury Arthur in the fall of that year.

Rowdy and Laughing by Bea, as B. L. Holmes, is a book of poems written during the initial turbulence of Bea's and Jan's love affair that began in 1974. Three new lesbian novels were published 1991; *Singin' the Sun Up* by Ocala Wings, *Hodag Winter* by Deborah Wiese and *Mega* by B. L. Holmes.

Senior Citizen, also by B. L. Holmes, is a musical comedy in two acts, and was published the same year. The recent release of the non-fiction book *And Then I Met This Woman, Previously Married Women's Journeys into Lesbian Relationships* by Barbee Cassingham and Sally O'Neil is selling strongly and looks like it will be a best seller for Mother Courage Press.

Their latest published book, *Amy Asks a Question, Grandma, What's a Lesbian* by Jan, is selling well after its release in 1996. Jan's book and *Mega* were honored to be nominated for Lambda Literary Awards: *Amy in* the children's category in 1997 and *Mega* in science fiction in 1991.

Speaking of best sellers, *Why Me* now has 55,000 copies in print and *Something Happened to Me* has 30,000 copies in print. Mother Courage's third best seller is *The Woman Inside.*

The eighth book Mother Courage published can be read as a history of the women's suffrage movement because the biography of Olympia Brown, the first ordained woman minister of any designated religious denomination in the U.S., chronicles her lifelong involvement in getting the vote for women. *Olympia Brown, the Battle for Equality* was written by Charlotte Cote.

In 1989, for comic relief, the Press came out with a cartoon-illustrated feminist dictionary, *Womb with Views*, a *Contradictionary of the Enguish Language* by Kate Musgrave.

In 1990 Mother Courage Press published the first of a series of women's true adventure books with the title *Women at the Helm* by Jeannine Talley, a chronicle of Jeannine's and Joy Smith's adventures cruising the Pacific Ocean on their leisurely circumnavigation of the globe. In the spring of 1992, Mother Courage published Jeannine's second book, *Banshee's Women, Capsized in the Coral Sea.*

The press began a line of spiritual/New Age books with *Welcome to the Home of Your Heart* and *Meditations and Blessings from a Different Dimension* by Dorothy "Mike" Brinkman, and they plan to do more books on women's spirituality.

Mother Courage's books are selling across the USA, including Hawaii, Alaska and Guam, and in Canada, Australia, New Zealand, Great Britain, Germany, The Netherlands, South Africa and other countries. Mother Courage supplies to every major book wholesaler and library jobber in the U.S. Foreign rights sales have been made to Germany, Mexico, Australia, The Netherlands and Israel.

Gay/lesbian booksellers and readers may be are interested to know that lesbian authors include the seven writers of Mother Courage's lesbian books as well as three more who have written books that are not lesbian in theme. The press also has ten authors who are straight women which shows an even balance and a commitment to women's issues.

From Mother Courage Press

All Books in
The Whistling Girls and Crowing Hens Series

Book 1 – *Not to be Denied* captures humorous, sad and, scary family life between 1900 and 1970: The Depression, wars and life at home, schizophrenia; tomboy girls and teen girlfriends, sexual encounters, children, husbands, and individuals' choices that shape them. Passion explodes for two women in their early '40s. Liberal religion and Transactional Analysis weekends bring them together. Their paths meld when these naïve lovers test their magnetic attraction after Jan asks, "What could it hurt if we just let it happen?" (January 2024)

Book 2—*Gullibles' Travels*, where divorced Bea tries not to be a lesbian and her lover Jan strives to keep her children, husband and Bea happy. Bea and friends test the Sexual Revolution of the '60s and '70s. Jan recalls living in Cold War Germany in the '50s and touring Greece, Leningrad and Moscow with her husband in the '70s. Jan defuses a labor/management conflict and Bea and Jan escape to Europe for a rowdy and risqué three-week escapade in '76. (April 2024)

Book 3—In *Secret Transgressions*, Jan's hospital PR job expands with Bea as her assistant. Jan's marriage turns raw. Divorce. Bea is subject to sexual harassment in the workplace, is fired, and Jan is emotionally harassed on the job. Travel helps them heal and they create Mother Courage Bookstore and Press. (July 2024)

Book 4—*Being Mother Courage* embodies a dream come true: creating a feminist bookstore and experiencing historic events and adventures in the women's movement and the gay/lesbian world. Women's spirituality circles and lesbian support groups in Bea and Jan's home inspire and support women. Jan confronts job harassment and Bea faces the bookstore's demise. Tension turns to courageous laughter when conflicts are overcome. Bea uses her skills to pioneer Apple's Mac desktop publishing and was a guest speaker/teacher at the International Women's Booksellers Conference in Barcelona, Spain. (August 2024)

Book 5—In *Grit & Gratification*, Sailor Bea commands the boat and Jan, her bungling crew. Bea and Jan muster strength after Bea's homophobe father and Jan's supportive father die and they rehab their inherited rundown properties. Their new Mother Courage Press creates a significant, successful book for sexual abuse victims. When their retail bookstore closes, they are free to travel. As lusty lovers, they tow their camper to New York City, Provincetown, America's Stonehenge and Niagara Falls. Then they experience Michigan Woman's Music Festivals. Jan accepts that her lost Door County acres can be found on women's festival land.

Book 6—In *Moving On and Up*, Jan's stress is healed through her uniquely devised feminist therapy regimen. Jan's boss eliminates her PR department and job, but her reputation earns her a better one at a major metropolitan hospital. Bea and Jan stay strong together. Mother Courage Press begins to thrive. Surviving scuba diving and wild camping trips, sneaking into Disney World, being inspired at women's music festivals and gatherings, traveling through the Great Northwest makes them feel on top of the world.

Book 7— In *Close to Fine* (1984 to 1995) Jan moves up to the 'Big Leagues' of hospital PR in an exciting but stressful job. Mother Courage Press is a success and they travel to New Zealand, guitar heaven in Northern California, then Australia. They create spiritual autobiographies and a woman's band.

Book 8—In *Intimate Passages* (1984 to 2013) Bea tests their long relationship as a new friend comforts Jan. Goddess searching journeys to England, Mexico, Malta, Egypt, Scotland and France sustain and inspire them

For additional information on the series, contact:
Publisher Jeanne Arnold
MotherCouragePress31@gmail.com
https://www.mothercouragepress.com
**Books are on Amazon, Google Books,
and available through Ingram for libraries and bookstores.**

ABOUT JAN ANTHONY

Jan may brag about being a battled-tested warrior queen, but she's really an optimistic crone who blends truthful and imaginative words to recreate two women's audacious journey together. Their frustrated search for happiness as married women with teenage children fails. They fall in love, discover the depths of women-creative cultures and fight for successful careers while challenging socially acceptable norms. Jan's storytelling takes you into their intimate lives that enhance sensual and spiritual memories with their bodacious, risk-taking adventures.

Mother Courage Press
https://www.mothercouragepress.com
MotherCouragePress31@gmail.com